Political Refugees

Political Refugees

A New Perspective

Armin Danesh and Alison Assiter

ROWMAN & LITTLEFIELD
Lanham • Boulder • New York • London

Published by Rowman & Littlefield
An imprint of The Rowman & Littlefield Publishing Group, Inc.
4501 Forbes Boulevard, Suite 200, Lanham, Maryland 20706
www.rowman.com

86-90 Paul Street, London EC2A 4NE

British Library Cataloguing in Publication Information Available

Library of Congress Cataloging-in-Publication Data

Names: Danesh, Armin, author. | Assiter, Alison, author.
Title: Political refugees : a new perspective / Armin Danesh and Alison Assiter.
Description: Lanham : Rowman & Littlefield Publishers, 2022. | Includes bibliographical
   references and index.
Identifiers: LCCN 2021055981 (print) | LCCN 2021055982 (ebook) |
   ISBN 9781538161388 (cloth) | ISBN 9781538167496 (paperback) |
   ISBN 9781538161395 (ebook)
Subjects: LCSH: Danesh, Armin. | Political refugees—Iran—Case studies.
Classification: LCC HV640.5.I73 D36 2022 (print) | LCC HV640.5.I73 (ebook) |
   DDC 325/.210955—dc23/eng/20220104
LC record available at https://lccn.loc.gov/2021055981
LC ebook record available at https://lccn.loc.gov/2021055982

How can I forget my late beloved mother Moira's enthusiasm and concern at ninety-seven as she followed each stage of my work, step by step? When she insisted on hearing me present the outline of my study to her, she fell fast asleep. She is always with me.

Contents

Acknowledgements

This book is the conversion of my doctoral thesis, which could not have been successfully completed without the care, support, and concern of others. I can find no words to express my gratitude. For me, this project meant far more than an academic journey; it was transformative.

I would like first to thank my son Ben, my daughters Marisa and Adrianna, and my extended family, especially Jane who was inspired by Sara's story to transform her life. They all gave me warm encouragement throughout the years of my study. My wife Alison, a professor of philosophy, respected my work and challenged me to reflect on it seriously. I am indebted to her especially. Our conversations stimulated and broadened my academic knowledge. She gives me confidence and strength. Her keen interest in my work led her to contribute chapter 1, bringing further weight to the project. The book became a family venture.

I am particularly grateful to Elisabeth Salverda, Sasha Smith, Dawn Farrow, Professor Emmy van Deurzen, Professor Digby Tantam, Professor Pam James, Dr Chloe Mitchell, Dr Rosemary Lodge, and Dr James Gordon. My extended family includes my dear friends Professor Nira Yuval-Davis and Professor Gill Hague who both urged me to develop my research into book form.

My nine participants' names could not be disclosed, but I acknowledge and appreciate their generous help and their trust and transparency during my research.

Many close friends supported and encouraged me from the beginning, especially Andrew Costeloe, Julian Haxby, Jill Grinstead, Mike Akbari, and Nivad Movagharzadeh.

Finally, I thank Professor Morwenna Griffiths. In 2012, when I discussed with her my desire to combine human rights discourse with psychotherapy, she thought carefully and then responded, "That is an amazing idea. You have to do it."

Preface

Armin Danesh

I am honoured and moved by my nine participants' generosity, trust, and honesty. Their humanitarian values inspired my work. I was aware that the project would be challenging and demanding, but I could not have foreseen the changes it would bring about in my personal and professional life. I carried this project in my mind for a long time; I wanted to give voice to their experience.

They were rejected and misrecognised in their homeland. Why was their existence under threat? How did they cope with all the risks they took? This human journey gave rise to many other questions—physical, psychological, social, and spiritual. My passion was to find answers. I searched every corner of this unknown region. My participants' journey helped me also understand my own.

By the end of the project, I felt my nine participants—representing many others—had risen from the ashes, reminding me of the symbolic phoenix that calls to everyone: change is possible, if you want it. The phoenix became a recurrent theme in my book.

The phoenix idea arose at the initial stage, when I presented my research in the Programme Planning Module meeting with Professor Emmy van Deurzen, Professor Digby Tantam and some potential supervisors. I had about twenty minutes for my presentation. At the end, I received very encouraging feedback. In particular, Professor van Deurzen said, "This is like the phoenix rising from the ashes!"

This resonant image caught my imagination and grew organically through my early writing on the project. It was then verified through Sina's lived experience.

The phoenix symbol has an integrative meaning for me personally. Some years ago, it inspired me to found the Phoenix Aid Centre—a charity providing therapeutic services to refugees and others in need. For me, it symbolises the power to overcome barriers, to face and regenerate oneself, and to bring about change. As Darius, one of my participants, said, "We can make a change if we want."[1] This was corroborated by other participants; however, I am aware of some political refugees, as Sara and Karimi mentioned, who failed to adapt to their new environment and committed suicide.

Some political refugees were able to take opportunities to develop new meaning in their lives. Their outlook was future focused.

All my participants had moments when they lacked a sense of self or control over what might happen to them in the escape process, as well as "phoenix moments" when they arrived. Sina said: "Here—in fact, in London—it is a different world. For me it was a new start. It was a new birth. . . . It wasn't just a feeling. You can see it; you can start again. . . . It was a discovery for me, that refugeeing brings a new birth and a new life, not necessarily physically."[2] Lida echoed that thought: "This was like a new birth for me. The very day of my birthday I received my leave to remain."[3]

This research gave me personally many phoenix moments: "Our greatest glory is not in never failing, but in rising every time we fall."[4]

NOTES

1. Darius, interviewed by A. Danesh, London, 25 August 2016.
2. Sina, interviewed by A. Danesh, London, 8 August 2015.
3. Lida, interviewed by A. Danesh, London, 7 October 2016.
4. Oliver Goldsmith, *Letters from a Citizen of the World to His Friends in the East* (London: Baynes and Son, 1825), 26.

Introduction

Alison Assiter and Armin Danesh

In her novel *Go, Went, Gone*, Jenny Erpenbeck aptly outlines the received characterisations of a "refugee." The novel features a retired academic in Germany who comes into close contact with refugees from various African countries.[1]

On the one hand, as outlined by Erpenbeck and as reflected in much of the literature on the subject, we have the description of refugees as a problem that needs removing. To quote from Erpenbeck: "someone on the internet calling himself "Don't Care" writes, on hearing about asylum seekers seeking arrival in Europe in boats in the Mediterranean, 'The only ones I really feel sorry for are the coast guard workers. Why should they have to keep going out there to drag bodies out of the water.'"[2] The novel also offers a compelling account of the paramount alternative view, the idea that refugees are "victims" needing help. In the novel, this takes the form of kindly well-meaning Germans who want to "help" the "Africans" but who have no idea which country they originate from, which language they speak, or even where in Africa the various refugees' countries of origin are located.

Indeed, while this is a novel, it captures something very important about the concept of the "refugee." As Peter Nyers has put it in his illuminating study of the subject, *Rethinking Refugees*, "Refugees and their movements regularly emerge as a 'problem' to world order."[3]

"What does 'foreigner' mean? Who is foreign? Who is the foreign man, who is the foreign woman? What is meant by 'going abroad,' 'coming from abroad'?"[4] Human individuals and groups have always moved to other lands to seek safety, food, and shelter for children or family; for ideological or religious freedom; or to escape war, political persecution, or torture. Most of the literature applies the general concept of "refugee" to those who cross international borders to seek safety and survival from

1

dangerous situations and human rights abuses.[5] Probably all refugees escape from a familiar environment to a strange one.[6]

In this book, through Armin Danesh's personal story and through his research on a number of Iranian political refugees, we seek to offer a different account of a refugee from the one assumed by Erpenbeck mentioned earlier and found in much of the literature on the subject. Rather than being either "victim" or "problem," refugees can be, we argue, people with great resources, fortitude, and conviction. In the cases we discuss, recognition by the host country is simply one necessary condition for them to continue their work.

We begin this introduction to the book by looking briefly at the history of the concept of a refugee in order to set our work in context.

BRIEF HISTORY OF THE REFUGEE

Since the early 2000s, the world has been experiencing the largest migrations ever recorded in modern history.[7] According to the United Nations (UN) World Migration Report, in 2020 there were 272 million migrants in the world, who made up 3.5 percent of the world's population.[8] This report states:

> Foremost have been the displacements of millions of people due to conflict (such as within and from the Syrian Arab Republic, Yemen, the Central African Republic, the Democratic Republic of the Congo and South Sudan), extreme violence (such as inflicted upon Rohingya forced to seek safety in Bangladesh) or severe economic and political instability (such as faced by millions of Venezuelans).[9]

The vast majority of migrants remain in countries close to their nation of origin, and these countries often have scarce resources to provide for them.[10] However, the United Nations High Commissioner for Refugees (UNHCR) insists that refugees are different from migrants.[11] Indeed, acquiring refugee status opens doors for a migrant that would otherwise be closed.[12]

Unlike the definition of the term *migrant*, the definition of the term *refugee* is very precise. It combines law and social science.[13] According to Peter Gatrell,[14] the term *refugee* first entered the vocabulary of English speakers to describe the expelling of the Huguenots from France in the seventeenth century. After the Second World War, the Allied powers negotiated the 1951 Convention Relating to the Status of Refugees, where a refugee became defined as

> someone who, owing to a well-founded fear of being persecuted for reasons of race, religion, nationality, membership of a particular social group or political opinion, is outside the country of his nationality and is unable or, owing to such fear, is unwilling to avail himself of the protection of that country; or who, not having a nationality and being outside the country of his former habitual residence as a result of such events, is unable or, owing to such fear, is unwilling to return to it.

According to the UNHCR Handbook,[15]

> A person is a refugee within the meaning of the 1951 Convention as soon as he fulfils the criteria contained in the definition. This would necessarily occur prior to the time at which his refugee status is formally determined. Recognition of his refugee status does not therefore make him a refugee but declares him to be one. He does not become a refugee because of recognition but is recognized because he is a refugee.

There are two elements that are worth noting in these definitions. First of all, and this is very important, although the above quotation proclaims the opposite, a refugee is effectively brought into being by being defined as such by the UN Convention. This is the case because a person is in fact not recognised as a refugee until they are legally accepted as one. Even if a person is claimed, by the clarification above, already to be a refugee prior to that recognition, no one will know or accept this until the legal status is bestowed upon them.

There is an assumption, underpinning the definition, then, that human rights are natural and inalienable. This is how they are recognised in the UN Universal Declaration of Human Rights. This is why the UNHCR Handbook claims that a person is in fact a refugee prior to the legal recognition; however, given the requirements of the law, this is actually not the case. We will argue, in chapter 1 of this book, that refugees have rights in accordance with the UN Declaration prior to the legal recognition.

Furthermore, being a victim of persecution is built into the definition of a refugee. One scholar, Benjamin Gray, suggests that the notion could have been derived from ancient Greek notions of "sanctuary" focused on political persecution.[16] As is well known, the context of the 1951 Convention was never to see again the mistreatment of Jews and others by the Nazis. Western powers adopted a classical liberal approach to the question of refugees based on civil or political rights. It has been claimed that if the definition had included social rights, such as the right to an adequate standard of living, that would have undermined the commitment on the part of the Allied powers to *laissez-faire* liberalism.[17] So, according to this view, then, certain rights are natural and inalienable but not the basic right to adequate means of survival.

The original 1951 Convention only applied to Europe; however, in 1967 it was extended to cover other states, and the United States and Canada joined in 1968 and 1969, respectively.[18] By 2015, 148 countries had signed. It was very important for acceptance of the protocol that the definition applied only to individuals who had crossed an international border. It is also significant that the definition concerns persecution by reason of race, religion, or nationality. This is significant today, as there have been legal cases of people displaced by climate change issues who have applied and been refused refugee status.[19] Clearly some think that it would be a stretch too far to claim them to be "persecuted" by flooding or fire.

According to David Scott FitzGerald and Rawan Arar, the original definition is crucial, therefore, in shaping who counts as a refugee and also in framing research into the issue. FitzGerald and Arar state:

The UNHCR is the primary producer of knowledge in the study of refugees. The agency assembles, curates, and distributes statistical data from its own operations and national governments. The UNHCR identifies who the refugees are, where they are coming from, where they are going, and how they are treated. Idiosyncratic definitions created in the early days of the refugee regime have become path dependent.[20]

FitzGerald and Arar also claim that there are groups of people who are sometimes omitted from research on refugees. One such group are the Palestinians who often fall outside the UNHCR Global Trends reports. So, the definition affects who falls within its scope. FitzGerald and Arar argue further that the Global Trends reports often exclude groups of displaced persons. Apart from the Palestinians, another such example they quote is those displaced as a result of the partition of India in 1947, around 13.5 million people. FitzGerald and Arar argue, therefore, that the exclusion of groups such as these from who counts as a refugee fuels fears that global migration is reaching unprecedented levels today.

Arriving at the total number of refugees globally, therefore, FitzGerald and Arar argue, is partly a political matter that is designed to shape aid agencies' responses or countries' admissions policies. The numbers can be used to justify restrictions on entry to countries.[21] Moreover, according to FitzGerald and Arar,

> The categorization of refugees is malleable both from above and from below. State labels are not necessarily transferable. The same person who is a "refugee" in Kenya could be a "guest" in Jordan, an "asylum seeker" in Germany, a "migrant worker" in the United Arab Emirates (UAE), or an "irregular arrival" in Canada. There is also a gap between the definitions imposed from states and international institutions and the self-definitions by displaced people who sometimes reject the refugee label or only use it situationally when interacting with authorities. For some, "exile" carries a more accurate and/or higher-class connotation.[22]

Laws were developed, B. S. Chimni argues, to enable forced repatriation of potential refugees either back to their countries of origin or to other "third world" nations.[23] Chimni argues that the definition of a refugee, delimiting who counts as such, was represented as a matter of simple fact, in a positivist manner, but, as already noted, it was actually political and ideological. It carried considerable weight for it derived from the dominant system of international law that resides in Europe. But it was set up in neutral language and viewed as an abstract system of rules that can be objectively interpreted.

The UK Human Rights Act means that the rights that applied in the European Convention are, at least at the moment, fully applicable in the United Kingdom. This gives refugees, in the United Kingdom, the additional protection of Article 3 of the European Convention on Human Rights (ECHR) that prohibits torture. It also prohibits a court from returning a person to a country where they could be at risk of torture.[24] This legislation, however, is under threat at the present time, and these threats need constant monitoring.

There are important organisations, such as Southall Black Sisters in the United Kingdom, as well as smaller organisations such as Hackney and Haringey migrant centres, that work with other agencies to monitor changes in the law and to work for beneficial changes in the law affecting refugees and migrants.[25]

One implication, then, of the definition of a refugee and of the reactions of people, both aspirant refugees and aid agencies, is that it is commonly assumed that refugees have less agency than others. Their movements are believed to be involuntary or forced.[26] These kinds of assumptions about refugees and migrants shape the thinking of those whose aim is to help asylum seekers gain asylum.[27] There is no doubt that the way asylum seekers are treated in some states encourages this way of thinking. They are often denied access to public funds or the right to work at the same time as being stigmatised for failing to work. The definition partially shapes how people in the countries capable of receiving refugees act. Chimni states: "First, activists and non-governmental organizations (NGOs) in the West concentrated their effort entirely on improving refugee determination procedures as opposed to being alert to, and developing the resources and capability to mobilize against the political strategies of states."[28]

Indeed, the characterisation of a refugee changes with practice in ways that are both negative and positive for groups of refugees. To quote once more from Chimni:

> In the second edition of his well-known work, *The Refugee in International Law*, Goodwin-Gill mentions "the extraordinary growth in refugee studies, literature and case law" in the period since 1983 when the first edition was published (Goodwin-Gill 1996: xi). It was in these years that the foundations for a paradigm shift in international refugee policy and law began to be laid *inter alia* through the creation of the myth of difference: the nature and character of refugee flows in the Third World were represented as being radically different from refugee flows in Europe since the end of the First World War. Thereby, an image of a "normal" refugee was constructed—white, male and anti-communist—which clashed sharply with individuals fleeing the Third World.[29]

Refugees within Europe were different in many respects from those within the global south. Nonetheless, refugees within Europe were also treated very badly. In the 1930s, for example, in France, refugees from the Spanish Civil War were kept in the most horrendous conditions on beaches, without proper shelter.

There have been, since 1951, many developments and additions to the 1951 Convention. One that has been mentioned is the Human Rights Act in the United Kingdom that came into full effect in 2000. Furthermore, there is, as noted, now a distinct academic field in refugee studies. The need for such a field stemmed partly from the belief, in the postwar world, that international states have a legal obligation to protect refugees.[30] Within the field, social anthropologists have given a perspective on the individual within an encompassing social system, such as kinship, economics, marriage, and politics. Others have suggested that it might be helpful to understand refugees through social capital theory.[31] Social capital theory argues in favour of a dependable environment, consisting of a stable social network, shared values, and community commitment. This includes access to reliable information.

THE PSYCHOLOGICAL LITERATURE ON REFUGEES

Therapeutic services for refugees aim to address the "physical and psychosocial needs of this potentially vulnerable group, many of whom have been exposed to multiple traumatic situations, profound loss, as well as long periods of deprivation."[32]

In much of the psychological literature on refugees, the focus is on trauma. It is claimed that most refugees suffer trauma.[33] In their paper on the mental health of refugees and asylum seekers, "Therapeutic Practice with Refugee Clients: A Qualitative Study of Therapist Experience," Robert Schweitzer, Sierra van Wyk, and Kate Murray emphasise trauma and vulnerability. According, moreover, to another set of writers: "A refugee, in the usual conception, is among the world's most unfortunate people. Besides being a victim—of persecution, war or natural disaster—a refugee has also been uprooted, forced to leave familiar territory because of that same oppression or destruction."[34] Another pair of writers purporting to describe the "psychosocial well-being of asylum seekers and refugees" characterises them as "anxious," "homeless," and "helpless." As they put it: "Exiles can often become convinced that they have almost no control over their circumstances and few options to improve the situation. This perception is not without substance."[35] In the psychiatric literature, it is sometimes assumed that many refugees will suffer from posttraumatic stress disorder (PTSD).[36] It is also recognised, in some of the literature, however, that this concept may be inappropriate for the experience of many refugees. As Angela Burnett and Kate Thompson put it, "some have argued that the focus on the medical aspects of trauma in PTSD ignores the political implications of traumatic experiences by creating an illness out of normal reactions to violence."[37]

It is generally assumed, then, that a refugee is traumatised by the experience of forced migration: it is said that, for example, a refugee is a helpless and dependent person who is socially isolated; who will have difficulty in adjusting to life in a new country because of "cultural differences"; and who needs across-the-board support.[38] Indeed it has also been claimed that the loss of "home" is a crucial feature of the trauma experienced by refugees. One article on this subject claims that "the fundamental sense of home forms part of the 'core substratum'" of the identity (of any person), and when it is taken away "a fundamental lack develops which imperceptibly takes hold of refugees, in addition to whatever other tangible losses they are aware of and that they consciously mourn for."[39]

These generalisations, however, about refugees are open to challenge. Indeed, there are various places where this is recognised. To take one example, in a collection edited by Renos K. Papadopoulos, in an article called "Misconceiving Refugees?" Peter Loizos recognises that "refugee is not a simple universal idea [. . .] but the outcome of sometimes arbitrary political and administrative decisions [. . .] Refugees often resist and resent the labels and policies of those who seek to help them."[40] Moreover, we should also recognise that the concepts of "trauma" and "home" are themselves many faceted, and their application to refugees as generic categories may be misleading. *Oikos* (home or household) for Aristotle, for example, was a generic term covering "family," "household," and "house," and it did not have exclusively the specific modern connotation of a dwelling place. Which of these is it that "refugees," in general, are supposed to mourn?

In Alexander Betts and Gil Loescher's view, the term *refugee* means different things in different contexts.[41] Dinesh Bhugra wrote how a refugee is conceptualised: "The definitions are often complicated and dictated by the legal system of the new country."[42] In Roger Zetter's view, the term *refugee* refers to the result of arbitrary administrative and political decisions.[43] It is also important to note that there are challenges to the view of refugees as either victims or problems. As Burnett and Thompson have noted, refugees and asylum seekers "are people who have known the most challenging experiences possible and who continue to live and function in the world."[44] To focus on (victimhood) at the expense of the "resilience" of refugees is to miss a fundamental point.

While it is no doubt the case, then, that many refugees face extreme and difficult challenges both in their countries of origin and then in dealing with the many pitfalls of their host countries' legal systems, the labelling of them as "victims" does not necessarily help. In recognition of this point, the language has been somewhat modified, recognising that they may be active agents in their lives in the face of adversity.[45] A further issue is that much of the literature on refugees focuses on the problems of refugees in the West, while in fact most refugee movements occur in the global south.[46]

In this book, we will set out to continue the challenge of this literature; however, our framework will be very different. We would like to question several assumptions. In chapter 1, we will offer an alternative theoretical framework from that offered by the brilliant theorist Nyers on this subject. We will also challenge several other characterisations of the concept of the refugee. We will end this chapter by introducing the concept of a "political refugee," a concept which we believe is important for what follows. In the existing literature, it is not easy to find a specific focus on political refugees. Our book will seek to offer a very different view of a refugee. Danesh's life experience itself offers a challenge to the notion of the refugee as either a "victim" or a "problem." His case studies offer further evidence of the conviction, resourcefulness, and dedication of a number of political refugees.

In chapter 1, we present a discussion of Nyers's theoretical view of the concept of a refugee. We suggest that his theoretical framework, while very interesting, may exacerbate the problems faced by refugees and, we argue, there is another way of looking at the issue.

Chapter 2 is a history of Iran prior to and during the 1979 Revolution, to set the context for the case studies of Iranian political refugees that will follow.

Chapter 3 outlines Armin Danesh's own life story—it documents his personal and political activities in Iran, his strong objections to the extreme misogyny of the mullah's regime, his escape from Iran, and his subsequent life in the United Kingdom. Chapter 4 begins to outline Danesh's existential-phenomenological study of nine Iranian political refugees. It considers his research strategy, the research process, the means of recruiting the participants, and, very importantly, the issue of trust, which figures heavily among Iranian refugees.

In chapters 5 and 6, we begin hearing the life stories of the nine participants interviewed for this study. Chapter 5 begins the story by describing the lives of the participants in Iran prior to their escape. Each one of them in his or her different way was politically active in Iran. The chapter then continues with the escape process, outlining each one in turn. In the following chapter—chapter 6—the stories continue with the "rebirth" of each participant as they arrive in the new country. It pinpoints the importance of recognition and respect for each person and outlines the ways in which the various participants felt that they had gained such respect. The chapter also outlines the significance of their networks to their survival and flourishing and deals, finally, with the notion of "survivor guilt."

The seventh and final chapter describes the clinical relevance of the study: what approaches to mental health might be beneficial for people like those in the case study and suggestions for ways of dealing with potential issues that might arise in the clinical process.

NOTES

1. Jenny Erpenbeck, *Go, Went, Gone* (London: Portobello, 2017).

2. Erpenbeck, *Go, Went, Gone*, 167.

3. Peter Nyers, *Rethinking Refugees: Beyond States of Emergency* (London: Routledge, 2006), 1.

4. Jacques Derrida, *Of Hospitality* (Stanford, CA: Stanford University Press, 2000), 90.

5. Alexander Betts and Gil Loescher, *Refugees in International Relations* (Oxford: Oxford University Press, 2011); Guus Van der Veer, *Therapy with Refugees and Victims of Trauma: Psychological Problems of Victims of War, Torture and Repression* (New York: Wiley, 1998); Renos K. Papadopoulos, ed., *Therapeutic Care for Refugees: No Place Like Home* (London: Karnac Books, 2002); Home Affairs Committee, "Khat: Eleventh Report of Session 2013–14," House of Commons (United Kigdom), November 29, 2013, https://publications.parliament .uk/pa/cm201314/cmselect/cmhaff/869/869.pdf.

6. Van der Veer, *Therapy with Refugees and Victims of Trauma*; James A. Banks and Cherry A. McGee Banks, *Handbook of Research on Multicultural Education* (New York: Wiley, 2001).

7. Celia Falicov, foreword to *Therapeutic Care for Refugees: No Place Like Home*, ed. R. K. Papadopoulos (London: Karnac Books, 2002), xv–xviii.

8. "UN World Migration Report," International Organisation for Migration, 2020, https://worldmigrationreport.iom.int/.

9. International Organisation for Migration, "UN World Migration Report," 2.

10. Angela Burnett and Kate Thompson, "Enhancing the Psycho-Social Well-Being of Refugees," in *Race, Culture, Psychology and Law*, ed. Kimberley Holt Barrett and William H. George (London: Sage, 2005), 206, http://dx.doi.org/10.4135/9781452233536.n14.

11. Erika Feller, "Refugees Are Not Migrants," *Refugee Survey Quarterly* 24, no. 4 (2005): 27–35, https://doi.org/10.1093/rsq/hdi077.

12. Andrew E Shacknove, "Who Is a Refugee?" *Ethics* 95, no. 2 (1985): 274–84.

13. Rebecca Hamlin, *Let Me Be a Refugee: Administrative Justice and the Politics of Asylum in the United States, Canada, and Australia* (New York and Oxford: Oxford University Press, 2014).

14. Peter Gatrell, "Refugees—What's Wrong with History?" *Journal of Refugee Studies* 30, no. 2 (June 2017): 170–89, https://doi.org/10.1093/jrs/few013.

15. UNHCR Handbook, 2011, ch. 1, para 28. https://www.asylumlawdatabase.eu/sites/default/files/aldfiles/UNHCR%20Handbook%20Reissued%2C%20December%202011.pdf.

16. Benjamin Gray, "Exile, Refuge and the Greek Polis: Between Justice and Humanity," *Journal of Refugee Studies* 30, no. 2 (June 2017): 190–219, https://doi.org/10.1093/jrs/few027; quoted in David Scott FitzGerald and Rawan Arar, "The Sociology of Refugee Migration," *Annual Review of Sociology* 44 (July 2018): 387–406, https://doi.org/10.1146/annurev-soc-073117-041204.

17. FitzGerald and Arar, "Sociology of Refugee Migration"; B. S. Chimni, "Global Compact on Refugees: One Step Forward: Two Steps Back," *International Journal of Refugee Law* 30, no. 4 (December 2018): 630–34.

18. UNHCR Handbook, 2011, ch. 1, para 28, and FitzGerald and Arar, "Sociology of Refugee Migration."

19. See Georgia Cole, "Cessation," in *The Oxford Handbook of International Refugee Law*, ed. Cathryn Costello, Michelle Foster, and Jane McAdam (Oxford: Oxford University Press, 2021).

20. FitzGerald and Arar, "Sociology of Refugee Migration," 390.

21. FitzGerald and Arar, "Sociology of Refugee Migration"; see also Jeff Crisp, "Who Has Counted the Refugees: UNHCR and the Politics of Numbers," *New Issues in Refugee Research*, UNHCR Working Paper no. 12 (June 1999), https://www.unhcr.org/uk/research/working/3ae6a0c22/counted-refugees-unhcr-politics-numbers-jeff-crisp.html.

22. FitzGerald and Arar, "Sociology of Refugee Migration," 391.

23. B. S. Chimni, "The Geopolitics of Refugee Studies: A View from the South," *Journal of Refugee Studies* 11, no. 4 (1998): 350–74, https://doi.org/10.1093/jrs/11.4.350-a.

24. See Anne Owers, "The Human Rights Act and Refugees in the UK," *Humanitarian Practice Network*, June 2003, https://odihpn.org/magazine/the-human-rights-act-and-refugees-in-the-uk/.

25. See https://southallblacksisters.org.uk/, and https://haringeymsc.org.

26. See William Peterson, "A General Typology of Migration," *American Sociological Review* 23, no. 3 (June 1958): 256–66.

27. Both of us have experience in working for refugee agencies.

28. Chimni, "Geopolitics of Refugee Studies," 354.

29. Chimni, "Geopolitics of Refugee Studies," 351.

30. Richard Black, "Environmental Refugees: Myth or Reality?" *New Issues in Refugee Research*, UNHCR Working Paper no. 34 (March 2001), https://www.unhcr.org/uk/research/working/3ae6a0d00/environmental-refugees-myth-reality-richard-black.html.

31. See, for example, Peter Loizos, "Are Refugees Social Capitalists?," in *Social Capital: Critical Perspectives*, ed. Stephen Baron, John Field, and Tom Schuller (Oxford: Oxford University Press, 2000), 124–41.

32. Robert Schweitzer, Sierra van Wyk, and Kate Murray, "Therapeutic Practice with Refugee Clients: A Qualitative Study of Therapist Experience," *Counselling & Psychotherapy Research: Linking Research with Practice* 15, no. 2 (June 2015): 109–18, https://doi.org/10.1002/capr.12018.

33. See, for example, Gilbert Reyes and Gerard A. Jacobs, *Handbook of International Disaster Psychology: Refugee Mental Health* (Portsmouth: Greenwood, 2006).

34. Thomas Alexander Aleinikoff, David A. Martin, and Hiroshi Motomura, *Immigration and Citizenship, Process and Policy* (St. Paul, MN: West Group, 1998), 615.

35. Burnett and Thompson, "Enhancing the Psycho-Social Well-Being of Refugees," 207.

36. See, for example, J. N. Glassman, "PTSD in Refugees," *American Journal of Psychiatry* 145, no. 11 (November 1988): 1486–87, and J. David Kinzie et al., "The Psychiatric Effects of Massive Trauma on Cambodian Children," *Journal of the American Academy of Child Psychiatry* 25, no. 3 (May 1986): 370–76, https://doi.org/10.1016/S0002-7138(09)60259-4.

37. Burnett and Thompson, "Enhancing the Psycho-Social Well-Being of Refugees," 215.

38. See Papadopoulos, *Therapeutic Care for Refugees.*

39. Papadopoulos, *Therapeutic Care for Refugees*, 170.

40. Peter Loizos, "Misconceiving Refugees?," in Papadopoulos, *Therapeutic Care for Refugees*, 41–57.

41. Betts and Loescher, *Refugees in International Relations.*

42. Dinesh Bhugra, Tom Craig, and Kamaldeep Bhui, eds., *Mental Health of Refugees and Asylum Seekers* (Oxford: Oxford University Press, 2010).

43. Roger Zetter, "Labelling Refugees: Forming and Transforming a Bureaucratic Identity," *Journal of Refugee Studies* 4, no. 1 (1991): 39–62, https://doi.org/10.1093/jrs/4.1.39.

44. Burnett and Thompson, "Enhancing the Psycho-Social Well-Being of Refugees," 208.

45. See Jackson, "The Migrant Crisis: Helping Syrian Refugees," *Therapy Today* 26, no. 8 (October 2015).

46. Chimni, "Geopolitics of Refugee Studies," 354.

1

The Refugee "Problem"

Alison Assiter

George Orwell's dystopian novel, *1984*, begins with Winston Smith ruminating about a film he has seen. "One very good one of a ship full of refugees being bombed somewhere in the Mediterranean," he writes. "Audience much amused by shots of a great huge fat man trying to swim away with a helicopter after him, first you saw him wallowing along in the water like a porpoise, then you saw him through the helicopters' gunsights, then he was full of holes and the sea round him turned pink and he sank as suddenly as though the holes had let in the water."[1] Our view, like that of Orwell, is that images and theories about refugees matter. They shape how non-refugees see them and how refugees see themselves.

In this opening chapter, we would like to offer a challenge to the theoretical framework assumed in much of the literature on refugees, a framework that is brilliantly outlined in the book *Rethinking Refugees* by Peter Nyers.[2] We devote a chapter to his work because we believe it is important in setting out to develop the ontological framework underpinning contemporary discourse on refugees.

A CHALLENGE TO NYERS

In his significant book, *Rethinking Refugees*, Nyers argues that refugees regularly are characterised as a "problem" to be solved. Nyers's book is important as he has offered a theoretical analysis, drawing on much contemporary literature, of the place of the asylum seeker and the refugee. He offers a convincing explanation of why the refugee is seen either as a problem or as a victim. In the introduction to his book, he writes: "I am not so much concerned with the ontology of sovereignty or refugeeness so much as their ontogenesis, their historical constitution through on-going political practice."[3] He aims to unpack the implications of this politics for global refugee movements.

We would like, in this chapter, both to explain and to challenge his thinking. We believe that, although he is setting out to recognise the agency and particularly the political agency of refugees, the ontological and political framework he outlines actually undermines this laudable aim. Our own aim in this book is also to recognise the agency of refugees, but we believe that this requires an alternative ontological framework.

To those concerned with the maintenance of order, Nyers claims, refugees constitute a "problem" to be solved. When refugees are described as a "humanitarian emergency," as they often are, they are characterised as representing a threat to world order and therefore "an immediate political concern."[4] Some scholars have pointed out that Euro-Western research on the subject is generally designed to solve problems, and so it often focuses on people's difficulties while ignoring their strengths and the contributions they do, or could, make to society.[5] Nyers argues that there are two potentially conflicting discourses that underlie the "refugee" issue: not only that of humanitarian concern for all humans—obviously including refugees—but also, and potentially in opposition to the former, a commitment to world order, based on the demands of competing nation-states. Referring to the work of Carl Schmitt, on sovereignty, Nyers points out that sovereign power is often construed in terms of its inclusiveness. The language of liberal political theory testifies to its theoretical commitment to all humans, without distinction of any particular quality; however, as Schmitt has pointed out, modern forms of power often function to determine the limits of the "normal" and therefore to exclude the "exceptional."[6] The nation, to put it differently, is founded on the principle of citizenship, and this excludes those who are not citizens.

As understood in many contemporary contexts, the sovereign relation characterises friends, enemies, citizens and foreigners, and insiders and outsiders. Extending this, and as noted by Nyers, Italian philosopher Giorgio Agamben deploys the concept of "bare life." Following the earlier work of Hannah Arendt, Agamben argues that life for many illegal immigrants, placed in detention centres or in refugee camps, constitutes nothing more than bare survival. Agamben notes that a person who has fled their country of origin is often reduced to "bare life"—to a life of the mere just-about satisfaction of basic needs—while their status and potential citizenship issues are discussed by sovereign powers, those who have the power to determine who is included and who is excluded. As the *New Statesman* put it in a recent article:

> The thousands of nameless, faceless and unwanted people who risk their lives trying to cross our borders, desperate to make a better life for themselves, constitute such "bare life." Their aspirations and legitimacy can be effectively negated by the power of a bureaucratic vote in Brussels. Meanwhile, goods, capital, and western citizens are flowing freely around the globe in the name of globalization.[7]

In the words of Nyers once more, "the refugee is a limit-concept that occupies the ambiguous divide between the binary citizenry-humanity. By 'limit concept' I mean a concept that expresses the limits of a certain logic of intelligibility—in this case, the political."[8] Indeed, to take it further, "refugee" is conventionally represented as the mirror image of the citizen, as lying outside the borders of the sovereign state. Refugees are, as Hannah Arendt puts it "the scum of the earth."[9] This is not a new or a recent phenomenon. Discourse about refugees has been surrounded with language of crisis and emergency. Refugees, as we have noted, have been seen as a problem that requires a solution. This then leads, according to Nyers's characterisation, to polarised interpretations of this "problem." On the one hand, it is a humanitarian crisis that requires a humanitarian solution, which generates refugee organisations (such as the ones we ourselves volunteered in for years) that set out to offer legal and other types of "help" to them; on the other hand, there is the xenophobic desire to "remove" or "eliminate" the problem.

I would like, following my work on human rights, *A New Theory of Human Rights: New Materialism and Zoroastrianism*,[10] to challenge Nyers's reading and to suggest that the discourse underpinning human rights, that itself feeds into the various categorisations of the refugee, needs to be rethought. Nyers claims, then, that the distinction that underpins much thinking about refugees and asylum seekers—between "humanitarian" activity (which has a normative and moral character) and political activity—is in fact shaped by the political discourse of sovereignty and citizenship. He suggests that the distinction between "humanitarian" activity that is concerned to "help" those in need in the world order and the political order that links with sovereignty and citizenship is built into Western political thought. He writes:

> When Augustine distinguished the City of God from the City of Man, it was understood that it was the former realm—that of eternity, heaven and life beyond the contingencies and indeterminacy of the temporal world—to which we were to hold our primary allegiance. Compared to these lofty heights, politics was an activity that was somehow fallen, inferior and amoral.[11]

Nyers argues that this distinction underpins "humanitarian" activity today. "The former president of the international committee of the Red Cross put the point thus: 'humanitarian endeavour and political action must go their separate ways if the neutrality and impartiality of humanitarian work is not to be jeopardised.'"[12]

Nyers argues that this notion of humanitarian action, with its focus on ethical matters, is intertwined with its obverse—the political—with its core notion of citizenship of states. Both, he argues, are derived from a Western liberal human rights tradition. Humanitarianism's core principles are derived from a Western imaginary that requires a strict line to be drawn between the "ethical" (and humanitarian) and the political (concerned with citizenship and sovereign states). Nyers claims, though, that it is, in fact, impossible to distinguish the concept of "humanity" from its engagement with sovereign states.

One of his illustrations of this point is the activity of the ICRC (International Committee of the Red Cross). This body, he argues, derives its principles from the 1991 United Nations (UN) resolution to the effect that "humanitarian assistance must be provided in accordance with the principles of humanity, neutrality and impartiality."[13] These principles of neutrality, according to Nyers, mean that the body should make no distinction of class, race, sex, or nationality, and it is to be guided solely by the individuals and by their needs. This means that the organisation does not "interfere" in the political affairs of individual states or comment on their political activities. Humanitarian actors, Nyers recognises, attempt to transcend the boundaries and borders of individual nations, and to effect a notion of a common humanity, a cosmopolitan notion of a world order. But, he writes, as Hegel has pointed out, although individuals are constituted as moral subjects in families and in civil society, Hegel also argued that war is necessary in the formation of individual nation-states.

When humanitarian norms are invoked outside this discourse, they are invariably couched in terms of the sacredness of life. However, as Hannah Arendt recognised and as Nyers, following Agamben, has noted, "to possess rights one has to be other than human (in the above discourse) one has to become the human's other, one has to become a citizen."[14] Nyers then continues by drawing on Agamben's characterisation of Aristotle—namely, his distinction between "zoe" (the fact of living common to all living things) and "bios" (the manner of living common to an individual or a group).[15] Bios, according to Agamben's Aristotle, is man's capacity for political existence.[16] Agamben adds to Aristotle's notion the claim that the "sovereign" or the "political," in this discursive construction, is built upon the exception. This exception, then, becomes the refugee or the asylum seeker. The refugee is condemned as lacking "bios" and as forced into a life of "zoe" or bare survival (if he or she is lucky).

Sovereign power, then, for Nyers, following Agamben, derives its force from its ability to suspend normal rules and to create "exceptions." What Agamben calls "bare life"—the characterisation of the individual as merely one of "zoe"—is "included in the political by virtue of its exclusion."[17] In ancient Roman law, according to Agamben, the figure of the *homo sacer* was a sacred person but one who could be killed without the law of homicide applying to them. Nyers argues that the challenges facing humanitarianism today are not dissimilar to the *homo sacer* of Agamben's project. Nyers argues that the principal reason why refugees constitute a problem is because they symbolise what is hidden—"bare life"—"they break the continuity between man and nativity and nationality, and they put the original fiction of modern sovereignty in crisis."[18] Sovereignty, then, is a violent relation, he argues, that works to keep things apart.[19]

Now, we would like to argue two things in this book. First, we present Danesh's studies of individual refugees who refuse the labels *victim, traumatised other*, or *problem*. These are individual refugees who demand human rights for all, and whose experience differs from the above characterisation of the refugee. But second, we would like, briefly in this first chapter, to offer a challenge to the theoretical perspective adumbrated above, which serves both to continue the process of subjugation of refugees and gives academic and theoretical backing to a practice that is detrimental to the interest of refugees, to those deemed *homo sacer* but also to many citizens of nation-states today.

This view of refugees and asylum seekers is implicit, if not fully spelled out, in much of the literature on the subject, which views refugees in the fashion of the early quote from Jenny Erpenbeck in her novel *Go, Went, Gone* outlined at the beginning of the introduction to this book. It shapes the view that refugees constitute a "problem" for the world order requiring a "humanitarian" or ethical and nonpolitical solution. It shapes the view that an individual nation has responsibilities primarily to its citizens and not to any "outsiders." This leads to a narrow form of nationalism that, in its turn, generates the xenophobia of those who see refugees and asylum seekers simply as a "problem" that has nothing to do with them and that leads to a waste of resources that ought to be devoted to their fellow citizens who are more deserving. It leads, therefore, to the view that there are no political obligations on individual states because refugees and asylum seekers have nothing to do with them. Refugees are the "exception" whose basic needs (if they are lucky—and often they are not) might just about be cared for, but for whom individual states have no obligations. Moreover, refugees and asylum seekers are also defined, in this view of them, as exemplifying the "exception" or mere "bare life," as lacking in political agency of their own, and it is this that we are very much concerned about in this book.

My work on human rights challenges the conventional reading of the origin and the theoretical underpinning of the notion of a human right. I have argued, first, that the theoretical view adumbrated above by Nyers and others, which draws a distinction between the normative or the ethical and the political, is an artificial one produced both by a selective reading of Aristotle and a Eurocentric view of the underpinning ontological assumptions of discourse on human rights. Rights, I have argued, as spelled out in the UN Universal Declaration of Human Rights, are universal and dependent upon a notion of universal humanity. Representatives from virtually every nation in the world were present in the discussion and in the drawing up of the Declaration. The whole point and purpose of it was that it would transcend individual nations. The UN itself was precisely set up to hold individual nations to account should they be seen to be violating individual rights. Whether or not the UN has been successful is a moot point. But that does not detract from the overall argument. Refugees, like citizens of a nation-state, are individuals with universal human rights—to life and to all the other core rights as set out in the Universal Declaration. As Gita Saghal has pointed out,[20] representatives from postcolonial nations were present at the signing of the UN Declaration. It was not drawn up solely by "Western" powers. The drafting of the Declaration included representatives of "Western" nations, but it also included Hansa Mehta from India, P. C. Chang of the Republic of China, Charles Malik from Lebanon, Hernán Santa Cruz from Chile, and Alexander Bogomolov from the Soviet Union.

Now, Nyers would no doubt respond to this point by saying that he accepts that the intention behind the UN Declaration was to develop a notion of a universal human right. However, he would claim, in fact, that this notion can only, in the present world order, be understood in terms of the above "moral" discourse of humanitarianism. As he puts it in his concluding chapter:

This humanity, however, is not a given but an identity that comes with a price. When refugees take flight from violence and persecution, their human life is stripped bare, with all political qualifiers (presence, voice, agency) erased from their identity. Refugees, therefore, are not so much human as "the site where the human stops."

He goes on to say, once more, that the effect of all this is the equation of "refugeeness" with "bare life."[21]

This critique can be turned into a general doubt about the possibility of characterising "universal humanity" in any meaningful way that means more than "bare life." Again, I have argued that the notion of universal humanity is more than this. I have outlined it in terms of a biological core, which encompasses the satisfaction of basic needs, but which includes powers and capacities that are actualised partially in a genome and in biological characteristics that are shared with other animals but which also include the capacity for freedom and for making sophisticated, responsible choices that are different from those of other animals. Rather than this constituting the derogatory "bare life," it is, in fact, a vital part of the core of the whole of humanity. We deny our continuity with other animal species, in the context of the present climate emergency, at our peril. We will continue and elaborate upon this point further in what follows.

Moreover, I have also argued that the common story about the origin of a right, in the European Enlightenment, is open to challenge. I have argued that one very important story of their origin, that ought not to be ignored, lies with Cyrus the Great and the ancient Persian Empire. The Cyrus Cylinder possibly represents the world's first statement of human rights. In its turn, this Cylinder may have been inspired by Zoroastrianism, a religion that itself influenced and shaped the work of Plato and Aristotle. So, Aristotle's notion of "bare life" can be read very differently from Agamben's interpretation; rather, humans, as living beings, are "ensouled" in just the manner of other living beings such as plants and animals. Humans have a particular type of soul that enables them to engage in alternative activities from other animals. But humans are a type of animal. There is a continuity between plants, animals, and humans—between all beings endowed with life. In other words, the distinction drawn by Nyers, between "ethical" or "humanitarian" activity and political work based on state sovereignty is open to challenge by these two theoretical points. Arguably one of the inspirations for the UN Declaration could be taken from this ancient Persian document, and it is also taken from aspects of Aristotle's thought. Moreover, the UN does have some legal teeth, and it is important that this is recognised and appreciated and not ignored, as it is in literature inspired by the framework of Agamben and others.

Moreover, it is also important to note that experts on Aristotle's work have argued that there is no distinction in his *Politics* between "zoe" and "bios." The distinction, according to one expert, is based on a reading of Aristotle that derives from Foucault and Arendt, a reading that is unfounded and does violence to Aristotle's meaning.[22] Arendt had claimed that "simple natural life," in her reading of Aristotle, is confined to the home, whereas "polis" constitutes political life. Schmitt also refers to "bare life"—the life, on his reading of Aristotle, of mere necessities. Agamben claims that "actually existing politics," which is the foundation of "Western democratic politics," is marked by this opposition between "zoe" and "bios." James Gordon Finlayson notes that Agamben makes some very large claims to the effect that the distinction between "zoe" and "bios" was "'pandemic' amongst the Greeks" and is "canonical for the political tradition of the west."[23]

Finlayson argues, however, that Agamben's reading of Aristotle is inaccurate. According to Finlayson's interpretation, Aristotle has two ways of understanding the highest form of the good life—it was either a life of contemplation or a life of practical virtue. These are two ways of living the good life peculiar to humans. A good life achieves the telos of eudaimonia—happiness.

Aristotle's notion of being "ensouled" is a radically different conception from that of the European Enlightenment thinkers, many of whom, following René Descartes, drew a radical distinction between humans (who possessed a soul or reasoning powers) and other animals, who did not and who were more like machines. So, if you read Aristotle through Descartes, humans without reasoning powers become nothing—"bare life"—or the exception to the sovereign state. But if they are seen as Aristotle saw them, they are creatures with a whole range of capacities and powers, some of which are shared with seals, pigs, dogs, and even bacteria. Indeed Aristotle, who was also a biologist, saw animals as well as humans as possessing "bios" or the ability to live a good life. The noun *zoon*, as Finlayson puts it, "literally means 'ensouled' or a living and animated being." It does not mean the derogatory interpretation that it has been given, as "lacking a soul,"[24]

Now it may be argued that there are simply two readings of Aristotle here, and some may take Agamben's reading as the accurate one. It is important, however, also to note some additional context. In the Enlightenment period, there was a groundswell of opinion against Aristotle. As one writer puts it: "In August 1642, over a thousand people gathered in a great Paris hall to hear a public disputation of fourteen theses against Aristotle. But the debate was prevented by official edict."[25] Scholasticism, then, as it was known, was strongly criticised in the seventeenth century; to some extent, that critique is embedded in contemporary Western conceptions of science, but it is also about rights and the social contract and about understanding Aristotle.

Finlayson's interpretation of Aristotle, indeed, is in line with the thinking of many contemporary biologists. In this way of thinking, humanitarianism is concerned with the deep and abiding and core principles of the human, and citizenship is a modern European invention that detracts from these core principles. We need, indeed, if we are to save humanity from the environmental crisis that envelops us, to rethink our core values along these lines.

Finlayson argues that "zoe" and "bios" are not mutually exclusive terms in Aristotle's *Politics*, as Agamben seems to assume they are. "Zoe" (what Agamben associated with "bare life") is not, according to Finlayson, excluded from political life, but it is rather a constituent part of it. "Zoe," moreover, also applies, for Aristotle, to the Gods who do not have basic needs. "Bios," furthermore, applies to any group of animals who group together—"animals that live politically are those that have any kind of activity in common, which is not true of all gregarious animals: of this sort are man, bee, wasp and crane."[26] "Bios," then, is not, in Aristotle's view, analogous to the modern concept of "citizenship." It is quite different and is rather an attribute of any collection of animals that group together.

So, to conclude this section of the argument, then, we would like to stress, contrary to the work of Nyers, who draws on Agamben, that the concept of a human right is universal and applies to all without distinction of class, race, nation, and such. In its turn, and this is also discussed at length in my book *A New Theory of Human Rights*, the concept of universality has come in for a huge amount of criticism in recent years—namely, that every attempt to outline what it means excludes some group. In our view, however, it is possible, as noted, in contradistinction to all of these critics, to develop a notion of universal humanity that draws upon our biological core, which is dynamic and changing but some of which is shared with other animals. Moreover, there is a critique of some "postcolonial" views of the "universal" from, for example, Chetan Bhatt, which argues that the characterisation of the "third world" person as "victim" leads to a denial of their agency and therefore to a form of Eurocentrism among those attempting to circumvent it. There is a parallel point about the refugee literature—it denies agency to the refugee in the very attempt to "help" them, and therefore, what is intended merely to "explain" the phenomenon may, in fact, be exacerbating it.

In contradistinction to Nyers and Agamben, then, there is a philosophical tradition, including the work of Friedrich Schelling, Baruch Spinoza, and Henri Bergson, as well as Aristotle, which sees the human as emerging from a natural world that pre-exists it. It is a view of our biological core that is based on powers and self-generating systems—autopoietic entities according to the work of biologists Humberto Maturana and Francisco Varela. Like Aristotle, this view sees humans as being continuous with other animals. As he noted, in his work *de Anima*, animals, like humans, possess what he called "souls" or powers that animate the body. This literature, then, to repeat the point, offers a less "abstract" and "bare" view of universal humanity than the critics, including Nyers, assume. Included in this view of universal humanity is, of course, the refugee.

Returning, then, to the concept of a refugee, we would like, once more, to quote the 1951 Convention definition:

> Someone who owing to a well-founded fear of being persecuted for reasons of race, religion, nationality, membership of a particular social group or political opinion, is outside the country of his nationality and is unable or, owing to such fear, is unwilling to avail himself of the protection of that country; or who, not having a nationality and being outside the country of his former habitual residence as a result of such events, is unable or, owing to such fear, is unwilling to return to it.

Nyers's theoretical reading of the refugee contributes and reinforces the view that refugees are outsiders or the exception to everything and for whom all that is required is charity. In fact, they have rights, not only rights to life but also to liberty and to other aspects of the rights of citizenship, as outlined in the UN Declaration. They deserve to have these rights recognised and appreciated. Moreover, as our study that follows in this book will show, many of them have much to offer whichever host country accepts them.

Nyers's theoretical perspective reproduces the view that refugees lack agency, particularly "political" agency of their own. While we do not deny that the legal systems that have teeth in the present world order are those of individual nations and they can exert some force in tackling the issue of large flows of migrants in the world, it is also very important to recognise that every single individual refugee or asylum seeker or migrant has human rights as defined by the UN Declaration. They also have individual experience and ought not to be simply reduced, as this literature does, to "the exception." The individual experiences highlighted in the study that follows in this book, conducted by Danesh, bring back together the two aspects pulled apart by Nyers—the humanitarian and the political. Danesh's studies bring back the psychological and the humanitarian into the characterisation of the refugee as a holder of rights.

It was precisely, to remind the reader, to attempt to avoid the complete dehumanisation of Jews and others in the Holocaust that the UN Declaration was set up. Not to offer humanitarian relief to those already dehumanised, but to avoid the dehumanisation in the first place. There is a risk, if we continue to uphold the above discourses on refugees, that we forget that the one single reason for setting up the UN Declaration in 1948 was to prevent the dehumanisation of any group of people. Therefore, when academics, in their zeal to attempt to explain the phenomenon, use sophisticated language that actually obliterates this key message, it is very important that other academics, such as ourselves, remind people of these very crucial and important matters.

We would like to end the chapter by referring to some work from postcolonial writers that continues the challenge to the earlier literatures, but from a different perspective. This work, like our own, seeks to challenge the picture of the refugee or the asylum seeker as a "problem" to be solved either by humanitarian intervention or by the actions of the nation-state.

As a result of this burgeoning recognition as well as other recent areas of growing interest, a new field of study has opened up, one which is usefully summarised in the article "'Refugee Literature': What Post-Colonial Theory Has to Say" by Claire Gallien.[27] This latest literature seeks to challenge the image, which is sometimes racist and at other times just false, of the refugee.

Gallien's article, to take one case, points out that the corpus on refugees is vast and it predates the current refugee crisis. She summarises some of the writing in literature and the arts by Middle Eastern and African writers that focuses on the refugee issue in the postcolonial context. Gallien set out to "intervene in and disrupt the power dynamics as embedded in discourse and as they regulate the politics of north and south."[28] She wants to confront the "problematic modes of representation" of politically displaced people and find alternative voices, discourses, and imaginaries. Gallien argues for the extension of the category of refugee to encompass "basic needs" so as to include those displaced by environmental destruction. One writer she quotes explores the problematic aspects of representational discourse, what Hannah Arendt called the "politics of pity" and Luc Boltanski called "distant suffering."[29] Valerie Anishchenkova offers video textual analysis of James Longley's documentary *Iraq in Fragments*.[30]

Gallien's summary of her volume ends on the following note: "the final brief reference needs to be made to the final article in this issue of *JPW*, by Hanan Ibrahim, an addition to but not part of the special issue on 'Refugee Literature,' titled 'The Question of Arab "Identity" in Amin Maalouf's *Les Désorientés*.'" Ibrahim examines this recent novel by Lebanese Arab writer Maalouf for the way its protagonist, an exiled intellectual who embraces positions such as Islamic extremism and Marxism, avoids envisioning any political resistance to the social oppression following the Arab Spring. His refusal to engage politically reflects the chaos in Lebanon and other Arab countries in the region in the aftermath of these insurgencies.[31] The subject of resilience was a notable theme. This confirms that, although significant proportions of refugees have been traumatised and suffer from mental disorders, they simultaneously may possess enormous strengths and coping strategies.[32]

This literature offers some uplifting stories of refugee survival and significant activity of various kinds. It is important to note, finally though, that within postcolonial literature there are strong critiques not only of the specific implementation of human rights legislation but also of the very concept of a human right as being Eurocentric and Westocentric. Most famously, Saba Mahmood has claimed that the concept is Western and indeed specifically Christian.

In the introduction to her book, *Religious Difference in a Secular Age: A Minority Report*, Mahmood[33] suggests that the norms of European nations, which were purportedly universal and areligious, were in fact substantively Christian. She argues, therefore, that the concept of a right is linked to the Christian revolution and that the crucifix should be regarded as a symbol of a value system that includes liberty, equality, human dignity, and religious tolerance—and also as a symbol of the secular state.

There are, however, a number of critiques of the work of Mahmood, including my own.[34] It is important to mention, for example, the work of Afiya Zia, which points to feminist activism in Pakistan that deploys the discourse of human rights to do so.[35] As noted earlier, my work on human rights offers a detailed challenge to Mahmood's argument and points specifically to the human rights activities of Pakistani feminists, in a postcolonial Muslim majority nation, against fundamentalist Islamists there.

We cannot repeat all of these arguments here. This book of ours describes the experiences of a number of refugees from Iran, a Muslim-majority nation; some of these refugees are themselves Muslim, who fought, in their country of origin, for human rights and for the rule of law. Not only did Danesh not see the concept as being associated with Christianity and with the European nation-state but many of those described here saw their/our Muslim friends die in their struggle for universal human rights thus for these rights to apply in Iran.

This work, therefore, seeks both to challenge the "Westocentric" conception of a refugee and the Eurocentric view of a human right, as well as the postcolonial critique that would do away altogether with the concept of a right. One of the risks, we argue, of abolishing the concept of a right, is that it opens the door to the very fundamentalism (as mentioned earlier) that many would-be refugees are escaping from. The following chapters focus on the combination of a personal story from Armin Danesh, an Iranian political refugee who now has status in the United Kingdom and Danesh's research into other Iranian political refugees. Most of them were political activists in their home nation, Iran, against the Islamic fundamentalist regime there. They are not lacking in agency; rather, they have achieved a great deal in exceptional and unusual ways. Moreover, they do not challenge the concept of a human right; instead, they were fighting in Iran for the right to have democracy and universal human rights.

NOTES

1. George Orwell, *1984*, (London: Secker and Warburg, 1949), 11.

2. Peter Nyers, *Rethinking Refugees: Beyond States of Emergency* (London: Routledge, 2006).

3. Nyers, *Rethinking Refugees*, x.

4. Nyers, *Rethinking Refugees*, 1.

5. Helen Lambert, "Refugee Status, Arbitrary Deprivation of Nationality, and Statelessness within the Context of Article 1A(2) of the 1951 Convention and Its 1967 Protocol Relating to the Status of Refugees," UNHCR Paper, Legal and Protection Policy Research Series, Division of International Protection, 1 October 2014, http://dx.doi.org/10.2139/ssrn.2521076.

6. Carl Schmitt, *Political Theology: Four Chapters on the Concept of Sovereignty* (1922), trans. G. Schwab (Chicago: University of Chicago Press, 2005).

7. "The Bare Life of Immigrants," *New Statesman*, 30 June 2008, https://www.newstatesman.com/politics/2008/06/illegal-immigrants-life.

8. Nyers, *Rethinking Refugees*, 3.

9. Hannah Arendt, *Imperialism*, part 2 of *The Origins of Totalitarianism* (New York: Harvest, 1968), 147.

10. Alison Assiter, *A New Theory of Human Rights: New Materialism and Zoroastrianism* (London: Rowman & Littlefield, 2021).

11. Nyers, *Rethinking Refugees*, 26.

12. Assiter, *A New Theory of Human Rights*.

13. Nyers, *Rethinking Refugees*, 20n15.

14. Nyers, *Rethinking Refugees*, 37.

15. Giorgio Agamben, *Homo Sacer: Sovereign Power and Bare Life*, trans. Daniel Heller-Roazen (Stanford, CA: Stanford University Press, 1998).

16. Agamben, Giorgio. Heller-Roazen, trans. *Homo Sacer: Sovereign Power and Bare Life* (Stanford, California: Stanford University Press, 1998).

17. Agamben, *Homo Sacer: Sovereign Power and Bare Life*, 103.

18. Nyers, *Rethinking Refugees*, 41.

19. Nyers, *Rethinking Refugees*, 41.

20. Gita Saghal, "Who Wrote the Universal Declaration of Human Rights?" *Open Democracy*, 10 December 2014, https://www.opendemocracy.net/en/5050/who-wrote-universal-declaration-of-human-rights/.

21. Nyers, *Rethinking Refugees*, 124.

22. See, for example, James Gordon Finlayson, "Bare Life and Politics in Agamben's Reading of Aristotle," *Review of Politics* 72 (2010): 97–126; Robert W. Cox, "Social Forces, States and World Orders: Beyond International Relations Theory," in *Neo-Realism and Its Critics*, ed. Robert O. Keohane (New York: Columbia University Press, 1986).

23. Finlayson, "Bare Life and Politics," quoting Agamben, *Homo Sacer*, 2.4, 106.

24. Finlayson, "Bare Life and Politics," 109.

25. Tom Sorell, *Descartes* (Oxford: Oxford University Press, 1987), 27.

26. Aristotle, *History of Animals*, 1.1.488a8–10, in Jonathan Barnes, *The Complete Works of Aristotle*: Revised Oxford Translation: Volume One: 96 (Bollington Series, 1984), 776–77, quoted in Finlayson, "Bare Life and Politics," 114.

27. Claire Gallien, "'Refugee Literature': What Post-Colonial Theory Has to Say," *Journal for Post-Colonial Writing* 54, no. 6 (2018): 721–26.

28. Gallien, "'Refugee Literature,'" 726.

29. Hannah Arendt, "The Social Question," in *On Revolution* (New York: Penguin, 1963), 59–114; Luc Boltanski, *Distant Suffering: Morality, Media, and Politics*, trans. Graham Burchell (Cambridge: Cambridge University Press, 2004).

30. Valerie Anishchenkova, "The Battle of Truth and Fiction: Documentary Storytelling and Middle Eastern Refugee Discourse," *Journal of Post-Colonial Writing* 54, no. 6 (April 2019): 809–20; James Longley, dir., *Iraq in Fragments* (New York: HBO Documentary Films, 2006).

31. Gallien, "Refugee Literature," 726; Amin Maalouf, *Les Désorientés* [The Disoriented] (Paris: Grasset, 2013).

32. See Matthew Hodes, "Three Key Issues for Young Refugees' Mental Health," *Transcultural Psychiatry* 39, no. 2 (2002): 196–213.

33. Saba Mahmood, *Religious Difference in a Secular Age: A Minority Report* (Princeton, NJ: Princeton University Press, 2016), 9.

34. Assiter, *A New Theory of Human Rights*.

35. Afiya Zia, *Faith and Feminism in Pakistan: Religious Agency or Secular Autonomy?* (Brighton: Sussex Academic Press, 2018).

2

My Perception of Political Refugees

Armin Danesh

The activities and beliefs of political refugees are often central to their identity. It is therefore useful to have some background knowledge of their homelands' politics and political history.[1]

This chapter presents my reflection on political refugees and will outline the history of Iran prior to the Revolution in 1979. I will examine the hopes of those who had been active against the shah and the disappointment of some when they saw the direction taken by the new clerical government and its followers. In particular, I will focus on the situation of women in present-day Iran. This is important because all my research participants mentioned a central reason for becoming politically active: they believed the regime in Iran to be based on discrimination against women. They were determined to stand against this misogyny. In order to clarify the situation of women there, I will also describe the clerical regime's ideological foundation. Control over women's identities, sexuality, and labour has been central to reinforcing state power. In the regime's portrayal of Islamised women as a symbol of Islam and de-Westernisation, it draws upon gender to define and redefine its own domestic and global objectives.[2] Therefore, defending women's rights became a central project for those who wanted to bring about democracy and equality in Iran. These overall aims were, in fact, the major objective of the 1979 Revolution. Finally, I will concentrate on Iranian refugees and offer a historical background and a new perspective through a critical review of the relevant literature.

HISTORICAL BACKGROUND

For nearly two and a half millennia, Iran was known to the Western world as Persia. The past century saw three major movements against dictatorship in Iran. The causes and historical background of these movements are a subject of debate among scholars. In this chapter I will offer a brief review of the history, based on its impact on my native country.

As a political refugee, I perceive these movements as sources of inspiration, pride, belonging, and identity. I was and am proud of genuine leaders and of people who stand against dictatorships and corrupt rulers. They desire to create possibilities for a decent life and to achieve freedom and equality. I remember when I was about fifteen years old, I decided to draw secret portraits of the leaders who became my heroes; in this way, I could show my connection to their progressive ideas, their meaning and purpose, and their determination, commitment, and devotion for others. They were alive in me then, and they continue to be so now.

The first revolutionary movement in my view was the Constitutional Movement in 1906, which gave impetus to the Iranian people's struggles for democracy and freedom. That revolution forced the shah to eventually sign a constitutional decree in 1906 establishing a parliament for the first time in Iran's history. The ruling system was transformed at least on the surface into a constitutional monarchy. Until then, Iranian politics and the governing body changed only from one king to another; the people had no voice. The second key movement was the National Front Party in the 1950s under the leadership of Mohammad Mossadegh. He nationalised the British-owned oil fields and established the only nationalist and democratic government in post–Constitutional Movement Iran. Finally, the Democratic Revolution, or what some may call Islamic Revolution, in 1978–1979 followed widespread uprisings; the Pahlavi dynasty's dictatorship was overthrown after fifty-seven years of corruption and repression. It was hard for me to believe the shah had been toppled; under his dictatorship, I was accustomed to carrying a combination of hope, fear, and uncertainty. I could see and feel during and immediately after the Revolution people's happiness, joy, and sense of unification and victory. The message for me was that unthinkable change is possible.

Reflecting on these three movements' results, I felt anger, sadness, and disappointment, my heart beating fast and loud. Many people died in the process of their challenges to the regime in each case. In 1908, the newly established parliament was bombarded with Russian and British support; many constitutionalist leaders were either arrested or executed.

In 1953, following a power struggle between the shah and his popular nationalist prime minister, Mohammad Mossadegh, the CIA and British intelligence services initiated Operation Ajax with conservative Iranians and some clerics to overthrow Mossadegh. From that point, the shah maintained a close relationship with the United States.[3]

In 1953, the shah, with the direct support of the CIA, began to assemble the nucleus of a new intelligence organisation. His goal was to strengthen his regime by placing political opponents under surveillance and repressing dissident movements. In 1956, this agency was given the name SAVAK ("the country's national security and intelligence"). This hated and feared institution tortured and murdered thousands of the shah's opponents. To the shame of our family, one of my uncles worked as an undercover part-time informer for SAVAK; we avoided him. From age twelve, I knew about and was frightened of SAVAK. The feeling of terror grew in me as my political activities progressed, and it continued for about two months after the 1979 Revolution.

Shia cleric Ayatollah Khomeini, the leader of the 1979 Revolution, first came to political prominence in 1963, opposing the shah and his programme of reforms known as the "white revolution." These reforms aimed to break up clerical influence, to allow women to vote, religious minorities to hold office, and finally grant women legal equality in marital issues. It all sounded promising but was, in fact, window-dressing to enable the shah to Westernise Iran, strengthen his power, and satisfy the United States. Seeing right through this facade, Khomeini declared that the shah had embarked on the destruction of Islam in Iran. In 1963, Khomeini was sent into exile where he remained for sixteen years until the 1979 Revolution. Despite political repression, Khomeini kept relatively silent until the uprising in Iran began.

A turning point came in 1977 with the inauguration of Jimmy Carter, the new US president. Wishing to prevent radicalisation of the regime's opponents and to maintain stability in the region, Carter opened up a foreign policy to exercise power in a more benevolent way. The shah began to allow the Red Cross to visit prisons and was forced by international pressure to loosen the grips of repression. Khomeini jumped at the opportunity to exploit the widespread social discontent and political vacuum created by the brutal clampdown on democratic opposition movements. Relying on religious demagoguery and the nationwide network of likeminded mullahs, Khomeini hijacked the leadership of the antimonarchical revolution.[4]

The determination of people all over the country to overthrow the shah was crystal clear; however, being accustomed to fifty-seven years of the shah's monarchical dictatorship, they had not managed to think of a viable plan for the alternative government they wished to establish. It was crucial to develop a clear governing programme guaranteeing social justice, freedom, democracy, equality, and economic progress. This was the first and greatest lesson they learned from the antimonarchical revolution. It was not enough for people to simply say they did not want the shah's dictatorship. Rather, it should be specified in precise terms what it is that they want and what must exist instead of dictatorship.

Another significant lesson they learned was to separate religion from government and to recognise gender equality. Without equality, how can democracy develop?

ROLE OF ISLAM IN THE REVOLUTION

For the millions of Iranians who took to the streets in 1978 to vent their anger and frustration against the shah's dictatorship, the word *azadi* (freedom) carried great resonance. The demand for freedom unified a wide spectrum of the populace and soon acquired a religious connotation or collective identity. In the eyes of the average Iranian, the brutal repression and endemic corruption under the shah's rule reflected his regime's antipathy towards Islam and basic Iranian values.

Muslims comprise more than 85 percent of the population of Iran. Throughout the history of Islam, from the early decades at the start of the seventh century CE to recent times, the Iranian intelligentsia played an active role in shaping the policies and cultural identity of Islamic society.

Given Iran's religious roots and no other alternative being then viable, the desire for democracy and to overthrow dictatorship developed an Islamic character, vulnerable to the efforts of religious reactionaries and fundamentalists to exploit the unrest. These agents were able to direct political and social development towards their own ends. They cite alienation from Islam as the cause of every problem in Islamic societies and a return to "pure Islam" as the blanket solution. Under the banner of Islam, the fundamentalists impose their own views, policies, and politics while benefiting from the legitimacy religion grants them in the hearts and minds of the Muslim masses. The most obvious example is Khomeini's usurpation of the leadership of Iran's antimonarchical revolution in 1978–1979.

At the time, foreign journalists interviewed a large number of protestors including youth, white-collar workers, housewives, and merchants, all of whom aspired for the revival of Islamic values in society. All insisted that Islam would meet these demands.

For much of the general public in 1979, Islam was symbolised by such figures as Imam Hussein, the Prophet's grandson.[5] Vastly outnumbered, Hussein was slain in 680 with seventy-one of his companions at Karbala in a revolt against a corrupt ruler. For centuries, people in every town and city gathered on the anniversary of Hussein's martyrdom to follow a white horse out of the city in symbolic ceremonies honouring his memory. Political themes within these rites were often directed against contemporary rulers. At the time of writing, memories of the collective atmosphere return. I found myself among the millions who were inspired by Imam Hussein's defiant revolt against injustice. In their writings, both devout Muslims and secular intellectuals praised his struggle for freedom from the despot.

ECONOMIC FACTORS

In considering what happened in 1979, it is important to acknowledge economic factors: the role of oil. The Persian region has 65 percent of the world's total oil reserves. Under the shah, Iran was the second-largest exporter in the world. This had a significant geopolitical impact. During the 1970s, Iran's oil revenues rose steadily, levelling off in the years towards the shah's dismissal. When the shah's regime suddenly found itself short of funds to continue its ambitious plans, inflation soared. Villagers' migration to the shantytowns skirting the major cities changed the urban and economic environment. Discontent rose sharply among the exploited populace. Meanwhile the shah's family and those loyal to them deposited billions of dollars of oil revenues in foreign accounts and spent lavishly in Iran. This fractured economic foundation ignited the Revolution.

FAILURE OF THE REGIME

The success of the 1979 Iranian Revolution is considered the result of a century-long revolutionary struggle. Two principal aims of the 1979 Revolution in Iran yet to be realised are "Independence!" and "Freedom!"[6] and to establish human rights and social justice for all people.[7] Unfortunately no institutions were in place to implement these slogans. The vast majority of authors within the literature, despite different emphases, take the view that the regime failed to implement these principles.[8] Among the regime's other failures can be counted the loss of legitimacy, trust, and economic health; however, forty-two years of clerical dictatorship has provided an opportunity for many Iranians, women in particular, to develop human values in their sustained stance against injustice.

THE WOMEN'S MOVEMENT IN IRAN

We learn from history written about Iran that the people would go to almost any lengths to bring about democratic change in their country, and Iranian women have a significant role in this respect,[9] which is borne out by their history of struggle. Women played a decisive role in all three major movements against dictatorship in Iran since the nineteenth century, but the present regime completely ignores the historical evidence.[10]

In April 1912, William Morgan Shuster wrote about the role of women in Iran's constitutional revolution at that time: "The Persian women, since 1907, had become almost the most progressive, not to say radical, in the world. The women did much to keep the spirit of liberty alive."[11]

During the shah's dictatorship, women joined the organisations of freedom fighters dedicated to the downfall of the monarchy. In 1976–1977, the families and supporters of political prisoners were among the first to stage street demonstrations, sit-ins, and gatherings to demand their freedom. At a later stage, millions of women and men participated in the street protests. The role of Iranian women in the Revolution has fascinated observers throughout the world. These movements are indicative of Iranian women's potential, which has reached a climax in the movement against the regime. Although women were a potent force behind the Revolution that deposed the shah of Iran, they lost ground soon afterwards and are still struggling to regain lost rights today.

On 7 March 1979, just two weeks after the overthrow of the shah and only one day before international Women's Day, Ayatollah Khomeini proclaimed that women must observe the Islamic criteria of dress. He decreed that Iran was now an Islamic state and that women must therefore adopt the full Hijab dress code.[12] The women's movement had been preparing to celebrate their international day, and the timing of Khomeini's statement was politically very pointed. This was the first indication of the regime's views about women. Women had not yet participated in the Revolution as "women" but, instead, as members of different political and social forces. Immediately after this they found themselves treated specifically as women. Yeganeh suggests that

> the Revolution of 1979 was itself an important breaking point transforming the whole conception of women's activities and women's organization. After the Revolution, since the first Government attack on women's status and the first demonstration by women against it, the "women's question" as such first came to the fore as a question to be considered, discussed, defended or rejected.[13]

On 13 March 1979, thousands of women publicly demonstrated their opposition to Khomeini's pronouncement. In the demonstration against compulsory veiling, Muslim women played an effective role. This was very remarkable given Khomeini's previously iconic status in the eyes of the majority of the people. It is worth noting that hundreds of thousands of Muslim women found that the new regime not only excluded them from social and political life but also threatened their new emancipation. This was a turning point for women in their relationship with the new Islamic state. As indicated previously, opposition that struck at the heart of official policies and attitudes could not be tolerated by the new regime, which consequently mobilised the military and police forces. There are now more than twenty-seven police forces whose role is to monitor women everywhere to ensure adherence to the Hijab code. The government also suspended Iran's family protection law and reduced the marriageable age of girls from eighteen to thirteen years old.[14]

Hundreds of thousands of women from different layers of society and female students from schools and universities joined the political opponents of the new regime in order to defend their rights. They were found on every street corner in the country in an unprecedented campaign from 1979 to 1981. Many women, in this two-year struggle for human rights, arrived at the following conclusions: first, a belief that all women face some form of oppression or exploitation; second, that commitment was needed to uncover and understand what causes and sustains oppression in all its forms; and third, the commitment to work to end all forms of oppression was required individually and collectively in everyday life.

In April 1981, 150,000 Iranian women staged a "mothers' demonstration," demanding change for women and presenting their commitment to end their plight. The main ideological problem between the people and the regime is the women's issue, because this regime is based on gender discrimination. I will elaborate on this later.

Once the absolute suppression and mass executions began, the armed movement was born, and a new chapter opened in the history of the women's struggle in Iran. Following the 20 June 1981 massacre of demonstrators in Tehran, the state-run dailies published photographs of young girls who had been executed the previous evening, without their identities even having been established.[15] The parents were asked to identify their children. This intolerable provocation forced women to choose between resistance and obedience.

The past four decades of the regime have thus given birth to a generation of women whose progress, maturity, and ability to take on their responsibilities are dependent on eliminating all reactionary restrictions. This is not a theoretical notion but a necessity that has emerged from struggle against the fundamentalist clerical dictatorship.

The women who joined the opposition parties have succeeded in developing their role by engaging in social and political struggle. A combination of experience and academic study within the movement has matured their understanding of the situation—in a society where the ideology of the ruling regime is based on denying women's humanity. After the suppression of the women's movement, I knew some women who decided that it was too dangerous to oppose the regime; they integrated themselves into the fundamentalist society that had been established. Others could not bring themselves to abandon their ideals and, in turn, had to become extreme in order to oppose an extremist government. The smaller groups have not survived the onset of repression. Their members either joined larger groups, integrated themselves into society, or left the country altogether.[16] I will focus on the Iranian refugees later. Moving on, in the next section I highlight the cultural issues that the regime used to justify human rights violations and to deny the universal notion of these rights.

UNIVERSALISM AND CULTURAL RELATIVISM IN IRAN

What can we learn from the literature about the human rights situation in Iran? What role does religion play in the discourse? Many scholars debate the notion of universalism versus cultural relativism.[17]

The Universal Declaration of Human Rights begins this way: "Whereas recognition of the inherent dignity and equal inalienable rights of all members of the human family is the foundation of freedom, justice and peace in the world."[18]

With its strategic location, natural resources, and historical and cultural role, Iran occupies a significant historical position in the Muslim world. Nowadays, discriminatory practices towards women are built into its constitution.[19] This marks the difference between the nation's cultural tradition and values and those represented by the present regime. Since 1981, the Iranian regime has led a struggle to modify the UN Declaration of Human Rights, on the grounds that it is a secular interpretation by the Judeo-Christian tradition. The regime rules that Muslims cannot accept this above "the divine law of the country."[20]

In 1984, the Islamic Republic of Iran announced that "Iran would not recognise the validity of any international principle that was contrary to Islam."[21] The founder of the Iranian regime, Ayatollah Khomeini, declared that "what they call human rights is nothing but a collection of corrupt rules worked out by the Zionists to destroy all true religions."[22]

According to United Nations (UN) records since 1979, the Iranian regime has been condemned sixty-five times by the UN General Assembly. The regime's version of Islam is a political movement conceptualised by Khomeini's own interpretation of the Qur'an.[23] His cultural relativism argues that there are no universal human rights; rights are culture specific and culturally determined. This remains a formidable and corrosive challenge to women's rights to equality and dignity.[24]

In his 1963 book, *Tahrir-al Vasileh*,[25] Khomeini states unequivocally:

> Women are sinister creatures. If a woman refrains from providing a favourable atmo-sphere to please her husband, he has the right to beat her, and he should make her sub-mit by beating her more every day. . . . A wife should not go out of her house without her husband's consent, even if she wants to visit her family or her father or to attend a funeral.

In this medieval atmosphere, women are of scant human value. Married women require their husbands' permission to apply for a passport, and there is no legal protection for victims of domestic violence, which is difficult to escape through divorce.[26] Is the suffering inflicted on the women and girls of Iran "cultural" or "criminal"?

THE IDEOLOGICAL FOUNDATION
OF THE IRANIAN REGIME

Islamic Fundamentalism

The term *fundamentalism* originated in the United States in the 1920s. As the pace of social change accelerated, Protestant Christians felt threatened by increas-ing criticism of the Bible and the spread of philosophical scepticism. *The Concise Oxford Dictionary* defines fundamentalism as the "strict maintenance of ancient or fundamental doctrines of any religion, especially Islam."[27] However problematic this formula, it does acknowledge that fundamentalism in Islam is today the most vis-ible and influential of all fundamentalisms. Increasingly these days, we hear about it from the Western media, the policy makers, and many an intellectual, as the term is widely used without a universally accepted definition.

What is fundamentalist Islam? Martin Kramer, an American scholar on the Middle East, writes:

> On the one hand, it manifests itself as a new religiosity, reaffirming faith in a transcen-dent God. On the other hand, it appears as a militant ideology, demanding political action now. [. . .] One day its spokesmen call for a jihad (sacred war) against the West, evoking the deepest historic resentments. Another day, its leaders appeal for reconcilia-tion with the West, emphasizing shared values.[28]

Their idea is simple: Islam must have power in this world. It is the true religion—the religion of God—and its truth is manifest in its power. Islam provides the one and only solution to all questions in this world, from public policy to private con-duct. It is not merely a religion in the Western sense of a system of belief in God. It possesses an immutable law, revealed by God, that covers every aspect of life, and it is an ideology, a complete system of belief about the organisation of the state and the world. This law and ideology can only be implemented through the establishment of a truly Islamic state, under the sovereignty of God. The empowerment of Islam, which is God's plan for mankind, is a sacred end.

Amos Perlmutter, who was a professor of political science at American University, writes: "Islamic fundamentalism is an aggressive revolutionary movement as militant and violent as the Bolshevik, Fascist, and Nazi movements of the past. It is authoritarian, anti-democratic, anti-secular, and its goal is the establishment of a 'totalitarian Islamic state' in the Middle East."[29]

From a historical perspective, the roots of Islamic fundamentalism go back to the first centuries of Islam. In modern times and during the twentieth century, too, fundamentalist movements sprang up in different parts of the world as isolated, weak movements. But what we call Islamic fundamentalism today came to prominence with the rise to power of Khomeini in Iran in 1979 and began to have an impact on the Middle East and the world. Iran enjoys a unique position in the world of Islam due to its strategic location, natural resources, and historical and cultural role in the development of Islamic civilization, among other factors. These factors provide the fundamentalist currents with inspirational, political, regional, and international support, similar to the way the October Revolution victory of Russia's Bolsheviks made that movement a global one. Until the demise of the Soviet Union, even those Marxist parties that had ideological differences with Moscow used to get their credibility from it.

It was Ruhollah Khomeini (1902–1989) who finally formulated the ideological basis for the first successful fundamentalist revolution in Islam. He transformed the idea of creating a global Islamic rule from an unachievable ideal to an achievable goal through many fundamentalist groups, which, in turn, gave these groups global backing. Khomeini was the first ruler of a Muslim state since 1258—the year of the conquest of Baghdad by the Mongol ruler Hulagu Khan—to wield both political and religious power. He made a breakthrough with his claim that only the individuals most learned in Islamic law can rule: "Since Islamic government is a government of law, knowledge of the law is necessary for the ruler, as has traditionally been laid down. The ruler must surpass all others in knowledge, and be more learned than everyone else."[30] Since no existing state had such a ruler, Khomeini's doctrine constituted an appeal for region-wide revolution, to overturn every extant form of authority and replace it with rule by Islamic jurists.[31] The major difference between the various types of Islamic fundamentalism and the Iranian version is that the latter considers *velayat-e faqih* as a pillar of Islamic fundamentalism, as we will consider in the following section.

Velayat-e Faqih

The Iranian regime is based on the principle of *velayat-e faqih*. It derives its justification and theoretical basis from *fiqh* (jurisprudence), which encompasses all aspects of individual and social life.[32] A review of this system demonstrates that the pillar of this school of thought is the idea that the male is the superior sex and hence the female is a slave at his service. This approach negates women.

Khomeini, in his letter to Ali Khamenei, wrote:

> The vali-e-faqih is empowered to abrogate the religious commitments he has undertaken with the people should he find them contrary to the interests of the nation and Islam. Governing is one dimension of the absolute authority of the velayat-e faqih and takes precedence over all secondary commandments, even prayer and fasting.[33]

The government of Khomeini and his successors is based on a theory of government called *velayat-e faqih*, literally meaning the guardianship of the religious jurist. The essence of the theory, developed and applied by Khomeini, is that one man with a thorough knowledge of Islamic law is designated as *vali-e faqih*, heir to the Prophet Muhammad. No public or private matter concerning a Muslim or anyone living in the Islamic world is beyond the *vali*'s jurisdiction.

Velayat-e faqih is, in fact, the essence of the Iranian mullahs' Islamic Republic. Incorporated into the constitution after the shah's overthrow, the immense powers bestowed on the *vali-e faqih* have been expanded since Khomeini's death. An understanding of exactly what the doctrine of *velayat-e faqih* is and how it functions is essential to understanding the theocracy in Iran and its drive to export fundamentalism.

The abolition in 1924 of the Ottoman Caliphate by Turkey's Great National Assembly was a turning point in contemporary Islamic history. For centuries, the Ottoman sultans had proclaimed themselves to be caliphs, the absolute civil and religious leaders of Muslims. Although the Ottomans governed only part of the Islamic world and their authority was challenged even within their empire, the abolition of the Caliphate generated profound debate among a wide spectrum of Islamic political thinkers. Various theories and hypotheses emerged on the role of religion in the Islamic community. In Egypt, for example, a group of Sunni fundamentalists put forward the thesis of the "Islamic state."

Nearly a half century later, in 1970, Khomeini published his absolutist views on the Islamic state. At the time, Khomeini could not have foreseen that he would one day be able to put his theory into practice. His book, titled *Velayat-e faqih* (Islamic Government), is essentially limited to a general discourse on the necessity of the Muslim *ummah* (nation) being ruled by "just theologians." Most of the Shi'ite clergy strongly opposed Khomeini's doctrine, saying it contradicted the principles of Islam. Among them were Shaiat Madari, Taleghani, and Montazeri, who held positions of significant clerical authority, equivalent to that of Ayatollah Khomeini himself. He stated: "In terms of his responsibility and status, the guardian of a nation is no different from the guardian of a minor."[34]

This dismissal of the notion of popular will characterised Khomeini's rule, during which he repeatedly declared that if the entire population advocated something to which he was opposed, he would nevertheless do as he saw fit. Misogyny is inherent to the theory of *velayat-e faqih* (the absolute supremacy of clerical rule), upon which the mullahs' dictatorship is based, and comprises the most fundamental characteristic of the system's internal policy.

Before the shah's overthrow, Khomeini had promised in Paris that the constitution of the future regime would be determined by a popularly elected constituent assembly. Well aware, however, that such an assembly would never support his absolutist doctrine, once in Tehran Khomeini replaced the promised constituent assembly with a smaller body called the Assembly of Experts, chiefly composed of mullahs close to his line of thinking. They drafted a constitution that incorporated the principle of *velayat-e faqih*.

The preamble to the constitution ratified by the Assembly of Experts notes: "Based on the principle of the Guardianship of the Islamic State and the leadership of the Muslim Nation, the Constitution provides a basis for the leadership of a fully qualified faqih whom the people consider as leader, to ensure that no institution deviates from its Islamic mandate."[35] Principle 4 elaborates on the mechanism by which the *vali-e faqih* has universal jurisdiction, providing quasi-legal justification to the supremacy of the *vali*'s will over the law: "All civil, penal, monetary, cultural, military, and political laws must be based on the Islamic principles."[36] Naturally, the interpretation of what is or is not an "Islamic principle" falls within the authority of the *vali-e faqih* and the Council of Guardians, another body of mullahs appointed by the *vali-e faqih*. Despite the superficial separation of the three branches of government, the constitution delegates their control entirely to the *vali-e faqih*. Principle 57 says: "The legislative, executive, and judicial branches in the Islamic Republic of Iran are under the supervision of the vali-e-faqih and the Imam of the Islamic ummah."[37] Since supreme religious and political authority rests in the hands of one person, the imam's power far exceeds that of any contemporary head of state. Principle 110 of the constitution specifies that the *vali-e faqih*'s absolute powers extend to every sphere—political, economic, legislative, executive, administrative, social, judicial, and military—and he indeed represents God on earth in the eyes of his supporters. Accordingly, no civil or military affair falls beyond the *vali-e faqih*'s jurisdiction.

A failure properly to understand this fact has caused many politicians, academics, and others to misinterpret differences displayed by various prominent representatives of the regime: these have been essentially nuances, or differences of style, and have not represented any substantive policy changes. It is of crucial importance to realise that, despite their disagreements and conflicts, they all share the same commitment and loyalty to *vali-e faqih*. This is why nobody within the regime can be relied on to bring about any real change in Iran, particularly when it comes to women's rights.

In conclusion, it is appropriate to refer to the words of Ahmad Azari-Qomi, a senior conservative cleric, who laid out the theoretical basis of such absolute rule in a series of newspaper editorials:

> The velayat-e-faqih means absolute religious and legal guardianship of the people by the faqih. This guardianship applies to the entire world and all that exists in it, whether

earthbound or flying creatures, inanimate objects, plants, animals, and anything in any way related to collective or individual human life, all human affairs, belongings, or assets. It also applies to God's religion, whether the primary and secondary commandments, worship, politics, social or family affairs and obligations, or what Islam recommends, tolerates or prohibits.[38]

THE DISCRIMINATORY GENDER
ATTITUDE OF THE IRANIAN REGIME

The version of *velayat-e faqih* practised for the past four decades in Iran is extreme in its treatment of women, since gender apartheid is a fundamental concept and principle. Gender discrimination is a driving force for the regime, for which reason any relaxation of the restrictions undermines the regime in its entirety.

The mullahs believe that women lack the mental capacity to make choices, thus denying them an undeniably human characteristic. On this basis, they deny women the right to make judgements, thereby excluding them from the bench (where verdicts are issued) and from the presidency.

From the fundamentalist mullahs' perspective, sexual vice and virtue are core principles. The most ignoble and unforgivable of all sins is sexual wrongdoing. Piety, chastity, and decency are basically measured by sex-related yardsticks. Seldom do they apply to the political or social realms. Purity or corruption is, in one way or another, related to sex. When such a value system evolves into the social norm, the walls of sexual segregation become even taller, thicker, and ubiquitous. For Khomeini and his retinue, gender is the primary distinction. They view woman as the embodiment of sexual desire, the source of sin, and the manifestation of Satan. She must be kept out of the public view at all times, reserving her for use, under the absolute domination of men, for sexual pleasure and reproduction. In this system of values, a woman is not considered a human being, although as a concession, she has been described on a par with children and the mentally unbalanced.

Inequality of men and women and violations of women's rights—and even their suppression—take place in many other parts of the world, but in Iran these have become systematic and legal. According to the Home Office report on violence against women, its causes, and consequences,

> Violence against women in Iran is ingrained in gender inequality, which is upheld and perpetuated by two factors: (a) patriarchal values and attitudes based on notions of male supremacy, and (b) a State-promoted institutional structure based on gender-biased, hard-line interpretations of Islamic principles.[39]

The discrimination starts from the regime's constitution and extends to its civil and penal codes. Consequently, women are subjected to constant and systematic pressure in all political, social, and private realms.

The constitution explicitly states, "the president can only be a man."[40] Prior to the June 2005 presidential elections, the Council of Guardians excluded all but eight of the 1,014 candidates who registered, including all women. Women are barred from serving as certain types of judges, as per Article 163 of the constitution, which states: "the qualifications required to become a judge are determined by law in accordance with religious norms."[41] The inclusion in the constitution of terms such as "religious norms" is a device that enables the regime to pass despotic laws discriminating against women. The denial of women's right to "issue verdicts" is an inviolable principle. One month after the victory of the antimonarchical revolution, a bill to reform the Ministry of Justice was passed; sweeping purges were launched accordingly, and many female judges were dismissed.

Many Islamic jurists, however, historically held the opposite view, such as Abi J'afar Muhammad ibn Jarir al-Tabari (ca. 839–923 CE), a prominent jurist and the author of the *Annals*, or history of the world, by far the most important historical source for the early history of Islam. Later Muslim historians made use of and built on Al-Tabari's *Annals*. He emphasises that since women are allowed to master *Ijtihad* (broadly speaking, *ijtihad* means an authority in matters of Islam) they can also become judges, just like men. Allamé Helli (d. 1405 CE), a key Shi'ite jurist of his time, wrote in *Nahjol-Haq* (The Path of Truth) that there is no consensus that judges must be male. Ayatollah Hossein Ali Montazeri, who is perhaps the highest-ranking Shi'ite cleric alive, also rejects any such consensus among Muslim clergy, saying: "In all the books of citations from the infallible Imams I have studied, I have not encountered such a matter."[42]

According to Article 102 of the Islamic Punishments Act, "During stoning, a man is put into a ditch up to his waist and a woman up to her chest." The significance of this distinction becomes clear in light of the fact that the law also says that if a person who is to be stoned manages to escape, he or she will be allowed to go free. Since it is easier for a man to escape, the discrimination is literally a matter of life and death. According to a report by Amnesty International USA, in 2008 nine Iranian women were under sentence of execution by stoning.[43]

IRANIAN WOMEN LEAD THE FORCE FOR CHANGE

In asking the question, "What is the solution to the problems in Iran?" it is essential to observe that the women's movement in Iran has already decided. It is necessary, then, to examine their solution, which was arrived at two years ago. As I mentioned earlier, Ayatollah Khomeini's pronouncement concerning the Hijab dress code came only two weeks after the Revolution had been successfully concluded. There were many acute problems in Iran at the time, but Khomeini's pronouncement addressed the core of his future plans for government. This demonstrates that the most important thing for any leader of the regime is the women's issue, and because of his powerful position he can shape the whole system on this basis. In other words, the women's issue is pivotal to policies of government. A fundamentalist regime with absolute power could only be set up if Iranians stopped attempting to promote their human rights. Gender discrimination is the pillar and defining characteristic of the mullah's regime.

Throughout the last century, Iranian women played major roles in all three movements from 1890 to 1979. In the Revolution against the shah of Iran,

> for the first time in the history of political struggles in Iran women took part side by side with men and in similar numbers . . . women have been the centre of attention for both the past-Revolutionary State and the oppositional forces. The massive participation of women in the Revolution of 1979 seems to be the main reason behind this interest.[44]

Women's exclusion from decision-making and political power was crucial for the establishment of the Islamic fundamentalist state. Hugely disappointed by this pronouncement, women actively sought a solution, a means of reversing the Ayatollah's decision. For two years, Iranian women adopted peaceful methods to promote their rights: they held seminars, published their ideas, and educated themselves so as to better understand the origins of the mullahs' attitude. Violation of women's rights on a daily basis and the extent of the repression helped the activists to understand the issue in a practical way.

Peaceful public demonstrations of dissent were organised, and women took every opportunity to promote their cause. Between the years 1979 and 1981, the two sides were entrenched. The mullahs regarded the women's views as incompatible with their notion of government, and the women persisted in their efforts to influence and change the political future. This period of political standoff ended on 20 June 1981, when Khomeini ordered his religious guards to open fire on a peaceful demonstration in Tehran. Half a million people had met to demonstrate that day, with mothers in the front line, to signify the determined but peaceful intention of the demonstration. After June 1981, Iranian women realised that their peaceful attempt to negotiate had failed, and the movement entered a new phase. Some felt forced to work under the rule of the mullahs in order to avoid prison torture and execution: their aim was to reform the fundamentalist law. Others felt that the mullahs would never give them the opportunity to promote women's rights and decided to change the situation radically to force the mullahs to change their discriminatory law completely. Since the women's movement divided in 1981, it is clear that the group who attempted to bring about reform from within have failed to do so. For example, in March 2006 Human Rights Watch reported: "Iranian police and plainclothes agents yesterday charged a peaceful assembly of women's rights activists in Tehran and beat hundreds of women and men who had gathered to commemorate International Women's Day."[45] According to the 2007 Home Office report,

> Activists on women's issues expressed concern that the woman selected by President Ahmadinejad to lead the Centre for Women's Participation, which is affiliated with the office of the president, does not have a background in women's issues. In addition

the government changed the name of the organization to the Centre for Women and Family, raising concern that the organization sought to reorient debate on women's problems to focus only on those related to the home.[46]

It is arguable that the position of women has been further undermined since 1981. However, according to the United Nations Special Rapporteur on violence against women, its causes, and consequences, in his report of the Mission to Iran dated 27 January 2006:

> This has been the source of divisive debates in the political arena between the hardliners and the reformists. The Sixth Majlis was reportedly a turning point for the articulation of reformist politics of gender in Iran. Within this process . . . some positive change has occurred in the laws and the administration of justice. However, gender-biased provisions and practices that prompt women's vulnerability to violence in the private as well as public spheres are still the norm.[47]

The age of marriage for girls is still thirteen, and stoning and hangings continue as before. The more radical women joined opposition groups already in existence. These of course were themselves traditional and, therefore, male dominated. By sacrificing their time and family, the women, working tirelessly and effectively, showed the opposition groups that they needed their help: without total and egalitarian cooperation, the determined political stance of the mullahs would be too strong to overturn. Women have thus gradually assumed a number of leadership positions. It is clearly impossible for groups in opposition to the mullahs—who espouse policies that discriminate against women—to adhere to such policies themselves. This has compelled the opposition groups to declare their support for women's rights, both now and in the future. Further, having attained positions of leadership women were able to attend meetings abroad. This in turn has led to an international promotion of the cause of women as well as Iranian freedom; the resulting publicity has attracted the attention of prominent political figures from various human rights groups around the world. Thus, the women's cause in Iran has obtained international support.

To achieve leadership, women had to break down many historical, psychological, and cultural barriers that traditionally humiliated and oppressed them. They were able to target the heart of misogyny—namely, the negation of women's human identity and qualifications to lead society—by maximising their sense of responsibility and commitment. Their convictions caused the men to abandon doubts about the competence of the women who fought alongside them for liberty. This was a major step towards equality, immediately followed by a massive eruption of energies. When these women overcame their historical humiliation and oppression, they released a tremendous, constructive force. They left behind the world of "the weaker sex": they believed that they were free, equal human beings; that they were not created for men, nor identified by them; that they were no one's possession; and that they owned their bodies, lives, and emotions. The corollary is that men attain their liberation by stepping down from their unjust domination and forgoing their aggressiveness. It is only then that men, as well as women, can achieve equality. In the opposition groups, the women's resolve, extreme sense of responsibility, willingness to learn, commitment to discipline, and selfless dedication brought a new sense of caring and humanity to the working environment. Their example has inspired many women in Iran and indeed throughout the world. The progress of women in decision-making and leadership positions in one part of the world will influence the rest. For example, people in numerous countries, including Iceland, Germany, Chile, Liberia, and Finland, have appointed a woman to lead their respective governments. Theirs is an achievement for all women. The experiences of the opposition movement in Iran are further proof of women's crucial role in the struggle against fundamentalism.

Since the Revolution, the mullahs have worked constantly to establish a fundamentalist society, ideally with majority public support. The persistent and large-scale opposition, however, means that, far from cementing a secure system, the mullahs have largely failed in their motherland, thanks to women. Iranian women have been historically exploited and suppressed, and their motivation and perseverance in the struggle to gain equality is unsurpassed. Their unwavering commitment confirms that women are the growing political force of our times.

Iran's ruling fundamentalists consider their doctrine universal—they therefore do not stop at oppressing and humiliating Iranian women and are the foremost advocates of misogyny around the world. The mullahs have tried to present their views as those of Islam versus the West. But the opposition movement in many cases led by women has ensured the establishment of an international network, which has redressed the problem as fundamentalism versus the democratic world. The women's movement in Iran has been able to communicate their collective experience to women's rights and human rights movements at a truly international level.

Women are now the centre of attention for both the regime and the opposition forces. Women comprise more than 50 percent of the leadership of many opposition parties against the Iranian regime. It is worth noting that some are Muslim. The achievements of Iranian women within the ranks of the movement against the ruling fundamentalists need to be studied. After all these years of struggle against the reactionaries, women hold key positions of leadership among the antifundamentalists. This growing force of women in leadership positions inspires women in Iranian society on a large scale to aspire to democratic change and transforms them into a major force to liberate Iran.

On 15 November 2019, the Religious Guards news agency, Fars, wrote about the role of women's leadership on the uprising of hundreds of thousands of Iranians from two hundred cities: "Women's special role in running and leading the recent riots seemed remarkable. In numerous places particularly in Tehran suburbs, women who were apparently between thirty to thirty-five years old, had a special role in leading the riots." The riots were triggered by the tripling of fuel prices and immediately mushroomed into political demands for regime change.[48]

At least fifteen hundred people were killed, four hundred of them women, while about eight thousand were injured and some twelve thousand arrested. Many of the wounded were arrested, and many of those arrested were tortured. Some detainees have even been sentenced to death. Many thousands of people were nonetheless able to escape to neighbouring countries such as Turkey in the hope of obtaining refugee status.

IRANIAN REFUGEES

At least 79.5 million people around the world have been forced to flee their homes. Among them are nearly twenty-six million refugees; roughly half of them are under the age of eighteen. There are also millions of stateless people, who have been denied a nationality and lack access to basic rights such as education, health care, employment, and freedom of movement.[49]

The world is now experiencing its biggest refugee crisis in recorded history.[50] The Middle East and North Africa region has become the focus of some significant intersecting topics in the contemporary scholarly discourse about refugees and their rights.[51] In Britain, the debate about asylum seekers and refugees is at the centre of political concerns.[52]

I began by asking these questions: What is a political refugee? What has been written about his or her experience? My initial intention was to study the literature in relation to four defined stages of my participants' experiences: life in Iran prior to their escape, the escape process, adaptation to resettlement in Britain, and finally their current situation and future plans. After extensive research, however, I was unable to find any academic study about Iranian political refugees' lived experiences in Britain. I therefore opened up my reading to include the experience of Iranian political refugees in other countries and refugees more generally. My main emphasis was on the psychological aspect of their overall experience.

Does the available literature give us a clear picture of the actual conditions for political refugees? In the light of phenomenology, how do they perceive themselves? How do they describe their experiences? What was it like for Iranian political refugees before they left their homeland? How did it feel when they first arrived in the United Kingdom, and what did they think their way of life might be? How would they describe their present situation, and what have they learned? What do they hope for in the years to come? Being a political refugee myself, I conducted my study as an insider and involved my participants' subjective experience. In the literature, however, most research studies are conducted from outside.

Mass movements of Iranian refugees have been recorded for many centuries. The best known of these was the Zoroastrian community's arrival in Gujarat in India following the Arab invasion in 936 CE.[53] Another collective group persecuted for their beliefs were the Bahá'ís who fled to Turkey in the mid-nineteenth century.[54]

Since the 1979 Revolution, which ended more than fifty years of the Pahlavi regime, around four million Iranians—mainly intellectuals, well-educated professionals, and human rights activists—were forced to escape their homeland.[55] This has continued up until the present day and is comprehensively documented within the social-political context. To what extent has this phenomenon been studied from a psychological perspective?

In much of the literature, the terms *asylum seeker* and *refugee* are used interchangeably. An asylum seeker has crossed international borders to seek safety and applies for refugee status under the 1951 UN Convention. A refugee is a person whose application has been successful.[56] In addition, most of the existing literature not only fails to recognise different types of refugee but also conflates those who have left Iran without differentiating refugees from emigrants.[57] For example, many who left their country were not necessarily motivated to change the political situation. Many intellectuals and professionals seeking a more congenial environment for their work were able to leave the country legally. In 2009, the International Monetary Fund reported the world's highest rate of brain drain from Iran: an emigration of 180,000 educated, skilled individuals.[58] Some suggest that, following the Revolution, political factors contributed greatly to this exodus.[59]

WHAT IMPELS SO MANY TO FLEE IRAN?

Within weeks of Khomeini's founding the new regime, his supporters and clerics took control of administrative, police, and judicial functions in the cities and in the state. Executions of high-ranking army officers and civilian officials from the shah's regime began. Those who played a significant role in the revolution against the shah faced persecution. This period saw the first waves of refugee exodus, mainly to the United States.

During the second year of the Islamic regime, the Iran-Iraq War began in September 1980 and lasted eight years, making it the longest conventional war of the twentieth century. Mobilisation for the war and other related emergency measures increased the undisputed dominance of Khomeini and helped firmly establish the new regime, which hoped by persistently pursuing the war to export the Revolution to neighbouring Muslim countries. The results were 680,000 dead and missing, more than 1.5 million wounded, nearly two million refugees, enormous loss of property, and complete disruption of the economy.[60] International writers have documented this extensively.

Over forty years, hundreds of thousands of political and human rights activists have been imprisoned and tortured; they include students, writers, journalists, teachers, lecturers, workers, clerics, artists, filmmakers, and members of religious and ethnic minorities. Their families were harassed, and their properties were confiscated and pensions suspended, leaving them destitute. It has become routine for people to be put behind bars without charge and without the right to defend themselves before a proper court of law. The number of individuals executed for their political beliefs totals more than 120,000, by conservative estimates. Public floggings, stoning to death, the cutting off of fingers, and the gouging of eyes are commonplace in the country.[61] Millions of Iranians have therefore risked their lives to escape from Iran and to gain freedom. Although the United Nations, Amnesty International, and the foreign ministries of European countries document these human rights violations, I found insufficient coverage of the experiences of individual victims.

This chapter provides a sociopolitical and historical background for Iranian political refugees' experiences, which will be explored in the following chapters. Over more than a century the Iranians' struggle for freedom, democracy, and equality included periods of victory. The Constitutional Revolution in 1906 established a parliament for the first time in Iran's history. In the 1950s, the movement under Mohammad Mossadegh nationalised British-owned oil companies and established a short-lived democratic government. The Revolution in 1979 overthrew fifty-seven years of shah dictatorship. Tyranny and human rights violations had prevailed, replacing the brief victories, which failed except for short periods. The struggle for democracy and equality rose repeatedly from the ashes. Regarding the recent history as a whole, I think valuable lessons were learned to differentiate progressive Islam from fundamentalism and to recognise the peril in mixing religion with government.

Furthermore, it is clear that many Iranians, particularly women, have been enabled to develop and sustain their commitment against injustice and to deepen the democratic ideal within the collective Iranian psyche. This resource may serve as a model for the Middle East region and worldwide.

The violation of human rights under the clerical regime cost millions of lives and created a massive refugee exodus.

NOTES

1. Dick Blackwell, *Counselling and Psychotherapy with Refugees* (London: Jessica Kingsley, 2005); Helen Taylor, *Refugees and the Meaning of Home: Cypriot Narratives of Loss, Longing and Daily Life in London* (Basingstoke: Palgrave Macmillan, 2015).

2. Hamideh Sedghi, *Women and Politics in Iran: Veiling, Unveiling, and Reveiling* (New York: Cambridge University Press, 2007).

3. Mark J. Gasiorowski and Malcolm Byrne, *Mohammad Mosaddeq and the 1953 Coup in Iran* (New York. Syracuse University Press, 2015); Stephen Kinzer, *All the Shah's Men: An American Coup and the Roots of Middle East Terror* (New York: Wiley, 2008).

4. Behrooz Ghamari-Tabrizi, *Foucault in Iran: Islamic Revolution after the Enlightenment* (Minneapolis: University of Minnesota Press, 2016); Mohammad Mohaddessin, *Islamic Fundamentalism: The New Global Threat* (Santa Ana, CA: Seven Lochs Press, 1993).

5. Amin Sharifi Isaloo, *Power, Legitimacy and the Public Sphere: The Iranian Ta'ziyeh Theatre Ritual* (London: Routledge, 2017).

6. Mehdi Semati, *Media, Culture and Society in Iran: Living with Globalization and the Islamic State* (London: Routledge, 2007).

7. Anoushiravan Ehteshami and Reza Molavi, *Iran and the International System* (London: Routledge, 2012).

8. Reza Afshari, *Human Rights in Iran: The Abuse of Cultural Relativism* (Pittsburgh: University of Pennsylvania Press, 2011); Ehteshami and Molavi, *Iran and the International System*; Haleh Esfandiari, *Reconstructed Lives: Women and Iran's Islamic Revolution* (Washington, DC: Woodrow Wilson Center Press, 1997); Manouchehr Ganji, *Defying the Iranian Revolution: From a Minister to the Shah to a Leader of Resistance* (Portsmouth, NH: Greenwood, 2002); Ali

Gheissari and Vali Nasr, *Democracy in Iran: History and the Quest for Liberty* (Oxford: Oxford University Press, 2009); Eric J. Hooglund, *Twenty Years of Islamic Revolution: Political and Social Transition in Iran since 1979* (New York: Syracuse University Press, 2002); Mohaddessin, *Islamic Fundamentalism*; Reza Pahlavi, *Winds of Change: The Future of Democracy in Iran* (Washington, DC: Regnery, 2001); Manshour Varasteh, *Understanding Iran's National Security Doctrine* (Beauchamp: Troubador, 2013).

9. Pahlavi, *Winds of Change*; Ali Mirsepassi, *Democracy in Modern Iran: Islam, Culture, and Political Change* (New York: New York University Press, 2010); Varasteh, *Understanding Iran's National Security Doctrine*; Barbara Ann Rieffer-Flanagan, *Evolving Iran: An Introduction to Politics and Problems in the Islamic Republic* (Washington, DC: Georgetown University Press, 2013).

10. Esfandiari, *Reconstructed Lives*; Kinzer, *All the Shah's Men*.

11. William Morgan Shuster, *The Strangling of Persia* (New York: Greenwood, 1968), 191.

12. April Fast, *Iran, the People* (New York: Crabtree, 2005); Sedghi, *Women and Politics in Iran*.

13. Nahid Yeganeh and Azar Tabari, *In the Shadow of Islam: The Women's Movement in Iran* (London: Zed Press, 1982), 35.

14. Mahmood Monshipouri, *Inside the Islamic Republic: Social Change in Post-Khomeini Iran* (Oxford: Oxford University Press, 2016).

15. Owen Bowcott, "Tribunal to Investigate 1980s Massacre of Political Prisoners in Iran," *Guardian*, 18 October 2012, https://www.theguardian.com/world/2012/oct/18/iran-tribunal-investigates-massacre.

16. Armin H. Danesh, "Gender Discrimination and Women's Movement for Equality in Iran" (MA thesis, North London University, 2007).

17. Edward Burnett Tylor, *Primitive Culture* (London: John Murray, 1992 [1871]); M. Martha C. Nussbaum, *Sex & Social Justice* (New York: Oxford University Press, 1999); Maryam Poya, "Double Exile, Iranian Women and Fundamentalism," in *Refusing Holy Orders: Women and Fundamentalism in Britain*, ed. Nira Yuval-Davis and Gita Sahgal (London: Virago, 2000); Alison Assiter, *Revisiting Universalism* (Basingstoke: Palgrave Macmillan, 2003); Gideon Calder, "Soft Universalisms: Beyond Young and Rorty on Difference," *Critical Review of International Social and Political Philosophy* 9, no. 1 (2006): 3–21; Hannah Arendt, *The Human Condition* (Chicago: University of Chicago Press, 2013); Jack Donnelly, *International Human Rights: Dilemmas in World Politics*, 4th ed. (New York: Westview, 2013).

18. "Universal Declaration of Human Rights," United Nations, 1948, https://www.un.org/en/about-us/universal-declaration-of-human-rights.

19. Hamid Algar, *Constitution of the Islamic Republic of Iran*, translated from Persian (Berkeley, CA: Mizan, 1980).

20. David G. Littman, "Human Rights and Human Wrongs," *National Review*, 19 January 2003, https://www.nationalreview.com/2003/01/human-rights-and-human-wrongs-david-g-littman/.

21. Michael Freeman, *Human Rights* (Cambridge: Polity Press, 2005), 53.

22. Barbara Ann Rieffer-Flanagan, *Evolving Iran* (Washington, DC: Georgetown University Press, 2013), 134.

23. Mohaddessin, *Islamic Fundamentalism*.

24. Assiter, *Revisiting Universalism*.

25. Ruhollah M. Khomeini, *Tahrir-al Vasileh* (Tehran: Islamic Publication, 1963), 305–6.

26. Yakin Ertürk, "Report of the Special Rapporteur on Violence against Women, Its Causes and Consequences: Mission of the Islamic Republic of Iran," UN Human Rights Council, 2006, https://digitallibrary.un.org/record/566706?ln=en; Freedom House, *Freedom in the World 2020: The Annual Survey on Political Rights and Civil Liberties* (London: Rowman & Littlefield, 2020).

27. *The Concise Oxford Dictionary of Current English* (1990), s.v. "fundamentalism."

28. Martin Kramer, "Fundamentalist Islam: The Drive for Power," Martin Kramer on the Middle East, https://martinkramer.org/reader/archives/fundamentalist-islam-the-drive-for-power/.

29. Amos Perlmutter, "Wishful Thinking about Islamic Fundamentalism," *Washington Post*, 19 January 1992.

30. Ruhollah Khomeini, *Islam and Revolution: Writings and Declarations of Imam Khomeini*, trans. Hamid Algar (Berkeley, CA: Mizan, 1981), 59.

31. Mohaddessin, *Islamic Fundamentalism*.

32. Arshin Adib-Moghaddam, *A Critical Introduction to Khomeini* (New York: Cambridge University Press, 2014).

33. Khomeini, 1988, quoted in Mohaddessin, *Islamic Fundamentalism*, 17.

34. Ruhollah M. Khomeini, *Velayat-e-faqih* (Najaf: Islamic Publication, 1971), 63.

35. *Constitution of the Islamic Republic of Iran* (Qom: Center for Islamic Publications, 1979), 9.

36. *Constitution of the Islamic Republic of Iran*, 17.

37. M. Mahmood, *The Political System of the Islamic Republic of Iran* (Delhi: Kalpaz Publications, 2006), 151.

38. Ole Høiris and Sefa Martin Yürükel, *Contrasts and Solutions in the Middle East* (Aarhus: Aarhus University Press, 1997), 228.

39. Border & Immigration Agency, "Country of Origin Information Report: Iran," Home Office, 4 May 2007, https://www.refworld.org/docid/465be2b72.html.

40. N. Rasa'i-nia, *Constitution of the Islamic Republic of Iran*, vol. 1 (Tehran: Saman Publications, 1996).

41. Rasa'i-nia, *Constitution of the Islamic Republic of Iran*.

42. National Council of Resistance of Iran: Committee on Women, Misogyny in Power: Iranian Women Challenge Two Decades of Mullahs 'Gender Apartheid (Paris: National Council of Resistance of Iran: Committee on Women), 26.

43. Amnesty International, "IRAN: End Executions by Stoning," 13 January 2008, https://www.amnesty.org/download/Documents/56000/mde130012008en.pdf.

44. Yeganeh and Tabari, *In the Shadow of Islam*, 26.

45. "Iran: Police Attack Women's Day Celebration," Human Rights Watch, 8 March 2006, https://www.hrw.org/news/2006/03/08/iran-police-attack-womens-day-celebration.

46. Border & Immigration Agency, "Country of Origin Information Report: Iran."

47. Border & Immigration Agency, "Country of Origin Information Report: Iran."

48. "Women's Role in Leading Iran's November Protests," Iran Focus, 17 November 2020, https://www.iranfocus.com/en/protests/45570-womens-role-in-leading-irans-november-2019-protests/; Reuters Staff, "Special Report: Iran's Leader Ordered Crackdown on Unrest—'Do Whatever It Takes to End It,'" Reuters, 23 December 2019, https://www.reuters.com/article/us-iran-protests-specialreport-idUSKBN1YR0QR.

49. "Figures at a Glance," United Nations High Commissioner for Refugees, 18 June 2020, https://www.unhcr.org/uk/figures-at-a-glance.html.

50. Sasha Chanoff and David Chanoff, *From Crisis to Calling: Finding Your Moral Center in the Toughest Decisions* (Oakland, CA: Berrett-Koehler, 2016).

51. Ahsan Ullah, *Refugee Politics in the Middle East and North Africa: Human Rights, Safety, and Identity* (New York: Springer, 2014).

52. Renos K. Papadopoulos, *Therapeutic Care for Refugees: No Place Like Home* (London: Karnac Books, 2002).

53. Mary Boyce, *Zoroastrians: Their Religious Beliefs and Practices* (London; Boston: Routledge; Kegan Paul, 1986), 157, 166.

54. Ahmad Kasravi, *Bahaii-gari* (Tehran: Peyman Press, 1943), 33–40; Edward Granville Browne, *A Year amongst the Persians* (London: Adam and Charles Black, 1959), 111–12, 226, 352.

55. Suleyman Elik, *Iran–Turkey Relations, 1979–2011: Conceptualising the Dynamics of Politics, Religion and Security in Middle-Power States* (Abingdon: Routledge, 2013).

56. Helen McColl, Kwame McKenzie, and Kamaldeep Bhui, "Mental Healthcare of Asylum-Seekers and Refugees," *Advances in Psychiatric Treatment* 14, no. 6 (November 2008): 452–59.

57. Linda Morrice, *Being a Refugee: Learning and Identity. A Longitudinal Study of Refugees in the UK* (London: Trentham Books, 2011); Mammad Aidani, "Displaced Narratives of Iranian Migrants and Refugees: Constructions of Self and the Struggle for Representation" (Doctoral diss., Victoria University, 2007).

58. Varasteh, *Understanding Iran's National Security Doctrine*; Amir Mohammad Sohrabian and Mohammad Amin Sohrabian, "Comparison Analysis of Financial Freedom of the Republic of Kazakhstan with the Islamic Republic of Iran," *European Scientific Journal* 10, no. 7 (2014): 92–101; Shirin Hakimzadeh, "Iran: A Vast Diaspora Abroad and Millions of Refugees at Home," *Migration Information Source*, 1 September 2006, https://www.migrationpolicy.org/article/iran-vast-diaspora-abroad-and-millions-refugees-home; Jerzy Zdanowski, *Middle Eastern Societies in the 20th Century* (Newcastle upon Tyne: Cambridge Scholars, 2014).

59. Akbar E. Torbat, "The Brain Drain from Iran to the United States," *Middle East Journal* 56, no. 2 (Spring 2002): 272–95.

60. Pierre Razoux, *The Iran–Iraq War*, trans. Nicholas Elliot (London: Harvard University Press, 2015).

61. Ganji, *Defying the Iranian Revolution*.

3

I Am a Political Refugee

Armin Danesh

I don't want to be seen as a victim or as a problem. I'm a human being! I love my country, I love my people, I didn't escape just for my own safety, I'm in the UK to continue my struggle for freedom and equality in Iran. I'm a political refugee!

—Karimi, 2014[1]

MY STORY

I've reached the Kurdish frontier! I'm at the border post. I have a cyanide capsule inside my cheek and a baby in my arms. I can't allow myself to be captured alive by the regime.

I feel intensely alive: I'm facing death. The Religious Guards at the border stand bored and watchful; they are armed and glance at the baby. They hardly notice me, waving me through with an automatic gesture.

Ahead lies the open road; behind me now, the deadly tension recedes. My new comrades in the resistance come to meet me. I'm still carrying my baby niece. I've spat my death pill out into the ditch—I can't stop laughing out loud. I'm shouting at the top of my voice, "Freedom! They couldn't catch me!"

This is my victory. I've defeated the regime: it's a moment of overwhelming joy. My awareness is extraordinarily focused. When the phoenix rises from the ashes it sings. This beautiful song is ringing in my ears. Nothing can stop me from surviving. In one great leap, I'm released from the regime's hands: free from religious fundamentalism, murder, torture, death. I will fulfil my destiny—to love life and to liberate myself and other human beings.

I've rejoined my spiritual and political family. How could I ever forget this unique moment of my life? My rebirth!

WHAT BROUGHT ME TO THIS POINT?

Since the 1979 Revolution, I've experienced many defeats in my life, and each time I've picked myself up. This strengthens my confidence and confirms that, if I'm again defeated, I'll try to rise up. This is my core message to my readers.

I've found through my life's work that love for humanity is the voice of liberation, and I have found this truth corroborated by others. It is the deep river into which my story and those of many others flow as tributaries. Our human quality manifests itself as a profound expression of our desire for justice and integrity.

My story is not written for myself alone, nor am I the hero. I want to investigate and shed light on a particular type of psychology and character, which is drawn to this kind of experience. In our struggle, both external and internal, we discovered that we share this experience, in our various individual ways. It is our common ground. We have lived our lives with all the stops out. The survival instinct and alertness to danger stretches every faculty, alters the perception of time, and awakens a heightened state of consciousness: the love for life. We accepted death as the flip-side of the coin. As we live, we spend our life. In my battles, I could see the beauty. The more you give in your life, the more you come to value it, by connecting to the whole existence and purpose of humanity. For many of us, our battle had this character of living "on the edge" with the whole of ourselves; and our removal from the battlefield was a severe existential loss.

As I think of this, I recall the sharpness of my mother's perception. Her close attention to all things, her care for her family and home, and her love prepared me for my revolutionary life. I recall with gratitude the parental strength and stability that nourished my early years.

I was born in Tehran in 1958, the fifth of a family of ten children—three sisters and seven brothers. My family were politically active against the shah, the king of Iran, overthrown in 1979, and during my early teens, my father (Agha) spent two years in prison.

My early background strongly focused my attention on human rights and working for others. Agha's influence and imprisonment inspired me to support his views. From about the age of ten, I would discuss with him philosophy and the meaning of life. Although he was a Marxist, I wanted to be a Muslim and had regular debates with him. Agha spoke very openly with me and deeply respected my serious approach. This established a foundation for my later life at university, when I became a representative for different student groups.

Although I came fifth among my siblings, my tendency was to take responsibility within my family. My parents felt confident enough to leave me in charge of the house when they went out. Among the children in my district, the same pattern appeared. We organised among ourselves a weekly contribution of money, which I collected. With my auntie's help, I bought a supply of toys, for all of our use, which made our parents happy. We created our own community. The pattern prevailed also at university and in my later life.

I learned these principles and ideals from Agha. He was enthusiastic about education and supported my studies. One of the main streets in Tehran was named after him during the Mossadegh era of the 1950s. Prime Minister Mossadegh was a national leader of secular democracy and nationalised the Anglo-Iranian oil company. Before the shah was reinstated in 1953, Mossadegh led a resistance movement against foreign domination.

My mother (Mama) was another strong personality. She was constantly busy with managing our large household and extended family and keeping her ten children tidy and presentable, and the whole house shone. I knew, however, that she was ill. As she too took pride in my studies, I felt affirmed by both my parents. Although I talked more with my father, Mama confided in me on matters of close concern to her. She and Agha inspired respect. Mama was sharp and would take no nonsense; she was also extremely kind and generous. We helped several families with financial problems. One family had two daughters who came every month to collect money from us. Mama treated them with respect and asked my younger sister to play with the girls. When on one occasion my sister refused, my mother spoke to her privately. She was angry: "Won't you play with them because they're poor? Shame on you!" Mama was also musical; she would sometimes ask me to lie down with her and sing her to sleep. This early atmosphere influenced my desire to help others and, later on, my charity work.

When I was fourteen, there came a turning point; Mama died. Giving birth ten times had exacerbated her heart condition. Because she came from the Azerbaijan district of Iran and spoke little Farsi, I would accompany her to the doctor, and I was at her bedside when she suffered her heart attack. It was about twenty minutes' walk from our house to the local surgery. As I ran, I thought, "I want to be a doctor and to help people."

Her death affected the whole family dynamic: my sisters and brothers were too upset to continue their studies, but I wanted to carry on. I had my own way of grieving. I bought tapes of songs in Azari, Mama's language; alone in my room, I listened to them hour after hour, sang with them, and cried loudly. In time, this singing became very therapeutic. When I later lost my wife, my friends, and my brothers, I would sing like this, and I still do whenever I'm upset, joyful, or deeply moved. The loss of my biological Mama when I was still a teenager found a deep healing when Moira Bradley entered my life in London and I became her son.

I felt responsible for my family, but I did not want to involve myself too much in family crises, particularly those in my mother's family. I felt instead that I should work harder and build my own life. I became a serious student and athlete and developed my political awareness. In my last year at school, I became head boy and was offered a scholarship to a private school.

Winning my place at Esfahan University was a great triumph for me, for my family, and for my numerous relatives. At the age of twenty-three, I obtained a doctorate in pharmaceutical science. Before that, my interest in the human psyche led me to gain a diploma in child psychology, which I taught for six months. Being much focused on sport, I became a gymnastics coach at the university. My goal, however, was to obtain my doctorate.

Iran's universities had traditionally been centres of opposition to the shah. In such an environment, my background and potential inevitably led me into politics. During my first year, I was buoyed up with the praise of my extended family—everyone in those days admired and respected students. It wasn't easy to get into university, and for those who succeeded, their future was guaranteed.

To begin with, I didn't follow any regular political movement but clung to my independence. I returned to my early pattern of taking responsibility for others; I naturally fell into organisational roles. So, when I joined a resistance movement, I quickly achieved seniority. In my present work as a psychotherapist in London, I have to learn each day how to listen and not give in to the old temptation of trying to mend other people. I'm still working on it!

At university, I met my first wife, a committed political and human rights activist. In 1979, when the shah was overthrown, I couldn't believe our freedom had come at last. A coalition of many classes, interests, and ideologies, together with a remarkable participation by women, had achieved our goal—the removal of a corrupt and despotic monarchy. The country would now belong to us, the people! Our dream was to rebuild the country and establish a democratic system. Along with millions of others, I was focused on a good life for myself, successful studies and a career, and a wife and family of my own. Thousands of liberation organisations mushroomed in Iran, sharing hope and freedom of speech; people cared for each other, and many returned to the country from overseas to help. During the Revolution, they shared everything; their common enemy was the shah.

We trusted the new religious leaders; we thought they would be honest, spiritual men. We soon realised the Revolution had been hijacked by Ayatollah Khomeini to establish Islamic fundamentalism in the region. It was a betrayal of everything we stood for. Our progressive, humane movement was stolen from us.

War broke out against the Turkmen and Kurdish peoples. Kurdistan had long been a stronghold against oppression. The people living there were kept in poverty and forbidden to speak their native language. Other ethnic and religious minorities, including Christians, Jews, and Bahá'ís were persecuted, and some of their leaders were killed.

The Resistance movement grew, particularly in the universities, to protect the Revolution's true purpose, which was freedom and democracy. I faced a moral dilemma shared by many: my commitment to the movement meant leaving my job, my belongings, and my family.

The protest against Ayatollah Khomeini began to grow among the people, particularly in the universities. Soon Khomeini, fearing loss of control, closed our universities under the guise of "cultural revolution." Most supporters of the new regime were uneducated. Although they attacked us brutally, we in the Resistance movement didn't want to confront them; many of us were beaten up. At that time, I worked as a postgraduate assistant lecturer, receiving a salary, until the university closed. We tried to stop the closure of the universities but didn't want to retaliate in kind; we wanted to act peacefully. Many of us were imprisoned, tortured, and even put to death at this early stage.

The shah had been a dictator of the classic kind, but the new regime was a clerical dictatorship. The ayatollahs brought the darkest part of our history and culture to the surface. People joined opposition parties to find a way forward. The new regime dragged us violently back into the dark and frozen past.

The regime was unable to tolerate opposition. Peaceful meetings of any kind were violently broken up. The regime quickly armed its supporters, forming a network of compliant mosques and setting up militia centres (Komitteh), which it controlled by force. The future of the country looked grim. The regime began to seize control of parliament, the economy, and industry. There were no fair elections. All opposition parties were excluded from the government and parliament.

The regime was unable to use the positive energy released by the Revolution. The outbreak of the Iran-Iraq War (1980–1988) created an opportunity to develop the regime's Religious Guards to crack down on opposition and justify human rights violations. Very soon the faint hopes that we had invested in the regime died; the idea of a democracy became inconceivable. Any questioning of their wrongdoing was considered anti-Islamic and subject to attack!

Our ideals were twisted around, forced back to front and hideously distorted. The existential loss was an unbearable nightmare; we were excluded from what we had achieved—if you open your mouth, you go to prison! We were desperate.

The dictatorship sustained itself by creating a rule of fear, to destroy unity and turn people against each other as informers. Schoolchildren were encouraged to spy on their parents—to say, for instance, whether their mother wore full Islamic dress. These divisions and mistrust became integral parts of the modern culture of Iran.

We have learned through suffering under it, that this long, painful process—more than four decades—to finally expel the regime has become necessary and inevitable. The people have paid the price throughout these long years. Our progressive purpose is to grow and transform our culture through our collective ordeal—like the phoenix rising from the ashes—as we confront and cleanse our history.

The Resistance encourages its members to examine their own natures individually. There needs to be an internal revolution, in each person's spiritual, psychological, and practical commitment. To change society, we must first change our internal conditions. This process releases a humanity that is genuine, relational, and positive, along with our all-too-visible imperfections. Our people are able to resist the regime with their humour and humanity.

THE SITUATION OF WOMEN IN IRAN AFTER 1979

My father named all my sisters after historical heroines and leaders.[2] He would ask me, "Why don't you wash your sister's clothes and help in the kitchen?" The ideal of equality was built into our family, and my parents visibly loved and valued each other.

When I was five years old, I once grabbed a kitchen knife to protect my sisters against some young men who were insulting them. The conditioned reflex was bred in my bones. It grew into my commitment to liberate women and fight for democracy in which their role was crucial. Today I note a timeless resonance with Persian history in my life's work and purpose.

During the Revolution, women's participation deeply refreshed and inspired my insight and understanding. I had retained some embedded cultural attitudes that our job as men was to look after women—that we men are superior in intelligence and strength. Women's active participation during the Revolution undermined this belief system. The role of the Resistance movement and other political parties that promoted gender equality forced me to use my own mind and to see the difference. For all the liberating influence in my upbringing, it was still a revelation to observe the active role of women and girls in the movement. No longer in theory but now in practice, men and women valued each other as companions. This phenomenon further distanced us from the ideology of our common enemy—the regime.

The women's issue has emerged as the most significant and decisive element under the regime. In fact, the attitude towards women deeply divides Islam in the historic schism of progressive and reactionary tensions. We witnessed women's capability as activists. We saw them as leaders of significant cultural change, and we learned from them. We men realised for the first time that their sacrifices and intelligence were equal to our own, and often deeper. They overcame barriers that we men did not even see; they proved themselves through their hard work. We were not blind.

In my experience, the essential fact in our fight with the regime was the women's situation. I believe we can test any progressive ideology, family, or society on the basis of its gender values.

Not complying with cultural expectation was a huge hurdle for women to overcome. They were at the heart of the division between two different types of Islam in the country's politics. They proved themselves during the Revolution, in the Resistance, in prison, under torture, and as political refugees. After managing to escape, they faced further huge challenges in adapting to a host society's way of life, while maintaining their leadership positions in the Resistance. Many of them were mothers also wanting the best for their children. They organised and led demonstrations; they worked as counsellors; they set up escape and information networks. Their integrity burned within them.

Gender equality and mutual respect: this deep revolution in the heart is the fruit, the main creative and positive outcome of our suffering. To measure the quality of a social matrix, we need only observe precisely how women see themselves in that context and how they are treated in consequence.

This is promising for the future, since it is women as mothers who educate their children. Sara said, "I want to be myself and take my stand against injustice; I don't want to just follow my husband." As soon as she had trained as a freedom fighter for the cause, she was no longer terrified. She made her conscious choice; she ceased to be a victim.

The sight of millions of women marching in the street challenged the attitudes I was born with. I started to recognise them and their role within the Revolution in a new way. I believe the victory in 1979 against the shah was made possible only through the large-scale active participation of Iranian women.

On 7 March 1979, Ayatollah Khomeini decreed that Iran was now an Islamic state and that women must therefore observe the Hijab dress code.[3] My first wife and my sisters were preparing, with tens of thousands of other women, to celebrate International Women's Day. Khomeini's statement was politically timed: it was the first indication of the regime's views. Having hitherto participated in the Revolution as members of different political and social forces, they now found themselves targeted specifically as women. Nahid Yeganeh and Azar Tabari, Iranian scholars and women's rights activists, wrote: "Since the Revolution, this was the first Government attack on women's status and the women demonstrating against it, the 'women's question' came to the forefront, to be considered, discussed, defended or rejected."[4]

In Iran, especially since the Ayatollah came to power, gender inequality and the suppression of women's rights have been systematic and institutionalised. In 1986, Rafsanjani, speaker of the Iranian parliament, stated: "One of the mistakes that Westerners make is to forget that the difference in the stature, vitality, voice, development, muscular quality and physical strength of men and women shows that men are stronger and more capable in all fields. Men's brains are larger."[5]

A husband can deny his wife any profession or job he considers would conflict with family interests or the wife's dignity.[6] Child custody laws are blatantly discriminatory (Constitutional Articles 1180 and 1043), and marriage for girls is conditional on the "consent of the father or grandfather." In his book of views and *fatwas*, *Tahrir-al Vasileh*, Khomeini deliberately degrades women to a level lower than that of slaves. He sanctions "temporary marriage," legitimising prostitution, specifying that women be paid for use of their body.[7] Polygamy is legal; men are permitted to have four wives and an unlimited number of temporary wives. Men make all family decisions, including those governing the movements of women and custody of children.

For activists, our passion to defend human rights values and democracy automatically places us in a desperate position.

In 1981, the Iranian regime became very aggressive towards its political opponents; a period of bloodshed began. Since those days, more than 120,000 people have been executed and more than 800,000 imprisoned and tortured for supporting free speech and political change. Among them were two of my brothers, my first wife, and one of my sisters, along with thousands of colleagues, friends, and fellow students.

The regime discriminated against women, but in prison they suffered torture equally. The regime perceived feminine resistance as a main enemy. The excessive severity of torture techniques, including rape, used against women was well known among political prisoners. Women's resistance inspired the men.

The brutal treatment of women prisoners stems not only from the fundamentalists' ideology but also from women's power and strength to resist it.

MY FRIENDS

Every day during 1981, listening to the news I heard of the executions of hundreds of people, some of them my close friends. I couldn't believe the regime could come to this point of executing even children in order to maintain their power in the name of "religion."

One of my closest friends was my classmate Dr Admashe. Two months after obtaining his degree, he was arrested and executed after refusing to confess to wrongdoing. He was an only child and extremely bright and popular at university. At school, we were in the same class; each term we alternated as head boy. In our friendly competition, I got the higher marks, but I knew he was the better student. When I heard about his execution, I was devastated. All the memories of our years of work and play together flooded through me. Everything changed so fast, beyond comprehension. Each day I read that fifty, seventy, or a hundred more were killed. It was unbearable. On the one hand, I tried to shut down my fear. I told myself that to show it would give credit to the regime. On the other hand, my cherished memories of each of my friends cut down in the bloodbath intensified my commitment to come into the open and fight. Later on, when I lost my connection with my resistance party for a while, the only reason I was able to survive psychologically and physically was my desire to find them again and to prove that I would never turn my back on all the tens of thousands of the best people of my homeland who gave their lives for freedom, democracy, and equality.

MY WIFE BEHNAZ

At the time my wife Behnaz and I got married, many people were being arrested, imprisoned, and killed. It was a time of intense slaughter. I admired her bravery, and I taught her some Judo defence techniques. One night I noticed she was crying. "What is the matter?" I asked. She replied, "I feel I'm too dependent on you. I love you and I want a life with you. Is that fair, with all my friends in prison?"

Another night I woke up and found her gone from the bed. Where was she? She had opened the window onto the terrace, and she was out in the heavy rain. She came in laughing and opened her arms wide—"I love the rain!" she cried.

As Muslims, my wife and I had no physical contact before marriage. One month after we married, we were in the car looking for a safe place for the night. She asked me, "Look, do you realise we *are* husband and wife?" and touched my hand for the first time.

On other occasions, we slept in the car in the countryside. Our life seemed to be a series of very short bursts of time spent together. During the presidential elections, the city was not safe for us. One night at 2 a.m., the local Religious Guards tapped on the car window; we were asleep. We had an advance plan for this eventuality. They searched us. We were friendly; we even joked and laughed to relax them. They called the main station in the city and were ordered to bring us in. If we arrived there, they would recognise us immediately. I drove my own car with my wife next to me; a Religious Guard sat in the back with a gun. The other two Religious Guards followed us in their car, along the country road. As we approached the city, I spotted a suitable place to run away. I stopped the car suddenly, jumped out and ran to the car behind shouting, "Your brother wanted to kill us!" That confused them. I doubled back zigzagging into the darkness, and none of the shots they fired at me hit their target; but what was happening to Behnaz? She jumped out of the other side of the car while they were focused on me! We stuck to our plan—never escape together but prearrange a place to find each other the following day.

Running and jumping along the bungalow roofs, I reached the city. I had thrown away my clothes so as not to be recognised. I knocked on a door and told the occupant that I had been asleep in a lorry when someone stole my shirt: could he give me one? He did, and I ran on—to the public baths. I took refuge in the steam for a few hours and prayed. When I came out, there stood a former friend of mine, now a commander of the Religious Guards. But I was focused and must have appeared formidable; he looked scared and ran away.

Later that day I found Behnaz at our rendezvous, and we laughed together. You cannot survive without being a fighter.

We could rarely stay in the same house together. We were careful not to go out or meet people. One sunny spring morning Behnaz went out and did not return. At that time, she and I shared a flat with three other members of the Resistance movement. The rule was this: if one of us didn't come back we must all leave the place at once in different directions. The regime's Religious Guards, particularly after arresting anyone, would put the rest of us under severe torture to get information. I had nowhere to go. I planned to go to another supporter's house; I discovered that it wasn't safe there either. I went outside and lay down in the square near the service station where travellers often stopped to rest. Many people slept on the ground there. At dawn, I got up and found a dog had taken one of my shoes. One bare foot might attract attention, so I hurried to the mosque early that morning and stole a shoe from there.

Behnaz suffered two months of prison and torture; she didn't recant, and she was executed.

Her mother visited her in the prison, where Behnaz pretended to be pregnant. She believed the Religious Guards would not torture or execute her until the baby's birth. They took no notice. Behnaz was tortured for a few days; her mother was not allowed to visit until the signs of the torture faded from her face. She gave her mother a message for me: "They are working hard to find you." I had left my driver's licence in the car, and they might identify me from the photo. She said, "Be careful."

I sent a message to her also. I said, "Whatever happens, I'm sure you will resist."

When I heard of Behnaz's execution, my immediate honest feeling was one of relief. Under torture she might have recanted and created a hell for herself for the rest of her life. I was proud of her. I would give no satisfaction to the regime by giving way to grief. For a few months I couldn't even believe she had been executed: our spiritual intimacy had been so strong. On one occasion, I found myself walking behind a woman wearing the same colour chador and clothes: "That's Behnaz!" I thought and ran up in front—of course, it wasn't her.

My father-in-law was a successful businessman. After his daughter's execution, he lost his way and could no longer work. He became disabled. On her mother's final visit to the prison, Behnaz, knowing she was going to her death, hugged her mother and told her, "My conscience is clear! They couldn't break me."

My wife's indestructible gift to me of these values gave me the strength to survive. Her spirit continued to guide me and strengthened my commitment to democracy and freedom. As I tell Behnaz's story, she lives and is present today in my life's work and purpose.

The regime was unable to break Behnaz's conscience. The culture of resistance became the norm among political prisoners.

FEAR, DEATH, AND DIGNITY

Now I want to face and examine my state of fear more deeply. Having made my conscious choice to defend democracy and freedom, I was aware of the risks I faced. I was afraid also of being captured, interrogated, and put to death.

The night after the Religious Guards took Behnaz, I was alert and acutely vulnerable. I was responsible for all the people in the house. Towards midnight, I went to lie down for a short time. We took turns keeping watch so that someone was always awake. The duty watch called me: something was happening outside. Armed Religious Guards surrounded our house; the road was a dead end. Our plan of action in case we were attacked was to escape over our neighbours' roofs. I recall this moment vividly. Peering through the window I couldn't control my body; my legs shook with terror. This had escalated with Behnaz's by now certain arrest.

As a freedom fighter, I didn't want to face this feeling. I would volunteer and deliberately put myself in the front line. I was intensely ashamed of my fear. It manifested my disloyalty to the cause and gave credit to the regime. My friends and relatives were dying! There was no room for fear, so I repressed that constant feeling within me.

I couldn't even mention it until one day in my psychotherapy training my classmate Steve pointed out: "you told us about your life; you had some terrible experiences—but you didn't say how frightened you were." Then I realised the extent of my difficulty. I was unable to separate my fear from myself. In Iran, I lived and acted under constant fear. I am aware that the element of fear will remain within me until its cause—the regime's existence—disappears. It is worth noting that my ongoing commitment to end the violation of human rights in Iran keeps me psychologically in the battlefield.

Writing this brings fresh insight, confirming that since I left Iran my fear takes a different form. To this day, although I live in the United Kingdom and am no longer in physical danger, fear and grief are triggered each time I monitor the situation in Iran, which I do several times a day. My response and commitment are embedded in my identity and influence each aspect of my ordinary life, with my extended family, my children, my friendships, and my work.

LOSS OF SPIRITUAL FAMILY AND COLLECTIVE IDENTITY

In general, there is a potential conflict between self-interest and the group commitment. I faced this conflict in my relationship with the movement. Within the group, the general discipline is to follow the leader's decision. This is crucial, for the group cannot function if individuals take matters into their own hands. I had a tendency, however, not to give up my ideas in favour of the group. I nearly always thought I could run things more efficiently. It was difficult for my leaders to deal with me. I honestly had the group's best interest in mind. I had volunteered and devoted my life and made personal sacrifices. I was also young and hot-headed, which caused friction within the Resistance movement. On three occasions, I was marginalised and lost my rank. I didn't appear to be sufficiently committed against the regime. This hurt me deeply.

I will now describe one of these occasions.

The Religious Guards routinely subjected arrested members to brutal torture until they either submitted information or died. Dozens of methods were used to break an individual and use him or her to make further arrests. For example, the Guards would drive victims through the streets with an armed escort to identify Resistance comrades. Or they would forcibly extract information about an upcoming meeting and surround the location in advance. They would go to any length to gain further access to members of the movement. It was extremely dangerous for a freedom fighter to appear in public. This constant state of siege forced our movement to be vigilant.

About a month after I found my widowed sister and baby niece and moved in with them, I experienced a traumatic incident. A meeting had been arranged with a senior member of the resistance movement. Like all such "casual" meetings in public, it had to appear unplanned.

I made the mistake of arriving five minutes late. In these situations, each minute counts. My superior was placing himself in great danger by waiting there for me. When he asked, "What's happened? Why are you late?" I didn't tell him the truth. I said, "I was just checking the street to see if it's safe. This took time."

He didn't believe me and ordered me to file a written report on my return to base. We wrote our reports on special paper that we folded up extremely small to conceal them in case the Religious Guards arrested us. I remember inserting a plastic-wrapped report into the bottom of a tube of toothpaste, then rolling up the tube. I gave it to a courier to take to my superior. A few days later, another member brought me a message.

Having read my report, and in view of their other disagreements with me, the movement decided that I feared for my own skin; I was weak and therefore a liability. They couldn't afford the risk. The party excluded me and ordered me to remove myself. I was allowed regular meetings with a mutual contact, but my sister and I had basically been expelled. I was devastated.

For many people, disconnection from ordinary life—their home, their loved ones, and their cultural roots—is a deathlike experience. For me, it was the expulsion from the movement that had nurtured my faith. My real trauma was not so much the loss of my wife, brother, family, and friends, for I had already chosen not to have an ordinary life—it was in the very ground of my faith. The movement had become my spiritual family to resist the regime and to help others survive, and within that family I held many responsibilities.

I felt destroyed. Where could we go? We had lost our protection. We couldn't stay where we were, or with any of my relatives and friends. I had to find a way to support my sister and her baby.

MY BABY NIECE, MY SISTER, AND MY BROTHER

The Religious Guards, always on the alert for activists, arrested tens of thousands of them in the streets. They closed residential districts and public transport and carried out random searches. For as long as possible, we avoided being seen in public. Because of my new circumstances and trying to support and seek safety for my sister and myself, I moved from the centre of Tehran to the suburbs, where I would attract less attention. Some camouflage was needed to allow me to go about my business. Carrying a child provided a natural protection. What activist would cause trouble with a baby? My baby niece became my bodyguard during my daily activities until I crossed the Kurdish border into safety. Her name was Saba. She was very thin and extremely beautiful with deep black eyes and dark hair. She was always solemn and quiet.

Her father had been an engineer and human rights activist during the shah's regime. He met my sister at Tehran University, and they married. In 1981, when Saba was about six months old, he was arrested and executed by the new regime. I managed to contact my sister, but we had nowhere to go, and we would not endanger our families; we were both in hiding. A relative of ours kept a market stall. It wasn't safe for me to speak directly to my sister, but I was able to find her through him. As he was not under suspicion, he still led an ordinary life. He arranged for us to meet in south Tehran. I arrived early to make sure the street was safe. Then I caught sight of my sister. Little Saba slept in her arms. To this day, I can still see the child's soft dark hair, her long eyelashes, and her pomegranate-coloured jacket decorated with small blue flowers. My heart overflowed with tenderness for her and for my sister. From that moment, I held Saba close to my heart.

We had to make plans quickly. My sister stayed with a friend for a few days but had nowhere to go. I told her, "I'll find a place. We'll go together."

It was then still safe enough for me to rent a flat. I spoke to some friends who agreed to share the accommodation. I pretended I was my sister's husband; my friends passed as members of her family, and we rented the second floor. The land-lord saw nothing unnatural in two families living together.

We kept watch around the clock. Often, we slept with our shoes on, ready to leap out of bed and flee. For every small errand, we had to make a detailed plan. Each day more people were being arrested and killed. We supported each other and kept our spirits up. Our focus on freedom kept us going through those hard times.

I found a job at a pharmacy: my qualifications helped me there, but it was too risky because there were so many customers. I decided to change jobs; it was unsafe to stay anywhere for more than one month at a time. I joined a sweets factory. The owner liked me because I brought new ideas to the job. I was offered a partnership after only a few weeks. But, again, I was tipped off with a warning. I found shelter in a south Tehran suburb. We knew it would be dangerous to carry our few items of furniture with us in the car; it might attract the Religious Guards' attention. Many members of the movement were on the run.

There's something I will never forget: one summer's day I was looking for work and took Saba with me. The child's presence protected me; we blended into the back-ground because we seemed so normal. We enjoyed our walks and games together. I visited various firms: "I have to support my family; I have no job." One of them was a garage: "We have no work now but come back in two weeks' time." As I was leaving, someone came after me and called out. I turned to see a man approaching; he offered me a handful of banknotes. "You've got a family, a little girl." There were tears in my eyes. My dedication was for the people; I couldn't accept the money. I was deeply moved.

You couldn't rent a flat unless you had a job. One day, while out job hunting, I entered a teashop. Being an educated person, I had to be careful how I spoke in a working-class area. I tried to develop a rough appearance, changing the way I dressed and the way I walked. After I'd ordered my tea, a group of young men entered, and I offered them my seat. When I went to pay, they said, "Someone already paid for you." They pointed to a man called Hashem. "You shouldn't do that!" I said. He replied, "Come, let's sit over here. What are you doing?" "I'm looking for a job." "What can you do?" "I do everything . . ." I noticed that Hashem listened to me carefully and seemed to engage deeply with my story.

Hashem was buying a small factory. "Come into it with me; we can be partners." I was overwhelmed. "I don't have any money, and you don't even know me." He replied: "I've never seen you before, but I don't find any reason not to trust you."

We became friends. We manufactured small kilns for baking tiles. He had the expertise; I did the paperwork. I earned three times as much as I had as a young uni-versity lecturer. With that job, I was able to rent accommodation for myself, Saba, and my sister. We had two rooms and a kitchen upstairs in a family home. Here, I got to know some of the locals. We lived there for a while, and I even bought a small car. One day a blind man called Akbar came into the teashop; I heard him telling customers that he hadn't heard from his great-nephew Hossein or his family. That happened to be one of my own names. He talked at length about Hossein and his family, and I learned a lot about them. I decided to seize the opportunity and later found his house. One day I went there and introduced myself as his nephew. Akbar was overjoyed. He hugged me and said, "Come in, have some tea." I also invited him to my house where we shared our meals. He became our uncle, and everything felt natural and safe; Akbar was very popular in the community. As he was not originally from Tehran but had grown up in northern Iran, nobody was likely to find me out.

Through Akbar also I bought a plot of land. I wanted to appear as a successful family man. Yet all of this was temporary: a cover.

I received a bad shock when the regime required all landlords to hand over their tenants' identity papers to the Religious Guards' headquarters, but I managed to produce some fake documents. To avoid arrest, I used at least five different names in different areas.

In that district, I had cultivated a number of friends. I even got along well with a senior member of the Religious Guards. During the Islamic holy months, I sang the religious songs and prayers in the mosque; the locals liked my voice and even offered to pay me, which I refused. I bought a book of the songs and chants and practised them at home. This helped our survival and our integration into the community.

Then I heard that my brother had been arrested. While still in Tehran, I'd heard he was going to marry another activist, but it was too dangerous for them to celebrate their wedding ceremony. I was able to meet him; however, that was the last time I saw my brother. Six months after they got married, he and his wife were arrested. He was given a three-year prison sentence; his wife fifteen years. While he served his sentence the Religious Guards found out about his activities in prison against the regime. They subjected him to torture and finally put him to death.

My brother was two years older than me. We'd been very close ever since child-hood. He didn't like to go anywhere without me. One day my father wanted to take him to the tailor for a new shirt, but he refused: "You should buy him one first!" My father hugged him.

My brother became an engineer and spoke English fluently. He was highly active during the 1979 Revolution and was much loved in our extended family. He did much work for the community and for his friends and relatives and was elected to represent more than nineteen thousand employees in his workplace. He was financially well off. One day I asked him, "Why don't you buy yourself a watch?" He smiled and said, "Lots of people have watches. If I want to know the time, I ask them! Instead, I can give something to the poor." He was a fastidious person; when we went to the public baths together, I had to wait for a long time while he washed his long hair thoroughly. He loved to sing and dance at summertime teenage gatherings in our street. The rest of us clapped the rhythm.

My other sister and my father went to visit him in prison. On my father's last visit, he wasn't allowed to see my brother. Instead, the Religious Guards gave him a photo of his dead body, to shock and break my father. They also told my other sister who was four months pregnant. When she heard the news, she miscarried and died.

In my last telephone conversation with my father after my brother's execution, he spoke out against the regime: "They just gave me his number in the graveyard. We weren't allowed to bury him or have a funeral, but over four thousand people came to celebrate your brother's life, they filled all the streets around the house."

I remember telling my brother before his arrest, "Don't worry about our sister and Saba, I will look after them." His home was no longer safe.

I've not touched this deep memory for a long time. I feel it surfacing like a long-forgotten clip from a film.

ORIGIN OF MY TRAUMA

A young man fought for freedom under the shah and helped overthrow the dictatorship. He enjoyed a brief taste of that freedom, which was no longer a mere theory. When the Ayatollah regime usurped the Revolution and that freedom was lost, the young man was inconsolable. What could he do on his own? He found an organised resistance movement, a political party, and joined it. He gave it his all, feeling not only protected but also profoundly empowered. He was now part of a greater body that gave him his new identity. When you fight for freedom, you become that freedom.

The Resistance represented his highest ideal. When his connection with it was severed, he felt he had lost his existential purpose. What could he do on his own? A single individual exiled from his collective body. He had identified completely with the movement.

Without daily contact with its ideals and his companions, the collective purity was no longer his. Feelings of betrayal, retribution, and banishment threw him into isolation. Like a single ant, bee, or bird separated from its fellows, he was a powerless unit, out of step, a creature with its shell torn off.

The Resistance was his existential purpose and his will to live. Suddenly he heard, "You are nothing. You have no existence." No book, literature, or theory can adequately describe the feeling of exposure and shock, the sense of being torn apart from inside. He might die, or a new life might emerge like a butterfly from the chrysalis. Human beings cannot bear isolation from their own kind.

After a period of despair and emptiness, I made a new conscious decision to defend myself. I had no choice but to be the phoenix and fly once more. I would join them again! I was not defeated. The regime was alive, but it could not kill my values and resources or extinguish the fire within me. I rose again with that. I threw everything I had into my escape to find and rejoin my ideological family. With the choice for freedom, I transformed the trauma and overcame my paralysis.

By then I also perceived my entire psychological journey within the context of human rights and politics. Finding my own agency, I was able to take the huge risk in escaping to defend my collective body and be reunited.

If we focus only on the individual interest, we will find conflict within the party, and it will be easy to blame the party and its power over us. Taking a broader view, with the party's existence and safety measured against the regime, its vigilance made sense. It had to adopt extreme positions in order to survive. In my long association with the movement, and having gained an independent view, my faith in its leaders and its principles remains unshaken. My trust in the movement deepened with my growing trust in myself. I feel I have gained much more than I lost.

THE ESCAPE PROCESS

I was desperate to retrieve my connection to my freedom-fighter comrades. My sister didn't know what had happened; I told her we were still in touch with them. I tried every opportunity to make contact. It was desperately difficult. At last, I decided I couldn't remain in limbo as a fugitive. I must work actively for the cause of freedom. At my brother-in-law's shop in a market in Tehran, I asked, "Do you know anyone from Kurdistan? I'm trying to escape." I knew the regime had relatively little control in Kurdistan. They agreed to help me. Another brother-in-law sheltered fugitives. He told me, "We will meet the cost of your escape. Don't stay here. It is too dangerous. You'll get arrested and they will find us also." He added, "I know someone there who sometimes brings stuff for sale."

I questioned this person carefully, meeting him and his friend several times. Could I trust them? I weighed the risk and decided that I could. I told them my intentions. They told me they were members of the Kurdish resistance party. They would arrange for me to escape with my sister and Saba. We met regularly over a period of two or three months. In fact, they became supporters of my resistance party and later worked for them.

Then I told my sister I had lost contact with the movement. I must go and try again to find it, and then come back for her. "You stay here—I can't risk your life and Saba." She pushed me inside the room and shut the door. "I won't let you go without us." During the long conversation that ensued, I explained, "It is very difficult for me to put your life and Saba's at risk." My sister was insistent and eventually convinced me that she could not possibly stay there without me. In the end, I said, "I just wanted to make sure you are serious—it is my responsibility." We agreed to leave together.

It was more natural for women to go out and about in those days, for it was mostly men who were under suspicion; women were regarded as not worthy of notice. I still didn't want the three of us to travel together—anything might happen. I sent my sister and Saba off first, towards a safe area in Kurdistan. They chose an unsuitable route, were prevented from crossing the border, and had to come back. We carefully discussed the options with the Kurds. We then decided on a different route and that we would all travel together—on a "family visit."

We boarded the same bus but sat separately. On buses, women were in any case segregated from men. I had changed my papers again to those of a murdered family member and bought my bus ticket. In case the Religious Guards were suspicious, I took materials with me to change it again. Before the border check, I did one more stealthy identity switch-over in a petrol station toilet. The ID was handwritten in ink; I'd brought a small quantity of bleach, some cotton buds, and a pen to erase and rewrite it. I dried the document and stained it with splashes of tea. We arrived in Kurdistan and stayed in a house our friends had provided; we changed into our Kurdish clothes and waited for our local people to check the border into the safe region. When they sent us the go-ahead, we travelled by minibus as a family; I had the cyanide pill ready in my cheek and carried Saba in my arms. I would not be taken alive.

At the checkpoint, an armed young member of the Religious Guards glanced at the passengers in the minibus and waved us on. We travelled for about two hours and reached the town where a van awaited us. We loaded up all my sister's belongings and were driven for about forty-five minutes until the driver stopped the van and said, "Your friends will come to fetch you here." We waited about half an hour; then two members of the movement arrived to take us to a nearby village. As soon as I saw them, I shouted: "Freedom! The regime couldn't catch me!" They came towards me, and we hugged. For the first time in years, I gave my real name and my sister's, which they checked. On their walkie-talkies they reported our arrival in code and guided us to one of their bases.

After reaching relative safety and freedom, I spent some years in the mountains, living mostly in tents. We built networks for the constant stream of refugees into the safe zone. This planted seeds for my later activity for refugees in general. It would become the focus of my studies and profession in psychotherapy. We also set up several surgeries to help local people improve their health and quality of life. In due course, the area was surrounded by the regime, and I had to escape again. Via Turkey I eventually arrived in the United Kingdom.

My sister became a committed freedom fighter, raised Saba in the Resistance community, and eventually moved to France.

MY ARRIVAL IN THE UNITED KINGDOM

My arrival in the United Kingdom was an opportunity to continue my human rights activities. My passion was to utilise every possibility there to bring freedom and democracy to my homeland. I was deeply relieved to meet my UK-based comrades in the Resistence movement for us to share the collective task. As soon as I saw them I felt at home! Some might think I had lost my homeland, but my home was within the movement regardless of country, city, or location. I felt no need to adapt myself to the ways of English society; within the movement we had fluent English speakers through whom we could communicate.

Living in the movement was distinctly different from life outside it. We carried the essence of our culture within it. There was no need for me to find a job or a place to live—the movement provided everything. My personal aim was to work for Iranian refugees all over the world and assist them to reach safety.

London itself was not where I would have chosen to be. In fact, I was indifferent. My very identity was enfolded in the movement.

I read in Erich Fromm's work, *Fear of Freedom*, that in the Middle Ages where thought and actions were ruled by the Catholic Church, an individual found his or her place in the design but had no sense of individual freedom. Of course, there was suffering as well as inward ecstasy in the confinement; the church indoctrinated that a person's suffering is for their sin. This created a dependency on the church.[8]

Was I dependent in this way? My safety, security, and shared aim in the movement was to change the regime.

Paradoxically, however, I had to focus on my adaptation process in the place where I was sent to. Everything was organised by the movement, and I went along with it. I didn't want to react or to feel anything. It was OK to live anywhere outside, so long as I remained in touch with my party from within. During my early years in London, I lived in a country within a country.

I felt conflicted. For instance, I had no desire to learn the English language. I needed to express myself in our Farsi language. I was afraid of undermining my identity. If I learned the English language and its ways, I might lose my eager desire to bring about the change in my homeland. Why so? I am anywhere a citizen of the world! Our active task to change the regime in Iran was a twenty-four-hour commitment. What else could we do?

I needed my British citizenship in order to be free to travel abroad to other resistance bases. I had no desire to travel, or to see the world. For me and my comrades, the idea of taking a holiday was a joke, even a taboo while our people remained under the regime's rule. The question of adaptation was irrelevant to me personally. I simply utilised each given circumstance to help me to fight effectively.

On the mountains in Kurdistan we had lived in tents, constantly clarifying and resolving the conflicts that arose between self and our community. Our shared tasks and targets were our well-being. Although we lived under command, we savoured our interior freedom of choice and commitment. We were happy because when your life is in focus you live and act your conscious choice; you are therefore free. I lived among others who shared this feeling. It drew us very close—more profoundly than with our biological families.

The personal interest is second to the collective interest; it is put to one side. To fight the regime, we needed interior peace. We would only disagree with one another in the methods for the task.

I saw the contrast between our lucid human values in the movement and the way people behaved outside it. It seemed they wasted their time and energy; they were victims of their circumstances and had apparently no contact with higher values. Initially I resented these "outsiders." From the depth of my heart, I tried to live according to the highest requirement. With my personal identity immersed and at rest, I could receive the harmonic strength of all the others in my party, as part of the whole.

When it came to establishing my identity to the Home Office, however, I faced a formidable barrier.

EXPERIENCES OF ADAPTATION AND RESETTLEMENT IN MY NEW HOME

In my new home, several factors contributed to and were crucial to my ongoing adaptation process. As well as my charity work and resuming further academic studies, I created a new extended family: wife, mother, uncle, sisters, and daughters.

The first thing I saw when I arrived and opened my eyes was the North Circular Road. The weather was terrible. The trees were dead and grey, and the district was depressed. Was this England? My Resistance friends had a base in London. I joined them. They advised me how to write my case for leave to remain.

Although I had studied professional English for three years at Isfahan University, I could not speak it. At the Home Office division in Croydon, a movement supporter came to explain for me. I was given a paper and told I must go in to sign each month. I went three times and was told to come back again. All I wanted was an ID card with my photo; I lost my patience and decided to confront the Home Office by myself. I didn't need advice; I'm a political refugee and deserve my identity; I will defend myself.

Back to ground zero again, I summoned my strength. I didn't consider making England my permanent home. I hoped my stay there would be temporary until I could return to my country of origin. In the Home Office I shouted at the top of my voice: "I won't go away till you give me that paper. Yes, call the police. I don't want to keep coming here."

This was my first "handshake" with the new country. Eventually my case came up, and I went to court. I refused help with the documents. "I'm a political refugee—why don't they give me my status?" My solicitor said, "One thing I ask you. Please keep your temper in court." Four witnesses who knew me in Iran supported my case. When the judge asked me point blank, "What will happen if you go back?" I said quietly, "They will kill me." The judge listened carefully, looked into my eyes, paused, and inclined his head. He was now convinced that my life was in danger. He gave me leave to remain, and a few years later I received my citizenship.

This was the turning point. My new identity began to take root from there.

Through the many years I have worked for human rights, the international issues we face have developed a profound meaning for me. This meaning soon travelled beyond my homeland in the reality of meeting others face to face. After I made my base in the United Kingdom I started to go from street to street and from house to house to raise support for tens of thousands of Iranian refugees, displaced children, and their families: with file in hand, I worked my way through London, Manchester, Leeds, Exeter, Brighton, Scotland, Wales, and Ireland. When I first started to communicate with people in the United Kingdom outside the movement, I was totally identified with the cause. Through their support, I derived much comfort and healing, and I felt our voice was beginning to be heard. The door was opening; we were not alone. I began to feel connected to my new country. I could never have expected this totally new experience. I worked tirelessly.

I discovered the universality of human rights and the kindness of those who welcomed me, and my heart opened further. In spring, summer, autumn, and winter, I sought out and found thousands, among the millions who live in this country, who generously supported our initiatives. In all levels and stages of life, innumerable staunch friends of human rights appeared. At times, I worked eighteen hours a day.

During the first fourteen years, these people helped me promote the awareness of human rights worldwide and save victims of tyranny in my homeland. They took care of me and helped me love others; they showed me the beauty of individual lives. It inspired me to befriend total strangers. It helped me recover, even from my fear of being a stranger. In helping others, my life renewed its purpose, and there can be no going back. To stand still would be to perish.

I learned to share my achievements with the people I befriended. They enabled me to change some of my own conditioning. I believe real change is possible in human life if we desire it. I learned to carry a strong hope for the future, and I would like to spread that hope. My deepest discovery, and liberation, is the essential humanity of men and women, regardless of race, gender, or ethnicity. My life is dedicated to human rights and guided by the law it serves, which in the end prevails. All bad things come to an end.

I began to accept and live with my trauma. I would like to summarise in a single sentence, all I have said so far. I have learned to love people more deeply, and I want to improve their quality of life. I founded a human rights organisation whose main objective is to promote women's freedom worldwide, particularly in the Middle East.

At the Kurdish frontier, my baby niece's innocence camouflaged me at the moment where I might have met my death. My friends and family all note my melting tenderness for the very young. I have tried to help the children ever since, especially those who suffer with their families in war zones or extreme poverty. In some cases, we are able to raise and sustain funds for the children to be educated and clothed, and for their communities to achieve self-sufficiency.

I decided some years ago that my work and my commitment to human rights and social justice could be further enhanced if I resume my studies. This course of further education played a significant role in my adaptation to my new home. I was able to obtain a master's degree in human rights. My research topic was "Gender Discrimination and the Women's Movement for Equality in Iran." This project broadened my early academic perspective. I find that the more research I carry out towards this aim, and the more I work with it, the deeper my motivation grows.

When I was younger, I had no faith in counselling or psychotherapy. I saw these as a symptom of social dysfunction. In my view, the individual didn't carry much weight. I believed that if we want to change individuals, we should change society first; that in any collective movement towards change, the individual would automatically follow.

The individual and society are interconnected, however; there is a dynamic relationship between the two.

My trauma shaped much of my more impulsive behaviour. The relationship with my English wife, a professor of philosophy, was initially based on shared ideals, principles, and value system. Alison was able to handle my more complex moods because she was articulate with her own feelings. This kept our relationship honest and down to earth. She had been recently widowed and had a teenage son, Ben. It was a major challenge to become a stepfather and to develop my relationship with him. Confronting my cultural history, background, and language, I saw how I must change, and that the real revolution starts with myself: to recognise some of my conditioned—and destructive—attitudes and turn them around.

I had some sessions with a counsellor, which I found helpful. My views began to change; Alison noticed a significant easing in my attitudes and ways of being, as I became calmer. This deepened our relationship and encouraged me to keep going.

With my growing desire to work with refugees with similar problems, I determined to study. My plan was to develop a counselling unit within the human rights organisation I was working in. Accordingly, I studied for four years to obtain my certificate, diploma, and a BACP-accredited advanced diploma in counselling and diploma in clinical supervision. Developing my own approach—humanistic existential—I engaged myself deeply in this new direction to understand myself better. Additionally, I established a charity offering therapeutic services to those unable to pay for counselling. At the National Health Service (NHS) surgery where I was in charge of therapy for eight years, I worked more than a thousand counselling hours and supervised the work of other counsellors.

I then decided to further my studies and obtain my doctorate, because I could see the beneficial impact study was having on my work. I found a suitable course and was fascinated by the working environment. The quality of relationships within the faculty encouraged me to enrol. Although Alison disapproved of the quality of the course, and I had to defend it, this reinforced my self-knowledge and my determination to master the hurdle. She was eventually convinced.

At the age of sixty, I obtained my doctorate in existential phenomenological psychotherapy with my research into Iranian political refugees' experiences in Britain.

MY DAUGHTER MARYAM

A Poem—My Little Girl

I have something to tell you, my dear daughter
To be with you, my freshest flower
There is so much to tell, of sadness, cold, and difficulties
How to choose
What can I bear to ignore?
When I talk to the children

I cannot describe the people who have wronged us.
Their dark deeds should not be paraded before such innocent faces.
I cannot speak of these people who have driven us apart
And made separation and sadness into a refuge.
Let us speak of the other people
Now distant but still honest
Whose love turns them from their own path
To smooth the cares from their children's brows.
What do they want most, these honest, caring people?
To feel the warm blossoming of a smile
Spreading like a flower
Across your face.

I feel I could write several books about every aspect of my relationship with Maryam. I haven't seen her for more than twenty years, but she has always been with me.

I remember her as a little girl, not much more than a baby. She had started to walk. During my clandestine meetings with human rights activists, she would come to watch what we were doing. When she had a toothache, I took her to the dentist. It was dangerous to go out, but she was in pain, and I did my best to keep us safe. For months afterwards Maryam played dentist to everyone she met. She asked them to open their mouth: "Look, you are eating too much chocolate! That's bad. You shouldn't eat so many sweets." She was very serious.

Maryam was a very bright child. Her eyes shone with smiles.

Why do I have such a strong connection with her? I have written poems and composed songs for her. She brought into my life the meaning of fatherhood and a sense of purpose. My feelings for her increased my desire to help children in need and led to my adopting two daughters in my new homeland. A natural capacity for the father-daughter relationship developed within me. As my new daughters felt my care and concern, they reciprocated by placing their trust in me as their father.

I desperately needed to be Maryam's father in action, and this is still my desire. I need to talk to her, to listen to her, to look after her, to play with her, and to think about her future. I have daydreams about her meeting her new siblings Ben, Marisa, and Adrianna. I was and remain psychologically connected with her. She became part of my identity and transformed my personality. My first email address was "maryamfather@ . . ." In correspondence, I write "Maryam's father" after my name.

I remember when I was studying academic writing at Kings College London one of my classmates, who was younger than me and did not have a good relationship with her dad, asked me to be her father. She confided to me her difficulties in life. One day the principal of the counselling school told me: "Armin, there are fourteen women in your class, some older than you, but in their personal reports they all wrote that they relate to you as their father."

My protectiveness towards Maryam has significantly strengthened my view on gender equality. I set up a charity to help orphans. Recently, Christina, a new family friend, asked me several times to be her father; she does not have one. In our neighbourhood, I have watched many little girls grow up into young women. All of them connect me to Maryam; there are many Maryams in my life. To protect her safety, at present I cannot write more about her. One day, when so many thousands of mothers and fathers in Iran are able to meet their beloved families freely, without risking anyone's life, I will see my daughter again.

I believe we will see the end of religious dictatorship there, and that I will see my daughter, hug and kiss her, and sing the song I composed for her.

MY MUM MOIRA

I first met Moira at a charity event in London in 1990. She was a chairperson of a Royal Air Force charity. She had visited Iran around 1970; her father had a German friend who worked in Iran as a structural engineer; my father used to work as an architect in the same company. Moira enjoyed her exciting and interesting trip to Iran and her discovery of the beauties of Isfahan, Mashhad, and Tabriz. She told me how touched she was by the rich culture and the people's kindness and hospitality in the various places she visited.

This elegant lady with dark hazel eyes communicated with me as if she had known me for a long time. She took me to meet other guests at the charity event; I felt shy because of my poor English and struggled to express myself. She asked me about the situation in Iran and listened carefully. When I told her about the human rights violations there, and my personal story, Moira was visibly moved; she felt sad and angry. She engaged deeply with my story and was particularly concerned to hear about the repression and abuse of women. I remember her saying, "That regime is afraid of women."

Moira gave me her home number and asked me to get in touch with her so we could meet. I called her later, and she invited me to her house. It was difficult for me to find her address; I didn't want to be late. To my surprise when I arrived, I found the dining table was laid with an Iranian handwoven cloth, Iranian sweets, and nuts. The warmth of the atmosphere and furnishings reminded me of my old family home.

Moira was extremely kind to me. She had prepared an Iranian dish, and in the kitchen, I saw an Iranian cookbook; she seemed to have gone to a lot of trouble for me. She asked about my life and listened carefully to my story when I told her I lost my mum when I was fourteen. Then she looked at me and said, "I can be your mother."

Moira had no children; she had never married, as she dedicated her life to look after her parents. Her mother passed away some years ago; her father became blind and passed away at the age of 108.

When we met, I was working as a volunteer project manager in a charity that helped orphan children. Moira involved herself in the charity, and we started to meet regularly. She had been in the air force during World War II. She was one of the readers in the local Catholic church. I accompanied her to mass, and we had regular discussions about religion. She thought I had a deep understanding of Christianity.

She was very keen on improving my English and dedicated hours of her time teaching me. Her own use of English was of a high standard. She read at least one book a week. She enjoyed a good whodunit, but she was also fascinated by world history and learning about different cultures; years later when her eyes were failing, she tackled *Seven Pillars of Wisdom* and *The New Silk Road.* She also loved a good racy novel; she was deeply interested in human character. She admired the Prince of Wales and read the Dimbleby biography and the one by Catherine Mayer. She said, "I never came across anyone with such ability to integrate a wide range of interconnected human interests, spiritual, ecological, and social. He is extraordinary."

We visited local libraries together to borrow books. It was a considerable task for me to find a book she hadn't yet read. The librarians all knew her as a serious reader.

One day she called me to come and help her with the shopping. I drove to the house and rang the bell but received no response. I called her neighbours; they had no idea. I panicked and climbed over the side gate of her house; I saw no sign of her. By now I was very upset and crying. The local police had no information. Eventually I found her at the hospital. She had fallen, and her collarbone was broken. At the nurse's station, I found out that Moira had given my name as her son and next of kin. When she saw me, she hugged me and said, "it's not serious, they say it was just a minor stroke—I'll be OK." After two weeks at the hospital, she urged me to take her home. I spoke to the consultant, and he agreed to discharge her; this was my first action as her son.

Caring for Moira after her stroke recalled my hospital visits to Mama all those years ago. I felt a deep desire to look after Moira. I couldn't bear to see her helpless and vulnerable. Every day at the hospital, if I were late, she would ask the nurses to call me. She introduced me to the staff and to other patients as her son. She recovered, and from that time on I committed myself to her well-being.

Moira never spoke of me to her father. He didn't like her to have anything to do with anyone apart from himself. She felt resentful towards his controlling nature, which kept her from her friends. She was crystal clear, however, about her duty to look after her parents; for this she had given up a promising career as an actress in theatre. She was beautiful and took great care with her appearance. She owned hundreds of pairs of shoes. She showed me the clothes she wanted to buy—did I like the style and colour? Gradually she became part of my life. We went to the cosmetics counter together to buy her lipsticks and creams. I knew all the best brands. I took her to the hairdresser every week. She loved to visit forests; we made an expedition each week, and I also took her to the church, where Moira spoke of me to the priest. I got along well with him, and we respected each other. He said, "In the church committee we put your name up as a collector for the offertory."

Moira loved to wear purple and other regal colours to offset her delicate English-rose complexion. We did all our shopping by catalogue and researched each season's collections. Her beauty increased with age, being small with fine bones, yet powerful; she ran around elegantly on her high heels, loved to play the hostess, and worked hard in her large garden. Before she became disabled, Moira joined me in supporting victims of domestic violence. She could also be very difficult! She was spirited and independent; to become physically dependent on others was a great trial for her. She became president of a charity we set up together to help distressed children and their families. Moira trusted and loved me totally.

Like many of her generation, Moira was highly disciplined. Her baths and all her meals had to be on time, and later I taught her carers to lay the table properly for afternoon tea and Sunday lunch.

From her stage training, Moira spoke in a way that carried presence. At all times, including when she was upset, her voice affected me emotionally. She was a deep thinker and an excellent listener. Her mind and her eyes opened wide to unusual ideas; she liked to enquire into life. I brought my friends to tea with her and nurtured these new relationships; her own friends had mostly passed away.

Moira encouraged me to study; she was very proud of my good results and liked to tell everyone she knew. She would complain, "You're not telling me about your patients." I said, "I'm not allowed to." "But you can tell me!" She followed up on all my essays, dissertation, and viva. One day she was cross with me—I hadn't talked to her about my viva. "Would you like me to present it to you?" I asked. I started, and in five minutes she was asleep. I completed my presentation and then asked, "What did you think?" She said: "It was excellent!" "But you fell fast asleep—right at the beginning." She had an answer for everything: "I closed my eyes so as to listen carefully."

It was essential for me to complete my doctorate before anything happened to Moira. When I passed my viva, she was in hospital again; I ran there to tell her. She was delighted and kissed me: "Well done—excellent."

Moira wanted everyone to know I was her son. One day a neighbour said, "We never knew you had children!" She replied sharply, "Was it my duty then to tell you?"

When I began my relationship with Alison, Moira seemed at first to accept the situation, but as she aged and grew physically disabled with arthritis, she needed me with her all the time. It was impossible for me to go on holiday. Keeping the peace between Alison and Moira became challenging. The circle of relationships with the carers, doctor, and dentist became a family matter.

When I took Moira to Kenwood House on Hampstead Heath, people admired her elegance and beauty; she rode her wheelchair like a queen under her stylish hat. She was in pain but would not allow it to spoil our outings. She inspired respect; she had considerable stage presence. Constantly I heard: "Oh, how elegant your mum is—isn't she beautiful!" I took great pride in her. I confided my problems and received her wise answers. She listened carefully, even to my arguments with Alison. She strove to be neutral and objective, and not just take my side.

Through Moira, I realised the importance of the elderly in our society—the contribution they make was a formative lesson in my life. She and I were interdependent. When she was ill, I had to be ready around the clock. Many times, a phone call came from the carers when they couldn't cope, and I went to her at any time of the day or night.

Four or five times towards the end of her life she almost lost consciousness. On one occasion this happened on the stair lift—as soon as she heard my voice she woke up. On three occasions, I woke her. She tolerated the pain in her life. I used to call her six times a day and went almost daily to meet her. Every week she planned a visit to the countryside. I arranged for a friend to read history to her and for someone to come and teach her Spanish. The beautician, hairdresser, and chiropodists came regularly, as well as a handsome young physiotherapist whose company she enjoyed.

Moira was fond of Adrianna, the daughter of one of her carers. She had known Adrianna since she was a baby, and I supported Adrianna's education financially. Neither of us knew what had happened with her father, and her mother was reluctant to speak of it. Moira used to look at me and say, "Why don't you adopt Adrianna?"

On her final admission to hospital, she told me, "I can't make it this time." She had heart and kidney failure. I had just received my second doctorate. From her hospital bed, she reached her frail hand up to my neck and tried to pull my face down to hers. She kissed me and said, "This is great." Her last words to me were, "You know I love you very much."

It was very difficult for me to let her go. One of our friends came to the hospital and told me quietly, "Moira is in pain; she is dying. She's waiting to make sure you are OK." I felt desperate. I walked up and down for twenty minutes. Then I decided to talk to Moira. I went to her bedside, took her hand in mine, and spoke clearly: "Physical life comes to an end. You and I believe in life after death. I don't want you to be in pain. It would be extremely difficult for me not to see and be with you, but I have to accept it. I will be OK."

Then I couldn't carry on; I came out again crying. But I think this gave Moira some sort of confirmation or permission. Father Linnegar said, "Moira lived for you, and she is now letting go." She was ninety-eight years old.

Later that day three angels arrived, smiled, and settled around the bed: her carers. Moira had waited to hear their voices, for she seemed to relax. They had looked after her around the clock, and it was quite challenging for me to make sure they kept the house and handled her in the way she wished. Often, she was grumpy, but all the carers loved her. They would say, unanimously, "She wanted only you. When she's difficult, as soon as you arrive, she's a different person."

With their presence, the scene was now complete; Moira's hand lay in mine, and quietly she passed away. I had a combination of feelings. I felt relieved that she was at last free from her physical pain, yet when I went home, I couldn't sleep. I had no sense of myself physically, but I wept out loud. I got up early to collect the death certificate from the hospital and discovered—my car had been stolen! Had Moira sent a thief to distract me from my grief? This brought a smile to my face. When I bought my new car, it had to be one that she would continue to enjoy riding in.

At the time of writing, now two years after her death, I reflect on the biggest loss in my life. When my biological mum passed away in my fifteenth year, I was not too affected, but Moira's death shook me to the core.

I feel her presence when I go to the cemetery. It is a comfort for me to talk to her there, to clean her headstone and renew the flowers and to tell her things, and to feel her quiet advice and counsel. I know she was delighted with the stylish funeral we gave her, with six white horses. All her carers came and released seven white doves.

About two months later, following her wishes, I established a human rights organisation under her name: Moira Bradley Foundation.

MY WIFE ALISON

The challenges I faced with Alison who became my wife were crucial in the adaptation to my new home. Initially our relationship was a culture shock. To be with me, Alison made some adjustments in her lifestyle and in her expectations; otherwise, I might have been unable to sustain the relationship. Her loyal care and love helped me view more objectively my trauma, my anger issues, and the way I had lived. I learned to observe myself, to engage deeply, and even to question my attitude and way of life.

Alison is a university professor of philosophy, a feminist, and a socialist. A quality of communication was required that I had not yet developed, for when I finished university in Iran, I became part of the Resistance movement. Living in a close-knit community of activists and freedom fighters, I had developed no experience of ordinary life.

On the surface, our culture, language, background, and ways of life seemed poles apart. Initially, we were all too aware of this. It was difficult for my ideological training and almost monastic discipline to accept the good-natured untidiness of a busy intellectual, surrounded by piles of documents, ideas for new books, and other activities. What brought us close and kept us together? Deep down we look through the same window. We share values. We care about people, about community, and about the environment; and we love each other.

Alison was a supporter of the charity where I worked as a volunteer project manager. Initially I would visit her in Wood Green twice a year to raise funds for orphan children. She engaged with me warmly; she listened very carefully and became close to the organisation. She attended all our events and brought her small son Ben with her. In those days, I didn't call her Alison; I called her Dr Assiter. In my culture, it was not courteous to call a woman by her first name.

One day, about sixteen years ago, I called Alison to make an appointment. She sounded subdued: "Hamid, I'm sorry, it's not a good time." She called me by my name. She said, "Unfortunately—my husband just died." I hadn't known Cyril was her husband. He was an elderly man, an eminent socialist. I had thought he was her father.

I used to play with their son Ben when he was four. I was very fond of him. Cyril was sometimes strict with Ben, but Ben was a good boy! We played with his toy train together.

I told a friend that Alison's husband passed away and suggested we go and convey our condolences. I bought a bunch of flowers, and we knocked on her door. Alison opened it: "Oh! Today it's Ben's birthday. Oh, thank you! Flowers for a funeral are now birthday flowers. Come on in." We were shy, but she insisted. In the house,

I was warmly welcomed by her friends, and I no longer felt shy: "Today it's Ben's birthday, so I want to sing!" I sat between Ben and his playmates and sang two Azari songs. Then I had to go, to keep an appointment.

After that, I began to call Alison regularly to make sure she was OK. A few days after Ben's birthday, I called her, but there was no reply. I called her sixteen times and then found out they were away on holiday. I became aware of my feelings for her. When Alison came home, I told her, "I feel love towards you." Throughout the previous ten years, our close friendship was based on mutual respect as colleagues in the work we were doing, and I always enjoyed playing with Ben; but our real connection started from this moment when Alison looked back at me. Over our next few meetings, she touched my hand. One day in Muswell Hill as we walked in a park near Fortismere School we hugged and kissed for the first time. I said, "You realise this is forever?"

Alison announced to her university friends that she was in love and took me to their parties. I had imagined that academics were serious people, but to my astonishment, they were all drunk and laughing loudly. This was unfamiliar to my upbringing.

I felt warm and proud when Alison recognised me as a stepfather for Ben. I was desperate to be his father; I was fond of the boy. I came into his life not of his choosing; I wanted to do everything I could for him—and to retrieve my own feelings of lost fatherhood. Ben was a gift for me. One day in a North Finchley coffee shop, I told him, "You know Ben, I came into your life, and you accepted me without hesitation. I was really touched. I can understand this might be a bit challenging for you, a man from a different culture and background in your life, but I just wanted to tell you this." Tears were in my eyes. Ben listened carefully. "Ben, you gave me the feeling of being a father." Ben stood up, opened his arms, and came to hug me. He said, "I'm proud to be your son!" He was then about sixteen. When I look back at this, I feel very emotional. My pure love for my son developed swiftly, and being his father is now part of my identity. I have been fond of all his girlfriends; he respects me deeply and listens seriously to my advice. Ben became a successful musician. Back home in Iran, this was not considered a serious profession: I wanted him to be a human rights lawyer. My loving engagement with his life enabled me to develop a more generous understanding of music and its value in human life. I now feel that music is intrinsic to the human condition: we are musical beings in the way we talk and the sounds we make. To understand Ben's world, I took piano lessons and even learnt to compose a little. Since childhood I had loved to sing.

From the beginning, Alison shared her many friendships with me. Overall, any area of conflict brings strong emotions. These became an expression of our deep connection and similarity. Although we argued frequently over our lifestyles, she never felt strange to me. We are extraordinarily close; she is a part of myself. Sometimes when Alison wants to make her point about something, I engage with her silently. She exclaims, "You're not saying anything!" In my natal culture, we are brought up to receive an opinion quietly and to think carefully before responding. When I do say something, Alison brings to it her intellectual training in combat and defence. In the movement, I developed the value of keeping quiet; not to react. This became my style. Always there is time and space to sit, discuss the difficulty, and find a way to overcome it. I have no hidden agenda. I try to listen and to get the full picture. I worked hard in engaging with other people's problems.

At first, I didn't want to waste precious time going away on holiday together, and Alison and I had arguments about that; nowadays I can relax and enjoy it more. We enrich each other's way of life. Alison became keen to learn Farsi; she spent a lot of time and energy mastering the language so we can speak it together. In her turn she has told me, "You brought fresh meaning and purpose into my life: we care about things in the same way. We do argue about everything, but our life is never boring!"

Alison is generous; she respects me deeply and helps me be myself as a whole person. This includes some of my rough edges, which she has the knack of drawing out. With her encouragement, I started to form my own charity organisations. Alison got me an introduction to the university where I obtained my master's degree in human rights and social justice. In the beginning, she would check my essays, but I had some difficulty with this; it seemed to affect our relationship. I preferred to do my own checking. My studies helped me find myself in the genre and express my strong feelings and ideas about education.

From the outset, Alison and I had no issues over our finances. When I had nothing of my own, Alison supported me. We were easy in this respect.

I am deeply proud of Alison's intellectual sharpness, her feminist values, and the way she cares for others. She embodies my ideals for human knowledge, education, and love of wisdom. We discuss ideas every day and polish them on each other.

I am lucky to have this woman of principle in my life. I could write forever about our daily life and all its adventures that lie beyond the scope of this book. If I let her read this chapter, we are sure to have another argument!

MY CHILDREN

As I became separated from my biological family—many of whom were killed by the regime—the urge was strong within me to create a new one and be a father to Ben, Marisa, and Adrianna. Moira was my mum, and Thomas Darby, a trustee of our charity, became like an uncle to me. Their acceptance of me as a family member, my capacity to love them as my own, and their reciprocation went a long way to heal my losses. Each person has a unique value in my life. I couldn't have imagined that I would develop such strong feelings for them, or how emotionally interdependent we would become. When Marisa cannot sleep because she lives on a noisy main street, it impacts my whole day. When Ben split up with his girlfriend, it deeply affected me. If Adrianna runs into difficulties at school, I feel profoundly concerned for her. I never stop thinking about their future and my role in it as their father. This very morning as I write, Alison (sounding a little astonished) told me how Ben admires, respects, and values me in his life and relies on me. How lucky I am. The love, care, and connection grow and grow. In my experience, we can create our family consciously and form an even deeper connection with these new loved ones.

My instinct to protect others is highly evolved. Within loss, there is a creation of possibilities. As the regime took my family, I created my extended family.

Marisa used to say, "From childhood, I longed to have a father." Our deep connection was clear when I first met her. I was the first mature man she was able to trust, and we decided to become like father and daughter. Through my presence in her life, she was able to find herself and to step beyond the difficulties she had experienced. She takes me seriously; she listens to my thoughts and my advice, and she began to flourish. From the beginning, I have felt proud to say, "My daughter Marisa worked very hard to overcome her life struggles and to obtain a first-class master's degree in law." In a recent serious conversation with her, she said, "I feel I depend on you, but I know that we are this way to each other."

My children are clear about my concern for their education and well-being. Ben eventually agreed to do his PhD and demonstrated his ability to obtain funding for his degree in music.

I have known Adrianna from when she was two months old. She came to my mum Moira's house with her mother who worked there as a cleaner. Adrianna has never met her biological father; her mother couldn't speak of him. Moira and I were parental figures for her from an early age. After my mum passed away, Adrianna and I decided to be father and daughter. In her Father's Day card to me, she wrote, "I could not ever have imagined that I have a father! I am blessed and I am lucky I have you."

All my children are part of my identity. They are with me all the time, in my heart and in my thoughts. They have brought enriched purpose and meaning into my life.

NOTES

1. Karimi is a political refugee who served a five-year prison sentence in Iran. Karimi escaped from Iran with his family and built a new life with his wife and six children in the United Kingdom. He qualified and works as an engineer. Karimi was one of my research participants.

2. To avoid any risk, these names are being kept confidential.

3. According to orthodox Islam, a woman's hair and her whole body must be covered to protect her modesty. Traditionally women must wear a long black robe called a chador, which covers them from head to toe.

4. Nahid Yeganeh and Azar Tabari, eds., *In the Shadow of Islam: The Women's Movement in Iran* (London: Zed Press, 1983).

5. National Council of Resistance of Iran Foreign Affairs Committee, *Women, Islam & Equality* (Paris: National Council of Resistance of Iran, 1995), 38.

6. J. Mansouri, *Civil Law of Islamic Republic of Iran*, vols. 1–3 (Tehran: Islamic Publication, 1997).

7. Ruhollah M. Khomeini, *Tahrir-al Vasileh* (Tehran: Islamic Publication, 1963).

8. Erich Fromm, *The Fear of Freedom* (London: Routledge, 2001).

4

The Research Strategy

Armin Danesh

Research is a quest. A quest is an evolutionary journey. The quest towards truth probes and liberates trapped patterns and transforms the attitude.[1]

Having relived and written my story, I invited nine other Iranian political refugees to share their own stories before and after moving to the United Kingdom. For confidentiality, they chose pseudonyms.

All my participants found my study meaningful and were willing to discuss their lived experience in depth; however, recruiting them was a challenge. It is common to find major issues of mistrust among Iranian political refugees. During our conversations, each mentioned his or her concern about the activities of the regime's spies in this country. Their suspicion of an Iranian unknown to them was natural. Accordingly, prior to the interviews I arranged to meet them informally. Once I had gained their trust, they became extremely open and helpful, and all offered me more of their time.

Much research has been carried out on refugees' issues from sociological, political, and anthropological perspectives. My study breaks new ground by investigating the possible impact on my participants' psyches and their quest for meaning.[2]

In my view, life has purpose. My worldview shapes all aspects of my life and actions, including my decision to study philosophical psychotherapy and counselling. Engaging with European philosophers such as Friedrich Nietzsche, Søren Kierkegaard, Edmund Husserl, Martin Heidegger, Jean-Paul Sartre, and Maurice Merleau-Ponty, I was able to relate them to my earlier Persian favourites: Avicenna, Gazzali, Rumi, Sopraverdi, and Mullah Sadra. These interactions bridging different ideas enriched my theoretical and philosophical foundation. At an East-West philosophy conference, Richard Bernstein was quoted as saying, "it is only through an engaged encounter with the other that one comes to a more informed, textured understanding of the traditions to which we belong."[3]

For the main question of my study, I used a qualitative research framework. The focus is on my participants' thoughts, inner meanings, and experiences through which they express their multilevel reality. I hoped to delve deeply into the subjective meanings that political refugees might attach to particular circumstances.

As a researcher, I engaged directly with my participants. I wanted to ensure that their views would remain in the forefront of the investigation, and that they would drive my findings.

I believe knowledge is more than a mere gathering of facts. Researchers perceiving reality in a fluid and dynamic way are able to "construct" knowledge. Multiple meanings can arise from the interaction. This process is often described as inductive. An inductive process by its very nature keeps the mind open to exploration, moving from specific observations and theory to develop a deeper understanding of my participants' lived experience.

After studying various qualitative methods such as narrative analysis, grounded theory, heuristic, and IPA (interpretative phenomenological analysis), I chose the latter to carry out my investigation.

I aimed to develop an in-depth subjective perspective, evolving from my participants' unique experiences. As I engaged with each individual story, doing justice to their voices, themes began to emerge, interweave, and interact to develop a collective voice (key theme). Each participant complemented and conversed with one another's stories as the narrative as a whole unfolded.

PARTICIPANTS AND RECRUITMENT

I did not recruit anyone I knew. I first approached academic institutions but without success. I knew it would be difficult for me, a stranger, to gain their trust; however, my personal network played an important role in my recruiting strategy. Through people who knew me well, I accessed those who did not. Recognising the sensitivity of political refugees' issues, trust was the essential element. For this reason, I recruited through third parties. Briefly: those who did not wish to be involved would not participate.

My first participant, Sina, said, "*one Iranian characteristic I have learned so far is Irano-phobia!*"[4] Iranians shun other Iranians—mistrust is very common.

When I asked Sina whether he had felt hesitant about my project, as he did not know me, he said, of course he had. He added that he trusted his British friend who introduced me to him. He had met her several times and asked her many questions. She told him a lot about me. Then he decided to give me his phone number. In our first conversation, he had felt really challenged and resolved not to contact me again. But after nearly a month, he felt bad. He thought of his British friend's impression of me and reached out.

Another participant, Karimi, said that the first interview helped him to trust me. He felt he respected me and was honoured to be able to take part. For him, the process was therapeutic and helped him understand himself better. He found my recognition of him as a refugee very helpful. My other participants echoed this sentiment several times.

Before her interview, a third participant, Gila, said, "*Although you were introduced to me by a person I trust, I do need to be sure.*" Afterwards, she said, "*I feel I trust you. At the beginning I hesitated.*"[5]

All my participants shared this initial doubt. They needed to assure themselves that I was in no way associated with the Iranian regime, and that I did not wish to undermine their political party. They said: The Iranian Government employ spies in the West, and use them to maintain their control by creating fear. Having worked with Iranian refugees for more than four decades, I found that often people in exile would neither express their views nor engage with any Iranian they did not know personally. They were aware that many Iranians who were not politically active thought it was safe to go to Iran, and when they did so the intelligence agency would arrest them; so fear of other Iranians is common among them. My initial approach, therefore, was to develop, through our initial meetings, a foundation of mutual confidence, which the interviews themselves enhanced.

It took me more than a year to recruit my nine participants.[6] Before starting the actual interviews, I met each of them informally at least twice to introduce myself and to develop the level of trust needed to gain rich data.

ISSUES OF TRUST

As our mutual trust evolved, my participants Sara, Karimi, and Gila helped me recruit the others. Gila and Lida in particular told me that, after the initial interview, their confidence in me moved to a higher level. Those who came forward to be interviewed about their experiences all shared a positive attitude about themselves and their achievement. I will later discuss in depth the nature of this limitation in my project.

It is crucial to maintain good working boundaries—a friendly relationship rather than a personal friendship. If both researcher and participant have some emotional investment in each other, it could colour what participants are talking about and distort the rich data to be obtained. The professional framework of safety and trust enabled the participants and me to concentrate on the study in depth rather than on ourselves. For political refugees, it is vital that they feel that they and their values are "recognised."

MY STUDY'S PHILOSOPHICAL FOUNDATION

To engage realistically with my participants' worldview, it is important for me to reflect on my own. In the context of my study, my worldview takes account of three fundamental phenomena: existence, human beings, and world history. Human beings desire to be, and to be something; to escape from pain and sorrow; and to achieve well-being and happiness. I believe our existence is a reality, independently from my perception, and evolving in its biological, sociological, and spiritual dimensions. The objective world, however, is entangled with human perception. Our "reality" is open to a multiplicity of interpretations and meanings.[7]

CHOOSING THE METHOD

Methodology is a strategic process or plan of action leading to the desired outcome. It influences and can determine the choice of research questions.[8]

The search for meaning is rooted in the human psyche. The research journey is a systematic discovery to advance our knowledge.

INTERPRETATIVE PHENOMENOLOGICAL ANALYSIS (IPA)

I adopted a phenomenological approach, which explores human interactions while preserving a lived relationship with reality.[9] The Greek word *phaenestia* means to flare up, to show itself. The origin is *phaino*, "to bring to light, to place in brightness, to show in itself, the totality of what lies before us in the light of day."[10] In Husserl's view, all scientific knowledge rests on inner evidence. In consciousness appear the phenomenal building blocks of human knowledge. Husserl states: "Any phenomenon is a starting point for investigation."[11]

Clark Moustakas refers to the experiential texture of situations, feelings, and ideas. "The task requires that I observe (them) . . . always with reference to textural qualities—rough and smooth; small and large; quiet and noisy; colourful and bland etc. . . . within an experiential context."[12] An enormous amount of information is accessed, leading us towards the essence.

In the 1990s, Jonathan Smith introduced interpretative phenomenological analysis as a qualitative research method to gather a detailed description of personal experience. Since then, IPA has been employed increasingly in psychotherapy and counselling research. IPA's philosophical foundation is based on the work of Husserl, Heidegger, Merleau-Ponty, and Sartre. "Stay with the phenomenon, in its appearance, view it from different angles. . . . When the evidence feels complete, the object is given to us adequately," says Husserl.[13]

Though based on existing psychological theory, IPA's main focus is to examine and analyse the content of each person's lived experience, rather than to make theoretical assumptions. Both participants and researcher share the cognitive factor as a central analytic concern, including a primary interest in the psychological process.[14]

IPA analysis is built around the interaction of the researcher's personal experience and psychological knowledge, with fresh information received from entering each participant's experiential world. The aim is to explore inner meaning. Through a series of leading questions to get an "insider view," the researcher plays an active role in the dialogue.

IPA allows the researcher to engage creatively with the participants, keeping the parameters open. The researcher may use empathy, or he or she may approach an emotional event in a more intellectual way, enclosing the episode in a suitable explanation or theory.

IPA is committed to a person's whole being. The researcher considers physical, affective, and cognitive aspects of a participant's emotional state and tries to "read between the lines."

IPA is conducted on small sample sizes. Aiming to collect a qualitative depth synthesis, I designed my questions to give scope for further questions to arise spontaneously, followed by comparison with other cases to broaden the analysis.[15]

IPA assumes and is rooted in the philosophies of both phenomenology and hermeneutics. Phenomenology is the study of perception, while hermeneutics studies interpretation. Although subjectivity is assumed, an IPA advocate works within the subjectivity of the person to interpret her psychological profile, never removing the arena of study from the person's perception of things.

One theorist, Carla Willig, draws our attention to certain limitations in IPA of which we should be aware: "These concern the role of language, the stability of the narrative, and explanation versus description."[16] Through their use of language, participants convey the sense of an experience to the researcher. Does it give a full picture of the event? The choice of words when describing a specific experience constructs a particular version of that experience. The same experience can be described in many different ways; therefore, we have to realise that it is almost impossible to access someone else's actual experience at the time it happened. IPA, however, enables both participant and researcher to make sense of it.

Speaking about her arrival in the United Kingdom, one of my participants, Parya, said:

> When we arrived, unbelievably, the police treated us with respect. It gave us hope. My God! I had tears in my eyes. I couldn't control my feelings. I felt, I've found my home, I've found my family. Can you believe it? A woman hugged me, she said: Don't worry. You can't imagine! We were dirty, like sick people, our skin was pale, yellow, we looked wasted and weak. She said: Don't worry—we will help you. She really empathised with us. I wanted to talk! To open up, to explore my feelings! I wanted to tell her everything! I told her we had had a terrible time. She was holding me, she contained me beautifully, in such a comforting way. When she hugged me warmly, I felt I was saved, rescued. I'll never forget that feeling.[17]

IPA's flexibility, and engaging with the transcript, also opened up my own past, which I had forgotten. On the basis of the mutual trust Parya and I had established, she told me her story, and I was able to imagine the eleven-year-old girl who had been repressed and interrogated at school for asking the wrong questions, and who had been unable to accept herself. She had not been allowed to speak. Her feelings were very powerful. In that moment, I travelled with her on her escape route through

Kenya, where she had tried to protect herself and her children from Ebola, and where she had given some of their food to starving children.[18]

Embracing her whole story, beyond the words, I empathised with her way of communicating a life-changing experience. It was her phoenix moment: she was rising from the ashes. When I related the woman's hug to what had happened to her when she was eleven, she agreed, *"Exactly."*[19]

Perhaps all IPA researchers know the moment when an interaction jumps out of the box: in this case, it was the physical and emotional image of the woman embracing Parya, who tearfully recalled the event and brought it right into the present. At the same moment, I embraced Parya's self-acceptance with my attention.

The language participants use to construct meanings might obstruct their past experience. In my project, however, my participants and I share the same language, history, background, and general worldview as political refugees. This is more likely to help bring those events into the present as we move closer to the centre of the phenomena and their meaning.

WORKING AS AN IPA RESEARCHER

From 2014, I started to conduct my study using IPA methodology. I learned that I could not limit my participants' humanity to being objects of my research. This enabled me to engage with them and to move within their world of human challenge. IPA allowed me to move beyond the research context and to access the unlimited sense of meaning in my participants' lived experience. In this journey, I observed my own life and my own story. I recalled forgotten episodes. Implementing the methodology in my study brought about changes in myself regarding my philosophy, my sense of authenticity, and my relationship with my wife. These changes could be summed up in a single word: *openness.*

As a human rights activist, I had fought in the battlefield against the violators of these basic rights. For me, the way forward was as clear as black or white. There was no room for grey areas in the battle to defeat the oppressors of human values. I feared that if I compromised, I would lose my edge and agency. IPA helped me perceive some shades of grey as possible alternatives, and I was able to both confront my fears and move into a broader perspective. Entering that space, my identity remained safe—and, in fact, clarified as I became more authentic. This was my inner change.

Jonathan Smith, the founder of IPA, contributed to the field of research by transforming personal ownership of the methodology to "public ownership." Researchers can now pool their own experiences. In this respect, I am aware of my responsibility.

As a researcher, I am aware that in order to be open and to receive fresh and meaningful data, I should not impose my technique, ideas, or theories on my participants, as there is no room in the inductive element of IPA for deductive processes. This requires that I understand my participants' unique situations and that I provide a safe, enclosed environment for them to explore their experiences. It elicits a way of communicating that works through their feelings and develops in me a high level of empathy.

Following the steps introduced by the IPA method, reading and rereading the transcripts, I meet my participants again and again afresh, through their narratives. Our interaction was not only cognitive but also reflective. This helped deepen my understanding, as did the act of writing my descriptive notes and rereading what my participants had told me. The themes flourish in this natural way, without being imposed. In this process, I feel I have known each participant for a long time—their struggle, their pain, their fear, and their achievements. They are alive within me.

SAMPLING

Keeping within the guidelines of IPA qualitative research, the number of participants is subject to the purpose of the enquiry. This depends on various factors: the degree of commitment to the case study, the level of analysis and reporting, the richness of the individual cases, and the constraints under which I operate. In contrast to the random or representative sampling strategies of quantitative research, IPA research methodology focuses on the detailed analysis of the experiences of small samples best suited to the research question.[20] As IPA allows their subjective thoughts and experiences to be investigated,[21] participants are recruited as experts in the phenomenon being explored. For example, IPA studies have been published with samples of one, four, nine, fifteen, and more, reflecting a recent trend for IPA studies to be conducted with a very small number of participants. A distinctive feature is IPA's commitment to a detailed interpretative account of the cases included, sacrificing breadth for depth.[22]

My sampling requirement was my nine participants' willingness to discuss the meaning of their own lived experience. This included their active interest in reflecting on these issues and making fresh discoveries. They shared an informed interest in my research topic, which I encouraged with my sample questions. The sample should be homogenous, in other words, consisting of those to whom the research questions are meaningful.

WHO ARE MY PARTICIPANTS?

Personally, I felt proud of them all because, despite what they had gone through, each was able to develop a new life. They kept their mission alive for human rights and social justice and, at the same time, became productive, respectable citizens in their new homeland.

I was able to bring only a small portion of their full experience to this research. This is partly because what happened to them lies in the past, and it is impossible for them to recall every detail. Additionally, their life patterns are very rich. To portray any of them adequately is beyond the scope of this project. My responsibility is to give as accurate an overall picture as I can. My connection with these individuals is linked to a collective movement for freedom and human values, regardless of time and place, and is ongoing.

Although I think of them as individuals, they moved from their personal space to join with others in fellowship. In their commitment and in the choices they made, they exemplify "self for others." They crossed the boundaries that alienate people and became "with others and for others." This became their life's purpose. Sara, Gila, Karimi, Darius, and all the others agree that, without helping other people, their lives would be meaningless.[23] At the beginning of the project, I was overconfident, full of my own experience of four decades of work with refugees since 1981. I had no idea that the project would bring so much new meaning into my life.

My participants helped me towards a better understanding of human values. For my part, their voice will not be limited to this project. They have enriched my life, and my mission is to continue to give them a voice. I carry all of them forward with honour, gratitude, and respect.

DEMOGRAPHY OF MY PARTICIPANTS

Sina

He is single, in his early thirties, and a member of an ethnic minority group in Iran. He lost many friends and relatives through their political and human rights activities, and the situation in his homeland became unbearable. He escaped in 2005 and studied anthropology at one of the London universities. In Iran, he had been barred from further education. His brother left Iran several years before him to live in England, where he is now completing his PhD. The rest of their family are still in Iran.[24] Sina is self-employed, loves his work, and enjoys intellectual activity and discussion.

Karimi

He is in his early fifties, married with six children—one son and five daughters. He and his family live in London. In Iran, Karimi was a political activist, a member of a proscribed party. Many of his friends, family members, and other relatives were executed. Because of his activities, he was imprisoned for five years where he was severely tortured and traumatised. After five years, he was released but remained under constant observation and interrogation. It was impossible for him to remain in Iran, so he escaped in 2005. After being granted asylum here, he managed to bring his family out. He studied engineering, and his children went to university. In Iran, they had been barred from further education.[25] Karimi is a very hard-working man, well respected and popular among his friends. He takes great pride in his work, in which he exercises his values.

Sara

Sara is in her mid-fifties, married, and comes from an ethnic minority in Iran. She and her husband were freedom fighters and members of a proscribed party. She has three children—one son and two daughters; her daughters went into medicine. Her son is not in work because of a psychological condition. Sara and her husband remain members of the proscribed party's European branch. She is an active member of women's rights organisations.[26] Sara has devoted her life to helping her people. She is well respected within her community.

Hiva

Hiva is a single man in his early forties. In 2008, he escaped from Iran. He was head of his family in Iran. After his parents died, he took care of his brother, who was an activist, and his sister, whose health was delicate. Hiva is the author of two books. Because of his activities—his house was used as a centre by opponents of the regime—he was arrested and imprisoned. After his release, he could no longer stay there and escaped. Hiva's application for asylum was refused by the United Kingdom's Home Office, and he is in the process of resubmitting his case. He was able to bring his brother and sister here, who were both granted asylum. He is disappointed with his own rejection by the Home Office. He has a strong personality and entrepreneurial gifts. He has created a successful business with more than forty employees.[27]

Watan

Now in his early thirties, Watan was a freedom fighter and member of a proscribed political party. Relatives and friends of his were executed. He was arrested and imprisoned but succeeded in escaping from prison in 2009. When he came here, his application for asylum was rejected. He married in England and is eager to study, but he cannot afford it without securing refugee status. He has developed several successful business activities and is resubmitting his application for asylum. Watan is popular in his community and remains politically active.[28]

Darius

Darius is single and in his early forties. In Iran, he worked as an English translator to support his family, until the intelligence service tried to force him to work for them. He refused, because to spy on people was against his conscience. The intelligence service attacked his father's house to try to capture him. Darius's life was in danger, and he had to escape. It took ten years for Darius to be granted leave to remain in the United Kingdom. During those hard times, he became a Buddhist and recently found work as a company administrator and translator. His contribution to the firm was appreciated, and after a few months, he was promoted.[29]

Gila

Gila, a widow in her mid-fifties, works in a supermarket. Her husband and brothers were executed in Iran. She was a political activist in a proscribed party and was arrested, imprisoned, and severely tortured. After her release from prison, she had to escape. Gila's three children are all high achievers in this country, and she herself is well respected as a political activist on the international scene. Through her activities for human rights and women's rights, she is well connected through the United Nations (UN) and the International Court of Justice (ICC) in The Hague.[30] She said, "*My purpose in life is to help people.*"[31]

Lida

Lida is in her mid-fifties, married twice, with three children. Two of them are in Iran with their own families. She was a political activist in a proscribed party. Her current husband is no longer politically active. Lida was being followed by Religious Guards who wanted to arrest her. Her party informed her of this and told her to escape at once. She fled with her eighteen-year-old son. Lida arrived here in 2013 and was immediately granted asylum. She is studying to improve her English and to write a novel. Her husband is psychologically fragile and suffers from being separated from his homeland.[32]

Parya

Parya is in her mid-thirties, married with two children—a daughter and a son. Her husband was a political activist; they were at risk in Iran and could not stay there. They escaped through Africa in 2013, where they risked catching Ebola. It was a highly traumatic journey for Parya in particular because of her small children. Parya was a school counsellor and always under surveillance because she had a mind of her own. From an early age, she held radical views about women's rights. This made it impossible for her to stay in Iran. Parya secured asylum for her family after her husband's application had failed. Although she enjoys her life here, her husband finds it very difficult to adapt. This has led to tension and serious family conflict. She is now the head of the family and breadwinner.[33]

INTERVIEWS

Those who fulfil the sampling criteria are invited to participate. I use semi-structured interviewing as my method of data collection, which requires careful preparation and planning. Semi-structured interviewing depends on the mutual rapport established between me and participants. For example, a researcher should not induce interviewees to reveal more than they may feel comfortable with after the event.[34]

My participants were generous with their time and appreciative. Hiva spoke for them all: *"I look to the future. I am very pleased to hear that people like you think about political refugees."*[35]

Conducting a good semi-structured interview requires the skill to cover the domain in a conversational manner and to offer unbiased probes.[36] Finding the right balance and maintaining control of the interview while not losing sight of the original research question is essential; at the same time, researchers should give the participant room to speak freely and openly. Additionally, researchers should consider the possible effects on the study of their own social identities in terms of gender, social class, ethnicity, politics, and age.

COLLECTING DATA

Through semi-structured one-on-one interviews, I hoped to elicit detailed stories, thoughts, and feelings from the participants. Initially, I collected demographic information: age, gender, education, social class, place of origin in Iran, profession in Iran and now in the United Kingdom, marital status, children and family, ethnicity, and religious beliefs. I also asked whether they had been arrested or imprisoned in Iran. I kept most of my questions open so as to avoid making assumptions about my participants or leading them towards particular answers. My main focus was then on analysing the data.

The interview schedule followed four primary domains of participants' experience: their life in Iran prior to their escape, the escape process, their experiences of adaptation and resettlement, and how they saw their current situation and future plans.

The following were my main questions:

1. Could you please describe what it was like for you in Iran before you left the country? (Prompt—What did you do there? What were your political activities?)
2. How did it feel when you first arrived in the United Kingdom? (Prompt— Were there any difficulties? If so, what helped you overcome them? If it was easy for you, can you describe what happened?)
3. What did you think your way of life might be? (Prompt—What were your plans?)
4. How would you describe your life at present? (Prompt—Positive and negative experiences, achievements, and meanings.)
5. What have you learned? What do you hope for in the years to come?

I relied on analysing the data following the interviews, to interpret it as it emerged. This gave my participants the freedom to explore their own stories. I was careful not to ask questions to which political refugees might be oversensitive, such as the practical and highly secret details of their escape. This allowed them to describe this crucial process freely, in terms of how they felt during it.

TRANSCRIBING—METHOD AND
PARTICIPANTS' APPROVAL

It is a highly concentrated intellectual and emotional exercise for me to listen to the recordings of my interviews with participants and make accurate transcriptions of each phrase of the conversation. I found it rather stressful and tiring to begin with. As I grew accustomed to the work, it became easier, particularly when I decided to tackle only one section at a time.

In Sina's case, with my first transcript, I wrote a rough draft of almost the entire interview, working through most of the day. I needed to know how long the process might take and felt encouraged. With the transcripts that followed, I was able to pace myself.

With a deep sense of engagement and empathy with my participants and their stories, I listened to the recordings repeatedly, while correcting the transcripts, focusing on the dialogue, and giving each section time and thought. I also included some observations on body language and tone of voice.

Sara, my second participant, spoke quite repetitively in her interview. In her case, too, I listened to the recording and corrected my transcript. Before we started, she had an urgent phone call and said she must leave soon, but that she had enough time. If we couldn't finish in the given hour, she would come back again. In fact, we spoke for an hour and a half, and I asked for a second meeting to clarify some points; she agreed to give her time. During this second meeting, I also showed her what I had transcribed so far. She read part of it and said she would like to read and sign each page of the full transcript next time.

Although during each of the interviews I asked my participants if they felt tired and would like to resume later, they were all fully engaged in the project and wanted to carry on.

DATA ANALYSIS

IPA does not prescribe a specific method for analysing data. The IPA approach recognises the central interpretative role of the researcher in analysing and making sense of the participants' accounts. IPA is applied flexibly to a set of common processes and principles. Analysis as an iterative and inductive process encourages the researcher to engage reflexively with the participant's narrative.[37] Although the analysis is a joint product of participant and researcher, IPA's primary concern is the participant's lived experience and the meaning that he or she constructs from it. The research finding is therefore based on the researcher thinking about the participant's thinking: a double hermeneutic. IPA analysis is subjective in its strength; nevertheless, that subjectivity is dialogical, systematic, and rigorous. Its application can be made available subsequently, for the reader to check.[38]

In my data analysis, the ideographic focus on each participant developed into a focus on the whole group. I explored the inner meanings derived from my participants' experience. My all-round picture for the analysis followed a step-by-step process. First, I immersed myself in the original data. While transcribing, hearing their tone of voice several times enhanced my sense of connection. Among other things, I considered their tone of voice, laughter, repetition, and metaphor.

For example, Lida, in her interviews, used watery images:

> I was like a bit of wood in the sea with all the waves, you don't know where to go. That is exactly how it felt. My God, where am I going—my son at that time was fifteen years old, he's now nineteen. . . . I kept my hope. The wood had reached the beach. The waves brought the wood to the coast, and I hoped I would then find my own way.[39]

Gila spoke forcefully about "keeping the blood in her husband's veins alive." She said, "*For as long as I have blood in my veins I will fight for freedom. I will never stop. This is my wish.*"[40]

Imagining their voices as I later read the transcripts helped me towards a more complete analysis. Using both my ears and my eyes, I also read the transcripts at different times of day for fresh points of emphasis and avoided doing so when I was tired. Through my reading, and as I assimilated their stories and drew close to their inner world, I felt emotionally connected to each participant in a way beyond cognitive understanding. The trust we initially established helped my participants engage with themselves and helped my in-depth interaction with them. Subsequently, writing, reading, and rereading the transcripts enabled me to meet my participants over and over again, experiencing each of their stories and their emotions for myself. It went far beyond engaging with written texts. Our openness to the unexpected flows into the encounter.

Nothing comes to life in the research without trust. The participants need to feel safe to use language freely and to remit the essence of their experience, though they may be selective and wary at first. Research is a search for truth. At different times and in different moods, I would reconnect, rather than reread, to discover new flavours of this relationship, the human journey.

I became inspired to start writing my own impressions—whatever came to mind spontaneously from reading the transcripts. This process increased my familiarity with the transcripts and identified the specific ways in which participants talked about their issues. As I moved through the transcripts, I noted similarities, differences, and contradictions.

By analysing my exploratory comments, I was able to identify emergent themes and to search for connections across them. I began to discern how the emergent themes linked together, forming patterns that clustered into key themes. As I assimilated the story of my first participant, Sina, I allowed my ideas to flow in response to his statements and began to notice their pattern and consistency.

The same process with the rest of the participants began to reveal the patterns across their narratives and how they suffered in their unique ways to serve the greater cause of freedom and equality. In my final collation of the key themes that arose, I was able to regard the nine participants as a single body. The conscious choice and struggle to bring about change united them as one voice:

> *In our country human rights were violated, threatening our self. Sustaining our value system and commitment, we risked our lives and loved ones to create possibilities. We overcame obstacles and conditioning to face a psychological rebirth. Through this we were able to rediscover ourselves in the arena of cultural shock and adaptation. The future in our hands is now relatively stable. The mission to bring freedom and democracy to our homeland remains our task.*[41]

CONCLUSION

I moved from the individual to the group as a whole, representing the individual, ideographic, and group character of my study. Recognising each participant's unique contribution enabled me to move on coherently to a view of the whole. Each participant, for whom the same theme carried different weight, guided me towards my deeper understanding of the others in the study. My grasp of thematic material in the interview with Sina, which formed my pilot study, grew significantly in the group analysis.

There is no single correct way to conduct an IPA study and to write up its results. This chapter follows the step-by-step process to make sense of what my nine participants said. I have discussed the recruitment process, which took more than a year. The research methodology was based on my own worldview.

Studying various methodologies in the qualitative approach, I found IPA worked best for me. My sampling was homogeneous. I analysed each participant's data individually to meet the ideographic principle, and I looked for patterns across the cases to identify recurrent themes and to develop superordinate themes for the group.

In my study, the analytical interpretation of my participants' accounts moved beyond their own meaning-making and conceptualisation. This process allowed me to link my understanding, in a creative way, with the theoretical framework of mainstream psychology, which I will discuss later.

My contribution to IPA is my emphasis on the need to develop a relationship of trust prior to interviewing participants. This is the primary step towards accessing rich data. I found the IPA process flexible, creative, and open to further development. Joining the IPA community has had a positive and open-ended impact on my personal life.

One of the interesting things to emerge from my study was how the political refugees' identities became a central concern, particularly during a major life transition. My research is in part an enquiry into the cultural aspect of my participants' lives. Their personal, spiritual, and physical dimensions were influenced by social or political lives. This dynamic is shaped within the whole transitional process. The philosophies of Heidegger, Sartre, Merleau-Ponty, and Husserl came to life, together with that of the great Islamic existential philosophers such as Mullah-Sadra.

In Heidegger's view, our interpretations of experience are shaped, enabled, and limited by language. He calls language "the house of being." His metaphor *Dasein*, being "thrown into the world," helped my understanding of my participants' relationship with culture and language. We are constrained within the existential boundaries of our physical, social, spiritual, and cultural world.

Consistently with Merleau-Ponty's view of embodied knowledge—we come to know the world partly through our bodily engagement with it—my participants' physical sensations before and during their escape remained with them vividly. As well as the daily threat and their experiences in prison, there were restrictions on dress and appearance. The body also represents a person's emotional nature. This is central to our experiential understanding and intersubjective actions. In other words, my participants' physical, cultural, and cognitive dimensions are equally important in this book.

In the next chapter, I will narrate and discuss the findings of my research in detail.

NOTES

1. Jane Adams, *The Master's Eye* (London: Broad Field, 2009), 5.

2. Emmy van Deurzen, *Everyday Mysteries: A Handbook of Existential Psychotherapy*, 2nd ed. (London: Routledge, 2009). Van Deurzen reintroduced the idea of examining psychological states in four domains: psychological/personal, social, physical, and spiritual.

3. John James Clarke, *The Tao of the West: Western Transformations of Taoist Thought* (London: Routledge, 2002), 11.

4. Armin H. Danesh, "Exploring Iranian Political Refugees' Experiences in Britain: The Phoenix Rises from the Ashes" (Doctoral diss., Middlesex University, 2019), 84.

5. Danesh, "Exploring Iranian Political Refugees' Experiences," 85.

6. Participants had to fall into one of the following categories: former political prisoners, human rights activists, members of women's rights movements, supporters of banned political parties, or members of student movements. Or they might be writers, authors, or journalists fighting for democracy. Additionally, participants had to be

1. between the ages of twenty-five and sixty;
2. settled in the United Kingdom for periods of three to twelve years;
3. fluent English speakers; and
4. more than twenty-one years of age at the time they moved to the United Kingdom.

Three to twelve years is an appropriate period for a refugee to settle down and to organise his or her memories and activities while they are fresh. Were I to sample a longer period, it could be difficult to obtain fresh information; memories become distorted over time.

7. Ernesto Spinelli, *The Interpreted World: An Introduction to Phenomenological Psychology* (London: Sage, 1989).

8. Jane Ritchie, Jane Lewis, Carol M. Nicholls, and Rachel Ormston, *Qualitative Research Practice: A Guide for Social Science Students and Researchers* (London: Sage, 2013); Francesco Berto and Matteo Plebani, *Ontology and Metaontology: A Contemporary Guide* (New York: Bloomsbury, 2015); Herman Cappelen, Tamar Szabó Gendler, and John Hawthorne, eds., *The Oxford Handbook of Philosophical Methodology* (Oxford: Oxford University Press, 2016).

9. Adrian Van Kaam, *Existential Foundations of Psychology* (New York: Doubleday, 1969).

10. Martin Heidegger, *Basic Writings*, ed. and trans. D. Krell (New York: Harper & Row, 1977), 74–75.

11. Edmund Husserl, *Ideas*, trans. W. R. Boyce Gibson (London: Allen & Unwin, 1931), 129.

12. Clark Moustakas, *Phenomenological Research Methods* (London: Sage, 1994), 90.

13. Husserl, *Ideas*, 117–18.

14. Susan T. Fiske and Shelley E. Taylor, *Social Cognition*, 2nd ed. (New York: McGraw-Hill, 1991).

15. Jonathan A. Smith, ed., *Qualitative Psychology: A Practical Guide to Research Methods* (London: Sage, 2013).

16. Carla Willig, *Introducing Qualitative Research in Psychology*, 3rd ed. (Maidenhead: Open University Press, 2013), 94.

17. Danesh, "Exploring Iranian Political Refugees' Experiences," 97.

18. Danesh, "Exploring Iranian Political Refugees' Experiences," 97.

19. Danesh, "Exploring Iranian Political Refugees' Experiences," 97.

20. Jonathan A. Smith and Mike Osborn, "Interpretative Phenomenological Analysis," in *Qualitative Psychology: A Practical Guide to Research Methods*, ed. Jonathan A. Smith (London: Sage, 2003), 51–80.

21. Katie Reid, Paul Flowers, and Michael Larkin, "Explored Lived Experience," *Psychologist* 18, no. 1 (2005): 20–23.

22. Reid, Flowers, and Larkin, "Explored Lived Experience," 20–23.

23. Danesh, "Exploring Iranian Political Refugees' Experiences."

24. Danesh, "Exploring Iranian Political Refugees' Experiences."

25. Danesh, "Exploring Iranian Political Refugees' Experiences."

26. Danesh, "Exploring Iranian Political Refugees' Experiences."

27. Danesh, "Exploring Iranian Political Refugees' Experiences."

28. Danesh, "Exploring Iranian Political Refugees' Experiences."

29. Danesh, "Exploring Iranian Political Refugees' Experiences."

30. Danesh, "Exploring Iranian Political Refugees' Experiences."

31. Danesh, "Exploring Iranian Political Refugees' Experiences," 110.

32. Danesh, "Exploring Iranian Political Refugees' Experiences."

33. Danesh, "Exploring Iranian Political Refugees' Experiences."

34. Willig, *Introducing Qualitative Research.*

35. Danesh, "Exploring Iranian Political Refugees' Experiences," 113.

36. Richard E. Ashcroft, Angus Dawson, Heather Draper, and John McMillan, eds., *Principles of Health Care Ethics* (New York: Wiley, 2007).

37. Jonathan A. Smith, Paul Flowers, and Michael Larkin, *Interpretative Phenomenological Analysis: Theory, Method and Research* (London: Sage, 2009).

38. Smith, Flowers, and Larkin, *Interpretative Phenomenological Analysis.*

39. Danesh, "Exploring Iranian Political Refugees' Experiences," 120.

40. Danesh, "Exploring Iranian Political Refugees' Experiences," 120.

41. Danesh, "Exploring Iranian Political Refugees' Experiences," 120.

5

The Participants' Voice

Armin Danesh

Dear Reader,

I am sharing with you in this chapter the life stories of nine people, inviting you to engage with them in their world. I hope this may benefit you as well. We all pursue the meanings close to our heart, holding them dear and seeking to practise them. The dilemmas we face require choices to be made; we need to be free to make these choices. I believe freedom is the essence of our humanity. The human struggle for liberation is universal and has no end.

As you engage and empathise with these people's experiences, you may find yourself not apart from them but with them, recognising as in a mirror your own challenges in life. This encounter crosses national, cultural, and individual boundaries, as you walk in harmony, side by side. I deeply believe that we belong to each other, to the same world and universe. Universal values are not only written; the truth within them draws us together and reminds us of our unity.

My study's main focus was to find out about Iranian political refugees' experiences in Britain. We also need to examine in some detail the conditions they had fled, whose nature might in various ways shape their new lives in their host country.

Here is an opportunity to let them speak directly, through the transcribed recordings. I noticed that, though physically apart, their voices seemed to speak through the interviews collectively, as one, as a team. I have therefore allowed their personal narratives to interweave, as though in conversation.

In the nine interviews I conducted, I designed my questions to investigate each of their psychological journeys in four stages:

1. Their lives in Iran before their escape
2. The process of escape.
3. Experiences of adaptation and resettlement in the United Kingdom.
4. How they see their current situation and their plans for the future.

LIFE IN IRAN PRIOR TO ESCAPE

I just wanted not to be there. I couldn't breathe, I was being suffocated.[1]
You don't want to leave your country unless it is killing you.[2]

Violation of Human Rights as a Threat to the Self Value System and Commitment

All nine of my participants found their existence under threat from the clerical regime's violation of human rights and women's rights. The regime used fear and terror as its weapon to maintain power and control. My nine participants chose not to stay silent but, instead, to defend humanity. In their youth, they had enquired into the meaning of life. Parya and Watan were victimised at school for asking forthright questions.

My participants' conscious choice to stand against the regime followed their hope for a more positive future. As they kept that hope burning, they passed through an unknown and uncertain portal. There was no going back. The situation forced them to create a new life.

Since his teenage years, Sina's concern and sense of self were rooted in his ethnicity and culture. He described conditions of corruption, poverty, and exploitation; his people were being eradicated. Being community oriented, Sina, Sara, Hiva, Lida, Parya, and Gila suffered not only human rights violations in general but also the deliberate refusal to recognise their ethnic identity: a double repression. Watan said: "*I suffered because of my ethnic origin.*"[3] In Carolyn Zerbe Enns and Elizabeth Nutt Williams's view, genuine recognition is possible only within a systematic charter of rights.[4]

The religious dictatorship in Iran has been controlling people, particularly women, through abuse of power. As the ideological foundation of the current regime is based on gender discrimination, the issue of women becomes pivotal. Sina, Karimi, and Hiva share strong views on gender equality. Sara complemented them by saying, "*As a woman, I must fight inequality!*"[5]

From my project's early days, Karimi—still a hard-working left-wing activist, now in his fifties and with a large family—was both willing and grateful to work with me. He explained that one has to fight for justice. There is no safety and security for people in Iran who want freedom.

Karimi wants his struggle and his years of imprisonment and severe torture to be recognised: he paid the price for his protest against the injustices he witnessed in his country.

You can't, actually—it's impossible to walk four steps without seeing some violation against working people . . . either you're deaf and dumb or you cooperate with their system. If you want to do something, defend your rights, you go to prison, you keep quiet, or you escape! . . . Iran was like heaven; they changed it into hell. . . . When government rules your wife's head covering, and her clothes and how she should behave, what can I say? Really it is hell. Headscarf, clothes, everything.[6]

If a woman had her hair uncovered, she was insulted and bullied by the Religious Guards. It was clear from what Karimi said that without recognition of women's rights, there are no human rights.

Karimi spent five or six years in jail, with eighteen months in solitary confinement. The torture he suffered, which permanently damaged his feet, reminds him of his vulnerability, and I sensed his need to be contained and healed. His existence in his homeland was not only threatened but being actively destroyed. Torture can destroy part of a person's personality for the rest of his life. In 1988, Karimi witnessed the massacre of forty political prisoners. *"I can never forget that night—2 a.m."*[7] In the community of political prisoners, he carries the memory of the "good, decent people" who were martyred. *"They are part of our history. They fought, and they taught us to fight. Their names will be written in golden letters in our history."*[8]

There was psychological and spiritual torture, as well as the physical torture in the prison. *"I mean, on a daily basis you are under torture."*[9] In fact, visualising his family while he was in prison helped him resist and gave him the power of inner truth, which enabled him to survive. In Viktor Frankl's words, "There is nothing in the world, I venture to say, that would so effectively help one to survive even the worst conditions, as the knowledge that there is a meaning in one's life."[10] No aspect of daily life was free from threat.

Regarding his family responsibilities, Karimi remarks, *"If you are alone, it is easier."*[11] Each day was another death threat. *"You don't want to leave your country unless it is killing you."*[12]

This is another way of saying, as Sina did, *"I couldn't be there; I was unable to breathe"*[13]—speaking for not only himself but also his tribal group and loved ones. They had no representation in Iran, and now they are never far from his mind. Later, Karimi said sadly, *"Beside the beautiful rivers in my homeland, I couldn't speak freely. What is the benefit of that?"*[14]

Karimi is a family man with dependents and continues to work for the oppressed. In Iran, he said, *"You cannot be yourself."*[15] His survival depended on standing against himself, with a false personality. He saw people being abused and beaten every day. It had become the norm, and no one was allowed to argue with it. Desensitization is a significant human rights abuse.[16] Those who stood up for an elderly greengrocer being beaten or who defended humanity in any way were tortured and imprisoned. The alternatives were escape or death.

Even now, it is impossible to forget the level of brutality used against *"respectable, decent people."*[17] Witnessing the slaughter of good people left deep, emotional scars. Karimi's connection with the martyrs and what they stood and fought for gives him some comfort and meaning.

It was hard for Karimi to make social connections after leaving prison, as he feared putting his family and others at risk. His political struggle and combat came to an end. *"With the money they have, they should provide health, wealth, education, libraries for people—but they buy weapons and they pay people to spy."*[18] Individuals in the regime's employ reported casual conversations. His neighbours had high expectations of a political prisoner and activist, but Karimi was now forced to censor himself when confronted with injustice. It was intolerable to lie to himself, to adopt a false personality, and to risk compromising his integrity. For Karimi, with his desire to defend others, *"Either you become mentally ill and stay at home, or you do something."*[19]

Karimi's anger causes him to adopt a clear posture against the regime. In some ways, he lives in his past. He believes he is still on the battlefield, though in a different way. Before his escape, he was aware that there would be freedom to move around and to be treated as a human being in the host country, but he had no idea what this might be like.

Sina is studying anthropology and is a cab driver. He enjoys political discussion, rich use of language, and freedom of movement. Before his escape to England, he belonged to a nomadic tribe in Iran. He explained how the regime crushes minorities and their right to speak and described its confiscation and nationalisation of forest and grazing lands. His tribe had to obtain permission to graze their sheep there. It hurt him deeply that his people had no representation. He told me very emotionally that he couldn't breathe there; he couldn't stay. The developing internet technology was used to repress people. Sina's heart is heavy with the memory of family members who were killed.

Speaking of these conditions in Iran, he said:

> *Do you know, this means the presence of the state in the tribal people's daily life. Culturally, I don't know, how can I describe. Now is the century of the iPhone and technology, but people couldn't access it; now they can. And now I must not speak or be familiar with my mother language. In my view, it doesn't mean anything but repression, which hurts me. . . . From the time central government started brandishing machine guns, the situation of my people has got worse, not better. Technological development didn't necessarily benefit people or their freedom. Yes, it was used to repress people.*[20]
>
> *I mean, am I part of this society? I am talking physically about myself. Do I belong here or not? When you have such a feeling and you are constantly under repression, this increases the pressure and forces you to act, to do something. Also, in this situation you are young and full of energy. . . . The next thing is, if there is a way to escape, to move out. Do you know, my good friend who was killed, if he had any opportunity, he would be sitting here now. He wouldn't have lost his life at such a young age. . . . There is no way to use your energy productively there, and they don't care if you exist or not! . . . This feeling even helps you to risk your life. In Iran, you either are or you are not—and we were not! Yes, I just wanted not to be there. It is not simply that I didn't want, and I had a choice: it was impossible. In Iran, I couldn't breathe; I was being suffocated.*[21]

Sina knew he had somewhere to escape to, because he had a brother who had reached England—his "social asset" as he called it. Like Gila and Hiva, it made no difference to him where he went.

The Resistance shaped Hiva's education. Along with Sina, the nomadic tribesman turned anthropology student, and Sara, a fugitive mother of three who took her courage in both hands to train as a soldier, Hiva declares: "*We were always under pressure from the system. I wasn't allowed to speak my mother tongue.*"[22]

Watan Azar, a young man of thirty, chose this symbolic name related to politics and "the country of fire" in the Zoroastrian tradition. He told me his uncle was a political activist, and that Zoroastrians in his hometown worship secretly, as the ancient Persian faith is forbidden by the regime. "*I use this name on many occasions! I like it.*"[23]

In Iran, Watan was a cab driver from a strong community of political activists, and his role models opposed the regime. He lost many relatives to the Revolution and was also imprisoned. On one occasion, when in town with his father, he saw a man hanged in public.

> *The scene is branded on my mind; I can never forget it. When I came back home, I talked with my uncle. He was politically active; he had been in prison and was tortured severely. I joined different political groups to oppose this injustice, and I was arrested.*[24]
>
> *When I was at school, always I asked this question: Why do they destroy the lives of my family, why are they against them? . . . At school, they tried to involve me in religious activities. I don't believe in religion.*[25]

Like my other participant, Parya—see the next section, "Motherhood and the Battlefield"—Watan was persecuted by his religious teachers for asking questions. Looking for work in southern Iran, he found he was unemployable because he was from an ethnic minority and not Shia (the regime's approved version of Islam). "*I suffered because of my ethnicity; I suffered because of my identity! I couldn't speak my mother tongue openly; I couldn't dress as I wanted. This is the situation in Iran—to defend and fight for my ethnic origin.*"[26]

Watan was arrested twice; he was questioned about the leaflets he carried and about his family's activities. After his second arrest, he managed to get away while being transferred to a different prison. Barefoot and in handcuffs, he leaped out of the truck into the night. He was shot at, but he knew that part of the country well; the people there were against the regime, and a relative took him in. He then walked for two days and two nights.

Darius is in his forties. In Iran, he obtained a degree in English and worked as a translator for an oil company. He was not part of a resistance group; he was one of many millions of Iranians who disagreed with the regime but didn't want to risk their lives.

> *The government tried to control everything, and never let the young people say what they want. . . . Walking in the street, you know they would catch you if you had short sleeves or long hair or a tee shirt . . . if someone didn't like your face or didn't like what you said, they could cause problems for you.*[27]

Darius's English qualification opened up a chance for him to live in a free country; he planned to work in Australia to support his family in Iran. The turning point in his life came when the intelligence service asked him to work for them, to spy on his colleagues. He was also being followed. "*They wanted me to cooperate, but I never did.*"[28]

My female participants concur. Gila said, "*For as long as I have blood in my veins, I will fight for freedom.*"[29] Parya said, "*I had no freedom to express my views.*"[30] Lida recalls her fight for justice and freedom. They all described their motivation to make a positive change and their early commitment to their values. Freedom defined their existence and their aspiration to defend human rights and remain loyal to their people. Paying the price for their resistance in daily life served to strengthen those values within them. Finally, they knew they "could not be there." Their lives were on the line.

For the regime, sexual vice and virtue are predominant criteria.[31] Women in Iran, however, take a leading position against the clerical dictatorship. Male activists cannot serve their ideal without supporting women's leadership. As Hiva said, regarding the attitude to women within his own resistance party, "*They gradually accepted women's rights and encouraged them to fight against the regime.*"[32]

In Karimi's world, human rights, freedom of speech, and the right to work in safety are his priority. In Iran, he joined an organised left-wing opposition party. He stressed the importance of unity against the regime. "*I still believe the freedom of the workers comes from their unity. . . . You can't enjoy freedom without fighting for it.*"[33] The battle in his homeland was for freedom of expression and for basic amenities. "*I couldn't ignore what was going on against the working people, who were marginalised.*"[34]

Sina spoke not only for himself but also for the whole exodus of refugees and the agony that preceded it. I noted his philanthropic nature and his resolve not to put himself before others. In nomadic cultures, life is hard, and people must work together for the communal good. "*I came away, but relatives and family members suffered. More than this, it is about those people who have become poorer. . . . I feel I am part of them, although I am here. It makes no difference.*"[35]

During the early interviews in my project, Sina spoke with profound sorrow of the segregation of women in Iran, and how they are molested at night. Karimi expressed the rage he felt when the Religious Guards bullied his wife. Both men intuitively recognised that freedom for women is crucial to the whole issue of human rights and social justice, and to their country's struggle for liberation.

MOTHERHOOD AND THE BATTLEFIELD

Sara's interview, following on from those with Karimi and Sina, gave me the opportunity to hear the women's story directly. The first thing Sara says about herself is, "*I was a housewife in Iran.*"[36] Because of her situation and her husband's political activities, they often had to move to different places.

Sara is now in her mid-fifties. At the time of the 1979 Revolution, she had two children. She powerfully describes her ethnicity and her position against the new government after the Revolution. She is not a religious person. Her husband was an active member of an organised left-wing party against the regime, and she was at first his follower. Then their third child was born.

Sartre told the story of his student's dilemma during the Second World War: whether to fight in the resistance or to care for his elderly and infirm mother.[37] Many political refugees face a dilemma over the impact of their activities on their family's safety. All my participants, with the exception of Darius, grew up in politically active families, so the situation was familiar and accepted. Motherhood played a special role in the battlefield; in my study, this experiential reality is now given voice.

Sara speaks with pride about the freedom fighters. They were well known within their communities because they risked their lives. She fled her home under fear of arrest, despite the uncertain future of her three children. Carrying the responsibility for her children's safety, as well as the safety of her husband and her ethnic group, Sara moved from village to village like a hunted animal. She told me,

> When the regime attacked our region, they established military bases everywhere. It was not safe for our freedom fighters to stay in one place. My house became a freedom fighters' centre in our city. It was dangerous for us to stay there. . . . I knew 100% I would be arrested.[38]

Leaving two children with her mother in the city, Sara took the baby. It was very hard for her to separate from them, and harder still to choose which child to take with her, but Sara's determination to defend the freedom of her people to exist came first. She lived under attack. Finally, she decided the baby should stay with her mother, who was too old to look after all three, so her son came to her.

> The whole area was a battlefield. . . . In each village where we had stayed, the regime established a new military base. Our life moved from village to village. . . . As a family of freedom fighters on the move, we had no security. They labelled us "anti-revolutionaries"—citing this as a justification for destroying us. We had no choice but to keep on the move. It wasn't my situation alone. I was one of many families.[39]

This family feeling was targeted by the regime. When I asked Sara to tell me more about herself personally, she identified herself with being hunted: the unknown future for her three children and her own survival from one day to the next. Being married to a freedom fighter marked her down to a daily death sentence. I noted Sara's need to repeat herself—to underline her ordeal as a mother and as a woman. "*I had no choice, and I had to carry on.*"[40]

Facing these difficulties, and with her maternal and home-making functions taken from her, a turning point came.

> I began to think, I want to do something myself, not just follow. I decided I too can be a freedom fighter. I too can fight against that suffering which the regime inflicts. . . . I received military training and political education.[41]

As Sara joined her husband's party, her position transformed from passive to active, from despair to new birth: a "phoenix moment." Her great pride was reflected in her voice, a pride she feels to this day. She was "no one" until she decided to join her husband's party proactively.

> *Reaching this point, I wanted to be an independent human being, not merely to follow. . . . I asked myself, why is our country, and the world, like that? It made me feel I must do something. I must start from somewhere against all inequality and injustice against women. . . . As a woman, I must fight inequality.*[42]

Sara trained as a doctor's assistant and made the freedom fighters' hospital her place of work. The party gave her this job to enable her to take care of her son.

> *I must be for myself, not only for my husband. Following him from village to village, from town to town had given me a lot of experience of life. I came to the point where I trusted myself and knew I must act. . . . For me, this was a new self-knowledge, a new understanding. . . . At first, I was too young to know.*[43]

Other women also made this stand. "*Our party opened the door for women and gave us our chance. They encouraged us.*"[44]

Caring for her son doubled Sara's workload. Her sister was in prison. Beginning to define herself as a person in her own right, she felt reaffirmed also as a mother. She repeated to me three times that she wanted to be someone herself, not just to follow. Taking positive action made her feel protected. Joining the party removed her fear and manifested her equality and potential. "*Although we were militant, we didn't want to shoot anyone. We had no choice. They were attacking us, and we had to defend ourselves. Every one of us who had weapons felt the way I did. I never actually killed anyone.*"[45]

As a fighter among other women, Sara faced multiple battles—for her ethnic rights, for freedom, and for her equality and status as a woman. To reach this point, a woman had to overcome many cultural and psychological barriers. The alternative was intolerable.

> *I think the 1979 Revolution helped people, and particularly women, towards a better knowledge and understanding of their potential. We became more confident. The culture started to change from that time, particularly in our area. This was when women decided to fight against the regime. At that point, our knowledge of ourselves changed dramatically.*[46]

Sara's husband supported her independence and training as a freedom fighter. "*He always supported my independence . . . he encouraged me not to be dependent on him. He was always like a teacher for me.*"[47] This was quite unusual and touches on how "women's rights" may work in a progressive and cooperative partnership within marriage in a formative way.

Sara spoke with deep feeling about the agonies of separation; she didn't see her older daughter for seven years. She describes her heartbreak when she had to send the little girl away to a safer place. The trauma they both experienced remains with her. After crying her eyes out, she joined a tough ten-hour march through the mountains to reach the battlefield. This poignant episode illustrates the painful collision between parental love and loyalty to human liberation: woman's sensitivity with the fighter's steel.

Sara's physical and spiritual determination to improve the human lot transcended her biological family ties. This key episode in her life was very hard. She still suffers nightmares about the wrench from her daughter (who is now a doctor). For a while, her commitments seemed torn apart; yet she continued to hold them together.

When asked how she managed to make these sacrifices, Sara replied:

My purpose in life. My values. These values empower people profoundly. Otherwise it would be unbearable. When you decide you have to change circumstances—why people suffer—these things empower you and make you strong.[48]

When I asked Sara what pressured her to escape, she replied that her decision to fight gave her energy: "*the fear was removed from my body.*"[49] But throughout the years of her combined responsibilities, the elder children were separated from her and grew up; then her mother died. The regime began to put pressure on her children, who were in peril. They needed a good education and some stability, and she was caught in a moral dilemma over whether to abandon the battlefield. Sara is now a working mother and leader of women's action groups.

My fourth participant, Hiva, is a published author and man of ideas. My participants are thinkers and want to promote their politics. I noticed that many of them were more eager to talk about their ideas than about themselves. During the interviews, I had to remind them to focus on their lived experience.

Persia has ancestral traditions of family warmth and loyalty. Parya made the point that the regime usurps this role in Iranian culture. She objected to being called "sister" at the school where she taught. "*They are not my relatives!*"[50] In the religious dictatorship, people's loyalty was rewarded by their being called "brother" or "sister" within the ideological family. If a person stepped out of line or failed to show loyalty, they were ostracised. The reality was that outside the home everyone mistrusted everyone else.

Parya, a mother of three, grew up in a large, politically aware family. In Iranian tradition, the oldest brother enjoys a special place. Her brother was a freedom fighter and member of a left-wing party. In 2013, Parya escaped from a situation in which she was trying to avoid arrest. Two of her sisters became freedom fighters and one had already escaped to Germany. Parya's family was therefore well known in the community. Their lives, in their networking with others, were under threat. Being a female freedom fighter like Sara, Gila, and Lida demonstrates intense commitment to gender equality and women's rights, as political activity is traditionally reserved for men.

It is culturally acceptable for a man to want to be a political activist. If a woman wants to be an activist, she has to overcome the cultural and psychological barriers which limit women. It makes everything really hard.[51]

Parya's battle was a comparatively solitary one because she did not formally join a group. At the age of eleven, she asked her teacher: *"During the Revolution my brother loved the Supreme Leader. But now he is fighting against him. What's happened?"*[52] From that day on, Parya experienced interrogation and harassment by the school authorities. She opposed the regime's ideology by defending her desire to be a teacher, which involved taking a religious exam on trivial domestic details with time-consuming and confusing questions.

Living in this cultural environment makes it very difficult for a woman to keep any position or job outside the family. Parya refused to be brainwashed, having already crossed the regime's boundaries and already been penalised. With her desire to contribute to society and to help children, she chose to become a school counsellor, but she was kept under surveillance. She told me,

> *You don't want to upset your parents, particularly as people then think badly of them. A woman constantly has this worry and stress—did I do the right thing? She believes in what she is doing, but the same time she is harassed. . . . It was always difficult for me to wear the chador, and the school authorities always pressured me because I didn't wear it properly. Basically, you mustn't show any of your hair.*[53]

The regime mistreated women by blaming them for anything bad that happened.

> *When I talked with the children in my room, a Religious Guard would spy on us. They reported what I said and what I talked about with the children. I took this qualification because I genuinely wanted to help children. The regime didn't value that at all. I couldn't carry on there.*[54]

Parya's respected older brother was afraid and stopped being a fighter. He withdrew, but her two sisters kept going. Women suffer acutely under the regime. Their profound desire to change society is common within Iran. Parya married at eighteen, in the hope that it would give her more independence and protection. She disobeyed when her husband forbade her to attend university. She was an independent thinker, *"Why do we have to put up with this nonsense? Is it because we don't have the strength to defend ourselves?"*[55] Like the other participants, Parya faced a brick wall and couldn't keep her job. *"I felt I couldn't breathe."*[56] Gradually, she reached a breaking point. As a mother, she had to be particularly careful. Her husband's position as an underground political activist put the whole family in jeopardy. This helped Parya plan her escape, but she wanted the decision to be her own. They were ready to go anywhere other than Iran.

Gila, an internationally respected activist in her fifties, works in a supermarket. She told me she stood up for freedom throughout Iran and that, though she is a member of an ethnic minority, her heart is open to all Iranians. Her husband was executed in 1980, a year after the Revolution, when she was twenty-three. Four days after his capture, the Religious Guards called through a megaphone, "Come and take your dead bodies."[57] In Iran, they were members of a proscribed party.

The regime attacked us and began to kill our people. The situation for us was like it is in Aleppo in Syria. It isn't easy for me to go back to these memories of what happened. When I hear the news about Syria, about Kobane, about Aleppo, it reminds me of what we went through. It depresses and deeply saddens me, and I cannot sleep. My memories come to life. They captured people and hanged them publicly—and dropped bombs on us.[58]

Like Sara and Sina, Gila's people were under constant attack.

Gila's ethnic origin is a deep identity issue for her. When she feels she is "someone," this "someone" can fight for freedom. Her fight for values and decency gave her energy and gave her life meaning. Like Sara, Gila was traumatised, as a mother of three children under seven in a life-threatening environment. She uses strong language—*"for as long as I have blood in my veins, I will fight for freedom; I will never stop."*[59] This helped her to rise above her terror: the will to continue and to do better. *"From that point, I struggled to keep my husband's blood alive."*[60]

After Gila's father was assassinated and their home was confiscated, Gila's mother lost heart and died. Gila took responsibility for all her remaining relatives. At the same time, she worked in the resistance party and tried to supervise her children's education. Education became her priority, so her children could grow up into good people who carry on the values to which their father sacrificed his life. *"I never stopped fighting the regime and distributing leaflets secretly among the people. I felt I had strength and power. My mother died of depression. I would never die that way."*[61]

Gila told me she that she had spent fifteen months in prison, where she was tortured severely for information: *"I didn't."*[62] In the prison with her little girl, she was aware of the continuing threat to her other children and relatives. The two older children were at university, and their lives were at risk. Even after her release from prison, she wanted to carry on the fight but was forced to escape with her family.

We had no freedom. . . . I knew my phone was being tapped; I couldn't talk freely in my own home. If we wanted to go anywhere, they followed us. It wasn't my choice to escape; I would rather have stayed there to carry on the fight. It was very difficult for me to leave my homeland, mainly because I had a little brother. I brought him up. He didn't want to come with us. But I had to flee Iran. Under a religious dictatorship, everyone is behind bars. They created a vast prison for us, and it was impossible to stay there.[63]

During her interview, Lida told me of the negative thoughts, depression, and fears that still pursue her from Iran:

When I was there, I had no hope. When I was there, I was invisible. I had never been understood or accepted. I didn't exist. You don't have any voice—you can't reach anyone. These things bring despair.[64]

Lida, who is in her mid-fifties, has three grown children; two of them live in Iran with their own families, and her nineteen-year-old son lives with her. She married twice, which shows unusual personal initiative; in many parts of Iran, a divorced woman is a nonentity. Lida grew up in a politically active family environment. From an early age, she studied and read to understand the situation; she was resolute on her path.

> *After I married, I seriously wanted to do something. I felt something was growing and trans-*
> *forming me. It reached a point where I had to get involved. . . . For example, if I wanted to*
> *go anywhere in my hometown, I wasn't allowed to wear my national costume or speak my*
> *own language.*[65]

Lida spoke forcefully:

> *These things made me so angry; I couldn't tolerate it. It was like a storm inside me. You want*
> *to join that flood of people who are fighting for justice and freedom. . . . A lot of innocent*
> *people and youngsters were being killed. They even killed babies. I couldn't stay silent . . .*[66]
>
> *The situation in Iran is misogynistic. A woman has no value as a human being. Women*
> *are under the control of men, always. All decisions are the man's. The woman is an object. I*
> *mean . . . er . . . for a woman there, the only responsibility she has is to be at home, to look*
> *after children and the husband. Men don't take much responsibility; they just do what they*
> *like. The man is not committed to his family; he's always right.*[67]

Lida's work in the organised resistance movement was to liaise between them and their supporters in the city.

> *We had house meetings and I distributed my party's CDs of lectures, news, and condensed*
> *information. Our activities were discovered by the intelligence service, and one of my friends*
> *was arrested. I got a message from my party saying, "You must leave at once, urgently. Don't*
> *stay here. You have to go." As soon as I got this message, I didn't even go home, I left every-*
> *thing. . . I just knew I had to get out.*[68]

Hiva is in his early forties and single. His political commitment took priority over marriage. At the beginning of our conversation, he told me, "*I have conducted some research myself, and I am interested. OK, I'm ready!*"[69] During this interview, he was able to reflect on his past, to think it through, and work some problems out for himself. This brought a new sense of self-connection. He observed, "*The doors are open in many aspects of life. You have to realise as a political refugee, you are an important person. Don't undermine yourself.*"[70]

In Iran, Hiva studied political science and joined an activist circle. To be a student in those days brought a great sense of achievement. The university was traditionally a centre of opposition against the shah's regime, and now it opposes the ayatollahs. "*As activists, we had new ideas! And the regime . . . wanted constantly to keep us under control. Several times, the Religious Guards summoned me for interrogation.*"[71]

The regime was very afraid of people coming together in an organised way. Hiva could not move without surveillance and was frequently arrested. "*I was always questioned about my movements and my connections.*"[72] Threat, fear, and violation of human rights were recurrent themes.

As the eldest of three orphaned siblings, Hiva became head of the family. Their home was targeted as a centre of political activity. Hiva was found guilty of five charges, including being "a threat to national security" and "insulting the Islamic religion and the Supreme Leader," and was given a four-year prison sentence. Hiva's younger sister was not politically active but suffered imprisonment as well. The family and relatives of political activists can be arrested simply by association. Hiva carries in his conscience the burden of his sister's psychological fragility. *"My political activities did not allow me to start a family. At the end of 2005, I was arrested and imprisoned."*[73]

Hiva is passionately loyal to his people. Human rights, values, and the central government's injustices were embedded in his psyche from childhood.

I felt it through my whole body, and in my bones. I remember when I was thirteen, fourteen, I had a dream—to bring justice to our society. My ethnicity, my identity, was under threat. This awareness and what I saw happening, forced me to take responsibility. I represented the people's suffering; I had to defend them.[74]

With the same outrage, Karimi had witnessed working people being beaten in the streets. The participants in my study see themselves representing their communities, rather than acting in their own interest alone.

Hiva describes his sense of purpose and meaning:

When I became politically active, the main barrier I had to overcome was to risk my life. But when I thought about the justice and values and meaning we would bring to the people, it was very inspiring and helped me to conquer my fear. Many before me had chosen this path, and they also inspired us. Our martyrs inspired us.[75]

Hiva was not alone in his thinking. Karimi described "the worst day of his life,"[76] when forty fellow prisoners were executed. For Karimi, the memory of these martyrs is a valued source of inspiration.

Following on from Sara's story of how she and her sisters in the Resistance transformed traditional attitudes in themselves and others, Hiva echoed his observation of women's rights within his activist group:

Those groups I was involved with, they followed the traditional view of women. The groups and the parties in my area were for the men. Women had no significant role. But gradually this changed. Gradually, they accepted women's potential and were inspired by them. Basically, peoples' attitudes began to change, in my area. This was a significant achievement—an opportunity for women to fight.[77]

Hiva—an urban fighter—mirrors almost word for word Sara's account of herself in the mountains where she learned to become a fighter. He went on: *"When women began to join the political activists, they brought a new culture, and even a new literature. The gender equality issue developed and became progressive for the whole of society."*[78] Hiva, a university graduate, highlights here the flowering of a literature that empowered women's intellectual and cultural contribution. Gender equality is a progressive issue.

On the battlefield of his urban community and environment, the young Hiva committed himself to creating history within the collective movement. Speaking objectively, he said that his literary and political activities exacted a high price, between life or death for the cause, which is why he would not marry. Clearly, activists have little option, with the reaction to their political activity being unpredictable. Both Hiva and Gila wanted to stay in the country but were forced to escape. Hiva echoes Sina's statement: "he couldn't be there"; he was too well known to the regime.

> *Those who escape might aim to carry on their political activities. If they stay, they cannot be active, lest they lose their life. Some are only scared of that, so they escape. . . . I preferred to stay in my own area, because that was the centre of the problem, and I wanted to be involved. But there was no way for me to stay and to carry on. . . . Then an opportunity came for me to leave the country.*[79]

Darius's determination not to compromise his own values endangered his life in Iran and drove him to escape. A strong inner life may accommodate hardship and human rights abuse, as long as it can access its own values. He really wanted to stay close to his family, to try to help them and to keep a low profile. For Darius, a lover of philosophy, literature, and music, his intellectual refinement made it hard for him to uproot himself. He lived in fear for several months, avoiding direct meetings, deflecting the regime's pressure with evasive promises, and playing for time.

Freedom of speech is the ability to express a normal, simple life and to interact and care for others without looking over your shoulder. The most basic human rights infringement is when this simple liberty is violated.

Before Darius was forced to escape, he was planning to emigrate to Australia, whence he would be able to visit his family safely and to enjoy relative freedom of movement. The regime confiscated his papers and cut off that escape route. Alone and isolated, Darius addressed his own will to make a conscious radical stand against the regime: to make that change in his life. The individual struggle is no less significant than the collective one.

Karimi said, "*It is not only yourself. It's your family who are under threat.*"[80] Sina left, but relatives and family members suffered. Darius's initiative to support his family by getting work in Australia was blocked when the regime confiscated his passport. Hiva's first asylum application to the UK Home Office failed because he was too distracted by the stress of having left his brother and sister behind. Sara's situation was particularly difficult as she had to combine her responsibility in the party with being a mother. Watan's family lost many relatives to the regime's prisons. Parya spoke for all my participants: "*My children—particularly my son—I couldn't see any future for him in Iran.*"[81] Lida worried constantly that her family was at risk. Gila's responsibility to her sisters and to her children increased her need to look after everyone, even after she settled in the United Kingdom.

From the age of seventeen, Sina asked himself, "*Who am I? What am I for?*"[82] He wants to defend himself, and he constantly analyses himself in relation to the regime.

Does he belong to his country? Or to this one? Does he have a role in society? With this sensibility, he feels under pressure, seeking recognition. Is he wanted anywhere? With his deep sense of purpose and destiny, Sina looks towards the future, wondering where he can play a significant role. He states again the importance of his community and tribal identity. Could this strong quest for where he belongs come between him and his host country? Nothing can replace his roots within the community of his birth; he is never unaware of that loss.

Darius asked himself, "*Will you be able to see your family again, or . . . not?*"[83] When Hiva arrived in London, he felt overwhelmed by the loss of his old life. "*How can I start all over again?*"[84]

In Iran, where his wife was bullied by the Religious Guards, Karimi felt he lost control as head of the family. That loss was brought home to him again in the United Kingdom, where he had to confront and adapt to gender equality.

Sara recalls the long years during which she did not see her eldest daughter, while she was fighting the regime. "*Seven years!*" Watan's family sustained huge losses, with many of his relatives imprisoned or killed.

After taking on responsibility for her family, Parya lost any remaining harmony with her husband and found herself without support. "*I do all the jobs, with the children, everything. It isn't easy living here.*"[85]

On arriving in the United Kingdom, Lida found herself a stranger, a foreigner. She had lost all her belongings from her former life because she could not return home before escaping.

Few writers have addressed the significant interior transformation to which many refugees dedicate themselves long before being driven to escape. As we discover from my participants' accounts, they feared losing their integrity more deeply than they feared losing family or property. They feared losing their spiritual commitment to the cause and to their resistance party, companionship in the struggle. Conscious solidarity enabled them to withstand torture and solitary confinement. It heightened their sense of self and connection with the martyrs to the cause. With their comrades in prison, they were not alone. In prison, the women laughed at their jailors, sang, and wrote poetry. This higher dimension empowered them.

PROCESS OF ESCAPE

Taking Risks to Create Possibilities

Political refugees generally do not discuss the details of their escape to protect the routes for others to use. I was sensitive to avoid this area, which they could not disclose, but I was able to ask them about their feelings during the process. Parya and Darius, however, did voluntarily disclose some unexpected information about their journey.

Most political refugees think, feel, and act collectively, especially members of an organised party with a common purpose. Their training protects them to some extent from fear and deepens their loyalty. Some, like Karimi and Gila, did not disclose sensitive information, even under severe torture. It was essential during the interviews for me the researcher to understand the implications of this in our confidential relationship. For instance, Lida was ordered to leave everything and escape at once, not only for her own safety but also for that of her party. Some resistance parties impose a rule on their members to resist for a certain number of hours after being arrested, giving the party a chance to clear the network.

The feeling of not being accepted as human is itself life threatening, which drove Sina to risk his life: "*Do I belong here or not?*"[86] When an opportunity for survival appeared, he had no choice but to seize it. He believed there was somewhere he could go, only because his brother was now there, wherever it was. Knowing that millions had survived kept the way open. His closest friend and many others didn't have that chance. Escaping is a complex project in itself, requiring others' support and the readiness to seize the first opportunity. "*The several million who escaped from Iran were those who could. They were able to escape from Iran because they knew people; they had money to buy a ticket.*"[87]

His own escape confirms Sina's commitment and desire to seek a meaningful life outside the regime's standards and system. He might not realise yet that the search for meaning doesn't end! "*I felt I was putting myself in danger.*"[88] Clearly, there were potential consequences for his friends and relatives. Paranoia prevails among people who live under dictatorship. They feel constantly threatened and under scrutiny. These anxieties continue and often complicate the escape process.[89] For Sina, an environment without fear was almost inconceivable.

Karimi concurs: "*You don't want to leave your country unless it is killing you.*"[90] He continues:

> Before coming here I knew you can't do anything without risk. Imagine! You're going to destroy a bird's nest. It's not easy for the bird to see that. I had to leave everything—my nest. Of course it was risky—with a wife and children, it isn't easy.[91]

He was forced at first to escape without them. Like Darius and Gila, Karimi loved his country and did not want to leave. Only the escape option might save his family. If he were killed, they would be left destitute. Ten years later, he sees the stark ultimatum he faced. He had to sell everything he had; he could no longer make his stand there as a political activist.

> I had no experience of it yet, but I knew I was going somewhere where I would be respected as a human being. I was escaping from hell. I had heard about others, but having it happen to you is totally different.[92]

Gila took the risk,

> Carrying the responsibility for my children, myself, my brother [was] very hard. From the moment I left my home in Iran I was crying. I cried for many hours. I escaped to Turkey. The intelligence service tried to capture me in Turkey. They tried to find out where I was. I

was very careful, so they couldn't. I got to London through many obstacles. It took more than nine months. I didn't just lose my husband, my father, and my mother—my three brothers also were executed. They were twenty-three, twenty-one, and nineteen years old.[93]

Hiva was held up for a long time at the border, unable to trust any of the routes offered, and caught in a dilemma with his siblings.

Some of my relatives helped me to cross the border. I had no ID. I wanted to bring my sister and my brother. It would be easier for me to escape by myself: with three people it was more problematic. We had to stay at the border for several months. We were also in financial difficulties because we had no time to sell our property. We lived at subsistence level. I found a way to get out myself, on foot.[94]

To avoid arrest, Darius said he went *"to live with [his] grandma, who was ill at the time. There, I could find a way, some channels just to cross the border."*[95] He cannot remember exactly what was going on at the time:

My hope was just to stay alive, you know, because it was a very bad time when I left—the agents and this and that on the way all with guns, and Kurdish agents, this agent, that agent, yes—very frightening when you imagine it. . . . My hope was just to stay alive, you know. . . . That hope kept me alive. There was some light maybe flickering there in the dark; there was still hope.[96]

For all my participants, crossing the border was not only a geographical but also a psychological challenge. In fact, the border within them had already been crossed: the adrenalin flowed.

Sina recalled: *"I couldn't believe they would let me leave the country so easily. For more than two days I was terrified. I couldn't believe it."*[97] Accustomed to a world of paralysing fear, Sina knew nothing of the freedom he was about to touch. There were no words to express his sense of liberation; he *"just wanted not to be there."* But he could not imagine what the future might hold. He was focused on the instinct or will to survive, which acts without any concept of "future" or "past."

Lida used this metaphor:

I was like a piece of wood in the sea, with all the waves; you don't know where to go. That is exactly how it felt. My God, where am I going—my son at that time was fifteen years old, he's now nineteen. What would happen to him? My husband had been to jail several times, he was used to it. The regime might put him in prison again—but what of my son? It was awful.[98]

She went on:

I am diabetic. I have to keep taking my medication. I stayed in one room in Turkey; I couldn't go out. I was waiting for people who would help us to escape; we didn't know when they would arrive. When we moved, I had only painkillers to help me feel better. When we arrived here, it was very cold. I had no contacts. My cousin lives in London, but I didn't have her phone number. I was in an appalling situation.[99]

Watan remembers, "*It was October when I got here. It was snowing. I didn't know we were in England—I thought at first it was another country. I couldn't believe there could be so much snow in October.*"[100]

Darius recollects:

> *At the time . . . I can't remember exactly how I felt, but I was somehow down, and it looked like depression, you know? You don't know what destination, where you are going, what's going to happen to you, some kind of suspension, some kind of . . . up in the air, without know-ing where you are going, your next destination, or your last destination. A kind of confusion, yes. The effects . . . the effects stayed with me for years. Some of them are still there. Uncer-tainty, yes. No control over your own life . . . or what is going to happen. . . . At the time, no one knew what was happening to people, and how many people might be killed on the way.*[101]

It is difficult for Darius to recall the details of his clandestine journey, but he viv-idly describes his feeling of numbness and loss even of his sense of self. Unlike most of the others, Darius was able and willing to give some physical details of his escape route. I had not expected to hear this from him:

> *I was not sure what was going to happen to me. I didn't know. I came in a lorry! I just jumped out of the lorry. There was the Italian driver who just saw me; he didn't know I was in his lorry. At midnight, we got in the lorry, between somewhere like Belgium and France. Yes, we crossed some farms, and things and—I didn't look—some parking—drivers, they were sleeping. But at the time you are not thinking about anything. You don't know. When I go back to that time, when I think about it, I can't imagine what exactly I felt at the time, you know. It's a lot of confusion and uncertainty, as you say, and fear. Most of it will live with me for a long time.*[102]

Parya, like Darius, was not a freedom fighter or party member and could also describe her ordeal openly:

> *It was a very difficult time. We were in Africa for about five or six months. It was very hard. We were in Mali for four-and-a-half months. We were also in Guinea, in Kenya, for about seven weeks. I was very worried. Every day, I had the feeling something bad would happen. I was scared for the children. There was Ebola virus at that time. I felt I was going mad. Every day I tried to disinfect the rooms and ourselves.*[103]
>
> *I also saw starving children, and it was painful to compare them with my own children. It was terrible. That time was the worst in my life. I can never forget it. Because of Ebola, because of the unknown. Worrying about where we were going: could we go anywhere? Our aim wasn't to live in Guinea. We just needed to leave Iran; we couldn't stay there. My rela-tives advised me to go back to Turkey, and from there to Europe. But I thought not. We must find a way to get to Europe from here. That was our situation—we didn't even have the money for basics. We spent what we had saved. Our friends outside Iran helped us, but it was really difficult for me to request that help.*[104]
>
> *Living conditions in Africa—I don't know, have you been to Africa? Horrific, horrific—believe me! The first time we went to buy food at the supermarket, more than a dozen children surrounded us. I have to say, from all my shopping, all I was able to bring home was a kilo of potatoes. I gave them the rest. I couldn't ignore them once I had seen them. I'd never seen such things before.*[105]

Bringing her two children through these chaotic conditions put intense pressure on Parya as a mother. A supportive network played a crucial role in her survival. During that period, the traditional family roles changed, and she became the decision maker: this challenge gave her the opportunity to exercise her intelligence.

Lida, whose presence in Iran put her party in danger, also used a network. She had no idea where she would go. "*I just had to get out. My son-in-law made sure I would reach a safe place, he organised it all, he paid the expenses; he's well off. It took three days. I escaped in a lorry. It was really hard.*"[106]

For Sara likewise, the escape process was well organised. Her husband went before her, and she had a relatively clear idea of what she would face, though she did not disclose the actual details. She spoke about her loneliness: "*In Iran, we had family, relatives, friends looking out for us. Arriving here, we had no one. Psychologically you feel utterly alone! Yet I was happy, because we were going to be safe.*"[107]

A DIFFERENT WORLD

On reaching the United Kingdom, all my participants encountered a specific point of transition towards a new life. Despite the sense of freedom, Hiva felt bewildered, having to begin his life all over again in the unknown.

> *When I arrived in the UK it was night-time. I had a friend here, so I called him. I could speak some English, but not fluently. I met an Indian man. I couldn't understand his English! I was like a baby, just born. Everything was new to me. It was a different world. I couldn't make contact or understand—and people looked so different. Everything was different—even the buildings. In the past, I'd read Jack London stories about Whitechapel. I'd already read about London, but when I arrived it was . . . I felt . . . I felt scared. At the time, I was thirty-three years old. I was politically very active in my homeland, and I was leading the others. But as soon as I arrived in London, I felt, how can I start all over again? I felt like a baby. My first connection was with this situation—I couldn't understand what was happening. I couldn't understand!*[108]

For Sara, it was the joy of discovering herself safe and secure in a cosmopolitan environment, where she would blend in and be accepted.

> *At the airport, I saw people of many nationalities. Particularly in England, you see people of different colours and types—they can all live together. This made me very happy. As soon as I arrived at the airport, I saw black people, Indian people, European people, all together! They could live together. What a good feeling! If only the whole world could be like that! This was my first impression—I wished everywhere were like this.*[109]

Sina felt reborn in a new environment, which still required him to free himself. Despite the extreme violation of his basic rights in his homeland, he would now gain recognition within his host country. He said:

> *When I arrived here, the first thing I saw was the symbol of this place, the double-decker red bus! Without knowing my future, what might happen to me, I felt comfortable and*

relaxed—I don't know why. It was a symbol, which said, you have gone somewhere, arrived somewhere. It was funny. The bus didn't have anything, was nothing special, but when you go back to the past, you look at the experience, and also the symbols. The red bus was a symbol of that moment for me. Red bus! I felt safe.[110]

"Were there buses, where you lived in Iran?" I asked. "What were the differences between those buses and this one, for you?" Sina smiled sadly, "*Unfortunately, those buses segregated human beings according to their sex. Can you imagine? Here, people sit wherever they want on the bus, yes. Even the colour of the buses here is bright! That bus was the first good feeling I found.*"[111]

Lida remained hopeful. "*The piece of wood had reached the shore. The waves had brought the wood to land, and I hoped I would then find my own way.*"[112]

When Parya landed from Africa with her children, it was nothing like she expected; it was like a dream. "*Were we really safe? Had we been rescued? Had we reached a safe place, one of the world's best countries? We would have been OK to go anywhere, so long as it wasn't Iran. I was very happy! I had a very good feeling.*"[113] At the UK border, a female officer hugged Parya warmly and told her not to worry any more. This humane acceptance and embrace took her right back to the little girl who was persecuted at school for asking questions; her sense of self was restored.

The stowaway Darius emerged from the lorry expecting to be beaten up. To his astonishment, the Border Agency offered him courtesy and sandwiches.

> *You never see such a thing in Iran, and in the process of coming here, moving, and fleeing, we never saw such behaviour as we did here. When you come specially to a country in a lorry . . . yes, they were very polite, and then they just interviewed us very briefly, then sent us to the Home Office. . . . They took photos and put us in a hostel after a month, and then they gave us a free solicitor.*[114]

All my participants received courtesy on arrival, which reassured their sense of self. In their new environment, they would face fresh challenges. For Darius, "*a lot of things, changes, were happening at the same time . . . one month, two months. But that hope that you talked about, it changes bit by bit.*"[115]

In the next chapter, my participants will tell their stories of what it was like to settle in their new home and the challenges they faced.

NOTES

1. Armin H. Danesh, "Exploring Iranian Political Refugees' Experiences in Britain: The Phoenix Rises from the Ashes" (Doctoral diss., Middlesex University, 2019), 158.
2. Danesh, "Exploring Iranian Political Refugees' Experiences," 140.
3. Danesh, "Exploring Iranian Political Refugees' Experiences," 150.
4. Carolyn Zerbe Enns and Elizabeth Nutt Williams, eds., *The Oxford Handbook of Feminist Counseling Psychology* (New York: Oxford University Press, 2012).
5. Danesh, "Exploring Iranian Political Refugees' Experiences," 142.

6. Karimi, interviewed by A. Danesh, London, 12 October 2015

7. Danesh, "Exploring Iranian Political Refugees' Experiences," 141.

8. Danesh, "Exploring Iranian Political Refugees' Experiences," 141.

9. Danesh, "Exploring Iranian Political Refugees' Experiences," 141.

10. Viktor E. Frankl, *Man's Search for Meaning: The Classic Tribute to Hope from the Holocaust* (London: Random House, 2004), 126.

11. Karimi, interviewed by A. Danesh, London, 12 October 2015.

12. Karimi, interviewed by A. Danesh, London, 12 October 2015.

13. Karimi, interviewed by A. Danesh, London, 12 October 2015.

14. Karimi, interviewed by A. Danesh, London, 12 October 2015.

15. Karimi, interviewed by A. Danesh, London, 12 October 2015.

16. Thomas Cushman, ed., *Handbook of Human Rights* (London: Routledge, 2012).

17. Danesh, "Exploring Iranian Political Refugees' Experiences," 190.

18. Karimi, interviewed by A. Danesh, London, 12 October 2015.

19. Karimi, interviewed by A. Danesh, London, 12 October 2015.

20. Sina, interviewed by A. Danesh, London, 8 August 2015.

21. Sina, interviewed by A. Danesh, London, 8 August 2015.

22. Hiva, interviewed by A. Danesh, London, 29 June 2016.

23. Watan, interviewed by A. Danesh, London, 27 June 2016.

24. Danesh, "Exploring Iranian Political Refugees' Experiences," 142.

25. Watan, interviewed by A. Danesh, London, 27 June 2016.

26. Watan, interviewed by A. Danesh, London, 27 June 2016.

27. Darius, interviewed by A. Danesh, London, 25 August 2016.

28. Darius, interviewed by A. Danesh, London, 25 August 2016.

29. Danesh, "Exploring Iranian Political Refugees' Experiences," 159.

30. Danesh, "Exploring Iranian Political Refugees' Experiences," 159.

31. Maryam Rajavi, *Women, Islam & Equality* (Paris: Islamkotob, 1995).

32. Danesh, "Exploring Iranian Political Refugees' Experiences," 370.

33. Karimi, interviewed by A. Danesh, London, 12 October 2015.

34. Karimi, interviewed by A. Danesh, London, 12 October 2015.

35. Danesh, "Exploring Iranian Political Refugees' Experiences," 152.

36. Danesh, "Exploring Iranian Political Refugees' Experiences," 145.

37. Peter Railton, *Facts, Values, and Norms: Essays toward a Morality of Consequence* (Cambridge: Cambridge University Press, 2003).

38. Danesh, "Exploring Iranian Political Refugees' Experiences," 154.

39. Sara, interviewed by A. Danesh, London, 7 November 2015.

40. Sara, interviewed by A. Danesh, London, 7 November 2015.

41. Danesh, "Exploring Iranian Political Refugees' Experiences," 374.

42. Sara, interviewed by A. Danesh, London, 7 November 2015.

43. Sara, interviewed by A. Danesh, London, 7 November 2015.

44. Sara, interviewed by A. Danesh, London, 7 November 2015.

45. Sara, interviewed by A. Danesh, London, 7 November 2015.

46. Danesh, "Exploring Iranian Political Refugees' Experiences," 155.

47. Sara, interviewed by A. Danesh, London, 7 November 2015.

48. Danesh, "Exploring Iranian Political Refugees' Experiences," 156.

49. Sara, interviewed by A. Danesh, London, 7 November 2015.

50. Parya, interviewed by A. Danesh, London, 30 November 2016.

51. Parya, interviewed by A. Danesh, London, 30 November 2016.
52. Parya, interviewed by A. Danesh, London, 30 November 2016.
53. Parya, interviewed by A. Danesh, London, 30 November 2016.
54. Danesh, "Exploring Iranian Political Refugees' Experiences," 144.
55. Parya, interviewed by A. Danesh, London, 30 November 2016.
56. Danesh, "Exploring Iranian Political Refugees' Experiences," 145.
57. Gila, interviewed by A. Danesh, London, 23 August 2016.
58. Gila, interviewed by A. Danesh, London, 23 August 2016.
59. Danesh, "Exploring Iranian Political Refugees' Experiences," 1.
60. Danesh, "Exploring Iranian Political Refugees' Experiences," 1.
61. Danesh, "Exploring Iranian Political Refugees' Experiences," 157.
62. Gila, interviewed by A. Danesh, London, 23 August 2016.
63. Gila, interviewed by A. Danesh, London, 23 August 2016.
64. Danesh, "Exploring Iranian Political Refugees' Experiences," 145.
65. Danesh, "Exploring Iranian Political Refugees' Experiences," 157.
66. Lida, interviewed by A. Danesh, London, 7 October 2016.
67. Lida, interviewed by A. Danesh, London, 7 October 2016.
68. Lida, interviewed by A. Danesh, London, 7 October 2016.
69. Hiva, interviewed by A. Danesh, London, 29 June 2016.
70. Hiva, interviewed by A. Danesh, London, 29 June 2016.
71. Danesh, "Exploring Iranian Political Refugees' Experiences," 149.
72. Hiva, interviewed by A. Danesh, London, 29 June 2016.
73. Hiva, interviewed by A. Danesh, London, 29 June 2016.
74. Hiva, interviewed by A. Danesh, London, 29 June 2016.
75. Hiva, interviewed by A. Danesh, London, 29 June 2016.
76. Danesh, "Exploring Iranian Political Refugees' Experiences," 152.
77. Danesh, "Exploring Iranian Political Refugees' Experiences," 146.
78. Hiva, interviewed by A. Danesh, London, 29 June 2016.
79. Hiva, interviewed by A. Danesh, London, 29 June 2016.
80. Danesh, "Exploring Iranian Political Refugees' Experiences," 158.
81. Danesh, "Exploring Iranian Political Refugees' Experiences," 158.
82. Sina, interviewed by A. Danesh, London, 8 August 2015.
83. Danesh, "Exploring Iranian Political Refugees' Experiences," 161.
84. Danesh, "Exploring Iranian Political Refugees' Experiences," 161.
85. Danesh, "Exploring Iranian Political Refugees' Experiences," 161.
86. Danesh, "Exploring Iranian Political Refugees' Experiences," 150.
87. Sina, interviewed by A. Danesh, London, 8 August 2015.
88. Danesh, "Exploring Iranian Political Refugees' Experiences," 333.
89. Dick Blackwell, *Counselling and Psychotherapy with Refugees* (London: Jessica Kingsley, 2005).
90. Danesh, "Exploring Iranian Political Refugees' Experiences," 140.
91. Danesh, "Exploring Iranian Political Refugees' Experiences," 162.
92. Karimi, interviewed by A. Danesh, London, 12 October 2015.
93. Gila, interviewed by A. Danesh, London, 23 August 2016.
94. Hiva, interviewed by A. Danesh, London, 29 June 2016.
95. Darius, interviewed by A. Danesh, London, 25 August 2016.
96. Darius, interviewed by A. Danesh, London, 25 August 2016.

97. Sina, interviewed by A. Danesh, London, 8 August 2015.
98. Danesh, "Exploring Iranian Political Refugees' Experiences," 117.
99. Lida, interviewed by A. Danesh, London, 7 October 2016.
100. Danesh, "Exploring Iranian Political Refugees' Experiences," 166.
101. Darius, interviewed by A. Danesh, London, 25 August 2016.
102. Danesh, "Exploring Iranian Political Refugees' Experiences," 166.
103. Danesh, "Exploring Iranian Political Refugees' Experiences," 166.
104. Parya, interviewed by A. Danesh, London, 30 November 2016.
105. Parya, interviewed by A. Danesh, London, 30 November 2016.
106. Danesh, "Exploring Iranian Political Refugees' Experiences," 167.
107. Danesh, "Exploring Iranian Political Refugees' Experiences," 167.
108. Hiva, interviewed by A. Danesh, London, 29 June 2016.
109. Sara, interviewed by A. Danesh, London, 7 November 2015.
110. Sina, interviewed by A. Danesh, London, 8 August 2015.
111. Sina, interviewed by A. Danesh, London, 8 August 2015.
112. Danesh, "Exploring Iranian Political Refugees' Experiences," 117.
113. Danesh, "Exploring Iranian Political Refugees' Experiences," 168.
114. Darius, , interviewed by A. Danesh, London, 25 August 2016.
115. Darius, interviewed by A. Danesh, London, 25 August 2016.

6

Experiences of Adaptation and Resettlement in the United Kingdom

Armin Danesh

> When I arrived here, the first thing I saw was the symbol of here, that double-decker red bus! Without knowing about my future or what might happen to me, I felt comfortable and relaxed. This was only a symbol, but I felt comfortable, I felt relaxed, and I felt safe and secure.[1]

PSYCHOLOGICAL REBIRTH THROUGH CHALLENGES

The New Birth

Can existence be conceived without birth? Our physical birth is a "given"; according to the Abrahamic religions, we may be born Christian, Muslim, or Jewish, but we also give birth to ourselves spiritually and psychologically in the way we act and interpret life.

In *The Human Condition*, Hannah Arendt "introduces natality as a conceptual moment when one is born into the political realm as the sphere where acting together can create the truly unexpected."[2] Arendt regards political action as a "second" birth or rebirth.[3] Our words and deeds reveal our unique personal character. She relates birth to political action. Although we must die, we are born to begin, and to change. With her focus on life and natality, rather than death and mortality, she opposes Martin Heidegger's view that since being born and dying are beyond our free choice we are thrown towards our deaths. In Hannah Arendt's theory, our birth is an opportunity to act and to be reborn psychologically or spiritually. We enter the world through birth: the root of our freedom.[4]

My participants' descriptions of their new birth as political refugees nearly always include how it feels for them individually to be recognised and respected as a human being during the period of resettlement. The theme of birth is almost inseparable from the idea of recognition and respect.

Beyond any doubt, Sina's arrival in this country was and continues to be for him an unexpected renascence. His personal survival embodies his tribal group consciousness. He repeats that it was not just a feeling but an actual "new birth,"[5] an intake of breath after being suffocated in his homeland. The opportunity to start again was miraculous for him. He says he had no preconceptions, nor could he ever have imagined this leap into the unknown; from existential suppression into having existence, purpose, and the freedom to circulate and to be. The phoenix rose from the ashes. In the United Kingdom, he found his values were respected. This continuing rebirth inspired him to adapt himself and to help others. The bright red London double-decker bus manifested a new safety, security, and community. In the drab-coloured Iranian buses, he said, women and men are segregated.

"*I felt,*" said Karimi, "*there are people who can understand you. This was very important. In your own country you are nothing. In another country where you weren't born there, they treat you as a citizen. It is a huge difference.*"[6] When Karimi reached the United Kingdom, his life was in tatters. On encountering humane treatment during a course of therapy for survivors of torture offered by the Medical Foundation,[7] his strength of purpose generated renewal for himself and his family; the rising of the phoenix entails an interior change. On observing his new neighbours, and for his wife and daughters' sake, Karimi began to think about and change some of his patriarchal conditioning, thus enhancing his family's resettlement. For some, this internal revolution may be even more significant than the social revolution they fight for. Is social change possible without individuals' willingness to change themselves, to be reborn?

Lida spoke of her feelings of despair in Iran, where "*your voice cannot reach anyone.*" Here is another example where the new birth brings recognition. She was given asylum within four days of her arrival in London:

The very day of my birthday I received my leave to remain. This was my new birth. I was very happy. They valued me. I was important. They recognised me as a human. They embraced me with kindness and warmth. That's very important! I will never forget it. When they believed me, they listened to me, they trusted me—I got my answer. Do you know how they treated me? After my first interview, the officer invited me to come to the window; he showed me where the post office was, and told me, "Go get a photo of yourself from there, for your asylum." It filled me with hope. This was REALLY my new birth. Yes, there is a new world! Yes, there are better people in this world! All people are not the same—therefore you can live differently.[8]

Parya was "reborn" when the female border officer embraced her. The teething problems were yet to come. In the process of confronting the hardships of adaptation she says, "*I think the beginning of any new life is problematic. It means you can't say, 'Now I arrived in this country, and everything is OK.' Sometimes you expect things which don't happen. . . . I thought everything would turn out the way I expected.*"[9] It took seven months for her family to be granted asylum. The first application, submitted by her husband, failed. The second, her own, was successful. Subsequently she lived with her husband's depression and homesickness, while she herself made new friends and became the family breadwinner.

> *When I was in Newcastle, I didn't know anyone. I got to know a few British families. I couldn't believe it—I fell in love with them. I can't believe that after only four or five meetings with them I became like their daughter, genuinely—a very, very good feeling. I met them at the gym. They invited me to their home; they had a music class. . . . When I told them I don't understand the songs, they said, "No, no it doesn't matter, you can come and listen."*[10]

Parya's resettlement and rebirth reclaimed flavours of her lost childhood. For her, as for Sina and for Darius, music (restricted in Iran) is an important part of their lives.

Gila's arrival and reception here further inspired her loyalty to both her homeland and her new country, as well as her desire for herself and her children to work hard and be useful. Sara, who rose to the challenge of learning English and making new friends, observed, "*In general, any existing conflict within the family between the men and the women, increases when they arrive in a new country.*"[11] As soon as she and her family were given a home, she made contact with her new neighbours by baking bread for them.

It is interesting to compare Darius's rebirth—his phoenix moment—with that of other participants who were activists. All variously reached a point where they could no longer breathe under the regime and abandoned their homeland. It took ten years—his dark night of the soul—for Darius to be granted asylum. During this extended period, he lived as a vagabond in the Midlands, finding casual work and sometimes sleeping rough. His encounter with Buddhist teachings kept "*the flickering light of hope alive.*"[12] The lengthy process of rebirth developed his philosophy and his aspiration "*to be a better person*" to the point where he profoundly appreciates what he has learned. Eventually, he gained his asylum by representing himself; by then he was free from the past. "*I told them: this is the story of my life . . . it changed things. After five, six months, I got my leave to remain. Then . . . I tried to change things. That's why I started working as an interpreter, a translator.*"[13] At present, Darius draws on his depth of experience to assist other refugees with their rebirth, as a volunteer counsellor and advisor.

Recognition by the host country can greatly help a political refugee establish his or her new identity. Watan remembers, "*I got away from a really horrible situation. I found my place—I can have a life here.*"[14] However, Hiva and Watan faced new difficulties. Their asylum applications were rejected by the UK Home Office; they had no status and were forced to live here unofficially. This felt almost as bad as the repression from which they had escaped, and it hindered their ability to leave the past behind. They both rose to the challenge, however, and developed successful businesses under new names; they are resubmitting their asylum applications and are confident they will be allowed to remain.

"I hoped I would find a better life,"[15] Hiva said. *"This was a new birth for me, and I was apprehensive, but I had hope. I felt I was reborn. But now, it is for me, like being in a regime prison here! I am imprisoned, but in the UK."*[16] He refers not to a physical prison but to the metaphysical limbo of misrecognition as a citizen of his new country. While continuing to trust that the new environment will not prevent him from finding a better life, Hiva cannot fully utilise his new freedom. While in prison in Iran he wrote two books. There his focus was on his political commitment; now he struggles with personal issues rather than working for others. For political refugees, their hardship in Iran was a creative spur.

Like Hiva, Watan was a hero in his homeland but lives here unrecognised. *"I found my place—I can have a life here. The first thing I thought of was—I can carry on, I can study! I was very keen on my studies and still am. But I didn't get a chance to do this here."*[17] Watan's anxiety about his brother and sister, who were still in Iran, caused him to bungle his asylum interview; he was too overwrought and had no representation. As a result, he, an intellectual, was forced to live in the shadows; he taught himself to grill meat for shish and, in due course, opened his own kebab restaurant using his business partner's identity. He could not yet afford to study.

There can be no birth without someone or somewhere to be born to. The most profound human connection is through birth to a parent, or to a new way of life. For some, this takes a moment; for others, it is spread over many years of adjustment or emerges (as with Hiva and Darius) through inner acceptance.

I note each participant's positive determination to live, to interact, and to try. They did not give up. A newborn baby appears helpless but has just won the first great battle for life. Birth holds some quality of the whole active life to come, which makes it difficult to determine at which point the refugee's new birth merges into his or her resettlement process. Each of my participants experienced rebirth and recognition through his or her contact with humanity in the new society. As Donald Wood Winnicott emphasises, a baby does not exist without its mother or caregiver; could a political refugee exist likewise in isolation?[18]

RECOGNITION AND RESPECT

Recognition is a vital human need.[19]

Like Sina's double-decker bus, Lida's symbol of freedom was red: a token of identity and relocation. *"They gave me a red card and a phone number, they asked me to contact that number for an appointment. . . . This gave me some comfort, someone knew I am here, I felt recognised."*[20] Shortly afterwards, Lida found a woman at a crowded railway station speaking her mother tongue; the woman helped her find her cousin's phone number in London. Suddenly she felt at home, with her native language, and could tell her family in Iran she was alive.

My participants all agreed that their first priority was to be able to communicate in English. In the matter of respect, Sara advises refugees not to use their children as interpreters or translators: "*Don't take them to the job centre or the doctor's surgery. That would be a great mistake. The children would think, not only do you not know the language, you're not capable—you don't have a brain! Gradually they will lose their respect for you and do whatever they like.*"[21] Her discovery that people in her new country "respect" one another—even animals—deeply interested her. Under a religious dictatorship, which profoundly fractures a society, the instinctive care among neighbours disappears because of mistrust and paranoia.

Sara recognised her volatile temper and learned to control it: "*We have to learn the way they do things here. It didn't come naturally—people had to battle for it historically—and we must recognise and respect this way. Really open our eyes and ears to learn. There are many humanitarian things we can learn.*"[22]

Karimi described what recognition and respect mean for him:

Here, we are regarded as human. This is very important. I have my own identity. My rights won't be violated. No one insults me. When you work, you receive respect, and you can be proud of the result. When you work for people, they respect you and feel grateful—then you can release your tiredness! Many people are encouraged to study; they are working and they are happy. I also am happy and I can help others.[23]

At the end of his interview, Watan said, "*I feel grateful. You are giving me a voice. This is why I accepted freely and voluntarily to come, and to give this interview. I owe you deep thanks!*"[24]

Sina told me,

The issue is no longer "they don't want me." Here everything is different; here the economy is not politically prejudiced. . . . It is my right to have an ordinary life. Here I have been given the right to live as a human being. I didn't have that possibility there. Do you know, I value the situation here, and what I have! I am grateful to people here, and to the system, from the bottom of my heart.[25]

Recognition is a process arising from deep within. Lida said, "*I felt something is growing and transforming me. It reached a point where I had to get involved.*" She recalls what it was like to have her human identity recognised, when "*the waves brought her piece of wood in the sea to the coast*":

They gave me this feeling: you are a human; you have your own voice—we can see you. Someone can see you. Someone can understand you. Those things gave me a lot of good feeling, which I never had before—it was the best. In Iran I felt like I was invisible; I didn't exist. This feeling here gave me confidence. I found myself. I found my position. These things are very valuable.[26]

On the other hand, recognition was a problem for those who were not quickly granted asylum. Watan's self-respect evolved through his natural ability for committed friendships, especially with women, and by working hard at the kebab grill (putting his symbolic fiery name to good use). He began to recognise his situation from a new perspective.

> *When I was in Iran there were many things in the political situation which I couldn't see, but I see clearly from here. . . . I think the way that I fight against the regime has changed. I feel there are many ways I can fight them—through reading, through studying, through writing—it goes on. . . . My feeling against the regime is stronger now than it was before. I am not now in the midst of battle like I was before. I have a chance to read, to reflect and to study the situation as a whole in Iran, and I have a clearer view of it. . . . I was part of the flood fighting the regime. But now I am outside I see and understand many things about the regime, about my own activity—sometimes I feel angry, and sometimes I just feel, this is the nature of politics.*[27]

This reflexive self-recognition is as significant as the recognition coming from others for making important interior connections. Recognition implies a dialogue within the individual or with others. For my thoughtful participants, especially Darius and Karimi, their reflexivity played a major role in their adjustment and resettlement. "*It's all uncertainty,*"[28] Darius told me,

> *because I don't know. . . . I don't know what would have happened at that time if I had stayed. I know I chose to do this, and not to cooperate with that government; but I went through a lot of bad times here, the worst I've had in my life. But when I look back now, and think about it, the only thing I am telling myself is that maybe it was necessary for me. Maybe that choice that I made, and all what happened to me, was needed for me to be what I am now, or who I am now. That's how I am thinking about it you know. I never criticise my past, because of that choice or because of what I didn't do. The idea that I went through this, and it's because I could have done this better or I could have done that better—I never think like that.*[29]

Gila remembers one of her neighbours in Iran, an old man who watched her fight for herself and others and who told her, "*Well done, we are proud of you. A lion is a lion, regardless of gender.*"[30] She carried this recognition to her new country—and to her political activities at The Hague: "*You came here; you have freedom here. Value it, and work. You can understand how women and men are equal, you can speak freely; try to be useful.*"[31]

At this point, Gila gave voice to her recognition of humanity:

> *When I see how the boys and girls are free here, there are tears in my eyes. When I walk in the street and I see old people walking along, they remind me of the old folk in my country. Old, young, they all remind me of my people in Iran. When I think of our young people in Iran—they don't have jobs, they can't express their views, they have no freedom, they can't marry, they can't get a place to live . . . all in my mind—because they have no freedom. I wish all Iranian people, all political parties, could join together to end this oppression, and to stop the killing machine. I'm always thinking of them, although I can't do anything. I did enough, and my conscience is clear, yet I always feel for my people. I think about what the*

regime is doing in Syria, using our people's money, to wage war on the Syrian people. I feel
very sad for those people who close their eyes to what is happening in Iran.[32]

Both Gila and Sara are highly respected internationally as activists. The recognition
and respect they receive from others are rooted in the way they take responsibility
for themselves.

I recognise the coming together of my participants as a team. Their concerted
voice for human rights and social justice reaches further than their individual voices,
none of which are subtracted from the whole. For all of them, their purpose spiritually and psychologically transcends self-interest. They express an openness to learn
and to try to do better in their new environment—and to face the inevitable conflicts
of adjustment and change.

PROCESS OF ADAPTATION AND THE NEED TO WORK

Through active employment and working for others, my participants became better
equipped to understand the differences they had with the new culture in which they
found themselves.

The primary conflict that many political refugees face is within their family relationships, together with the challenge of cultural adaptation. Sara states that any
residual dysfunction in a marriage will come to the surface with resettlement. For
Sara, Lida, and Parya, the adaptation process put pressure on their marriages and
increased underlying tensions. As Sara put it:

> *It depends on whom you live with. If you live with someone who believes in equality, it is*
> *different from those who follow the tradition. I have family friends who have been political*
> *refugees for a long time, but the man still finds this culture really strange. In Iran, the man*
> *had his authority as boss, as head of the house and family. When they arrived here, they found*
> *the opposite! It is much easier for a woman to adapt in this society than it is for a man. She*
> *can learn the language more easily. We are more sociable than the men. They stay at home*
> *and don't want to go out; their mind-set is still in Iran. They bring their basic attitude*
> *towards women to this country, and they can't accept the reality of women being equal.*[33]

Sara, Gila, and Karimi spoke of suicides and even honour killings within some
badly divided families. Many political refugees arriving here feel cut off and isolated.
"*Our culture is community oriented. Being with others is very important for us. This was*
the downside and it disturbed me—the lack of this kind of environment here. I felt all
on my own. I didn't know the roads, how to get to places. I didn't know the language."[34]
Sara noted that people here don't interact easily, but she got over this hurdle with a
nourishing, creative, and practical gesture: "*When I came to this country, I baked bread*
for my neighbours. They were surprised! Now they are my best friends."[35] She cooked and
shared; she did what women in her own ethnic community do.

Among the political refugee community,

even if the men try to make a change, they can only do it very, very slowly. I know many men who resist changing their cultural attitudes towards women; husbands suffer from serious depression, they are not happy. Women can adapt more easily, find a job, do physical activities, go to the gym, interact with this society.[36]

To begin with, Sara's husband stayed at home while she went out to work, but he remained supportive and shared his position of authority with her. Later he returned to the battlefield. Parya's husband also stayed at home; he fell into depression.

I had to carry everything on my shoulders. Everything. I do all the jobs, with the children. It isn't easy living here. I have to work all the time. There are always letters I must answer. He has to move!—to give me any hope. But he says, "I don't want to move . . . no I don't want to learn the language here."[37]

Lida described her husband's homesickness similarly: *"He can't meet his expectation of being here. That is why he's unhappy."*[38] And more generally: *"Men don't take much responsibility or commit to their family. Here it is not like that. I have learned to say no. In Iran a woman can't say no, but here, I can."*[39]

It seems that some women confront the problems of resettlement twice over. Sara soon became a full-time carer for her grandchild as well, when her daughter's marriage with an Egyptian boy fell apart. The cultural gap there was seemingly even greater than that between Iran and England.

From the man's point of view, Karimi's adaptation process brought realisations within himself:

Let me say something. This is not easy—I recognise that. It is not easy to accept all aspects of the new culture. For me, my own culture, I'm not interested in seeing women and men kissing each other in public. If you ask about what I do, what I feel, I don't think this is nice. But my first impression was: "there is freedom here." It was the sign of freedom for me. Here, there is a freedom, but I don't mean people should do whatever they want. I wasn't happy to see that— but my impression is: there is freedom here. To adapt to a new environment takes time.[40]

It was intense for him when his daughters brought their boyfriends home, and it did not feel easy to cede his traditional position of control in the family. He noted, however, that no one here forced him to go against his principles. This allowed him to learn from men and women whose values inspired him.

Karimi's first task when his family joined him in England was to retrain as an engineer. *"I didn't come here to receive benefits. I was a freedom fighter! If I want my freedom here, I must work. When you work, your family respect you."*[41]

With regard to the isolation felt by many, Sara said, *"Being with others is very important for us. This was the downside, and it disturbed me—the lack of a supportive environment here."*[42]

The conflicts faced were cultural and intra-personal, but Gila, a widow, also had to tackle the fear and paranoia still haunting her from her past imprisonment and torture. Lida also struggled to overcome and transform her depression. Part of Gila's mission is for her children to study and to lead decent lives. The fight for values creates an environment where children take themselves seriously. The tension in the family forces evolution and transcends self-indulgence.

My participants explained that many children of political refugees are now doctors, lawyers, and teachers, and they value their freedom to work. Gila made it her duty to strongly motivate her children. She refuses their financial assistance and works in a supermarket. Her strong language—"*for as long as I have blood in my veins*"[43]—challenges the persecution that almost dragged her under. Her fight for freedom and for her values helps her rise above her own difficulties and keep going. Against extremists, she became extreme in her views, so she and her children could survive.

Like Karimi and Watan, Gila refuses to take state benefits. She told me she fears Iranian regime spies in this country but trusts the police. She did not remarry.

> *I left my personal feelings behind, to be for my family and for others, to be for my people. My sister was a university student but was kicked out, and another sister, a teacher, was sacked. I had to think about them. I wanted to see they are OK. All of them are OK now. They are here. I never thought about getting married again.*[44]

Hiva and Sina agree that, having committed to upholding the values that brought them to this country, they could not make an extra commitment to a wife and family. At international human rights conferences, Gila meets many others who have lost family members. One day she and two other women counted eleven martyrs between them. Sara is a founding member of the women's rights group in which Parya, Gila, and Lida are active.

Watan's conflict with the Home Office continues, though he now owns a chain of restaurants.

> *In the first year, I concentrated on my case. I wasn't happy—it was very frustrating. I felt like just an object in the game they play—going to this place, then going that place. I needed my asylum. But even if I don't get my asylum, I can still work. Every week I pay £130, £140 in tax. I can carry on living here! I think I will get my asylum eventually.*[45]

Darius, Hiva, and Watan dealt with the difficulties resulting from their non-asylum status. Officially all three did not exist; inhabiting a limbo world, they had to work extra hard to support their families. "*What I've learned,*" Darius says, "*is that life and the universe will give you exactly whatever you have asked for. If you asked for good things, good things happen. If you think about bad things, think negatively, just think that you are doing your best, things won't change, or never change, and if you use negative words like "never," "no," and such-like, you are creating it like that.*"[46]

The adaptation process, facing and overcoming a string of troubles, fuels my participants' imperative need to be in work. "*No one stops me,*"[47] said Watan.

> *If you want, you will achieve. No one should underestimate themselves, in such circumstances. I believe in working. In whatever the circumstance, I believe I have to work. It helps*

me to carry on. I'm not here only to look after myself, I want to help others. Despite all the problems I've had, I help others. For example, a month ago, an Iranian who had citizenship here developed psychological problems. I paid for him to visit his family. I just heard of his difficulties—he's not my friend, I don't know him—but I paid his travel costs.[48]

A man experiencing difficulties came to Watan's restaurant one day, and Watan invited him to stay at his home. "*I trust him. I've been in the same boat myself. . . . I think I can do more, and I can be of more help. And I have to do more, for others.*"[49]

To "do more for others" helped my participants navigate the hurdles they faced, related to lifestyle, posttraumatic shock, lack of recognition, and personal relationships. It fuelled their adaptation through "conflict resolution." The fighter embraces ongoing challenges in the new country; against opposition, new meaning takes form. After his asylum application failed, Hiva lost his identity and status in "the ashes": the phoenix had to be born.

Receiving the right to remain can go a long way in helping political refugees to transfer their energy productively into the new environment. The Home Office's rejection of Hiva's, Watan's, and Darius's asylum applications confined their identity and way of life to a shadow status. For Hiva, this was another form of imprisonment. In Iran, he had been jailed for what he represented. He was a published author and a hero in Iran, but in the United Kingdom, his entire existence was denied. His focus in Iran was on a commitment to freedom, which could atrophy here under bureaucratic distractions. This contributes to Hiva's malaise.

Sara sums up the situation:

Ordinary jobs, like health care, local authority work and teaching, are done better by women. This is very difficult for men to accept. Some political refugees are less affected, but my own experience is that I did all the work, and my husband stayed at home. He basically gave his authority to me. He didn't have serious difficulties with that. But my experience with other families is that men can't easily accept these conditions easily. This is the general problem within family life.[50]

Perhaps the men are more accustomed to living in their heads and become locked up in their thoughts; the women take the children to school and connect with other parents.

Lida said, with deep feeling, "*I don't make it hard for my husband. If you see your wife as a human being, you won't find any problem relating to her. A couple can live together in harmony if they see each other as human beings. You are human—and she is human, too!*"[51]

Sara repeated that conflicts coming to light during the process of uprooting and resettlement, whether familial or individual, cannot be ignored. As a counsellor and active member of women's groups here, she practises conflict resolution. Political refugees' capacity to evaluate themselves afresh is a significant potential contribution by political refugees to their host society.

Adaptation to and resettlement in the new environment is hard work. Through active employment, my participants became better equipped to resolve their conflicts. Watan advises, "*Don't stay at home—go out to work. Work is essential. Staying at home means depression. A person who doesn't work is like a dying flower. They get weaker and weaker.*"[52]

Concerning his work as a driver and how he is able to communicate through it, Sina told me, "*It is the best job in the world! Financially I can stand on my own two feet, and I can be in touch with the rest of the world. I love my job! About my studies—part of my strength comes from my education. It helped me to become financially independent.*"[53] He enjoys his conversations at work and interacting with his customers, and he moves around in the open in the old nomadic way.

At this point in the interview with Sina, the phoenix started to fly. I witnessed an organic development through suffocation, rebirth, and now mobility. My question leading into Sina's expression of his present condition was carefully timed. Earlier, the nomad was still absorbed in feelings aroused by the past. His financial independence means a great deal to him. His job as a driver enables him to build upon his strength of purpose: his interest in people led him to take a degree in anthropology.

In a subsequent conversation, however, Sina was equally honest about the downsides and difficulties he felt in adjusting to his new world, whose values are hard to recognise: "*There is too much freedom here. There seem to be no boundaries, no legal restraint in place.*"[54] The cultural issue arose again when Sina said, "*Everything is available.*"[55] There seem to be so many avenues for a young man's sexuality in the West, and the challenge is to establish personal boundaries and to be responsible.

When I asked him what he may have lost, Sina replied,

> *I miss my tribal relationship. Everyone within the tribal group honours the tribal identity and thinks about the group—the group comes first. In many ways, they would try to sacrifice their individual interest to the group interest. This is the principle. Although things can sometimes get very aggressive within the tribe, when an individual feels pressured by the group identity, and there are conflicts between individual interests and the group. But despite the pressure we receive from the group, this is the society I grew up in. It is my life. The group was our priority—things were resolved in favour of it. This is my value system, my key to existence—including all the friction, the aggression, the pressure. I see clearly how the capitalist system maximises the benefit of the individual. If people thought more collectively here, it would undermine and threaten this system. This is very clear to me.*[56]

Things are not all rosy for Sina here. When I tried to delve deeper, he admitted his problem with "talking about himself, apart from his tribe"[57]; he feels he has not yet completed his task for them. It seems to him that many people living only for themselves lose their way, lose the meaning of life. He fears this could happen to him. It motivates him to keep thinking, to keep his integrity by educating himself.

Political refugees with a strong sense of purpose and meaning in their lives may tend to isolate themselves from society and be judgmental. They may feel superior to those who do not share their sense of purpose, particularly when they are young. This should be borne in mind when we consider how far political refugees can integrate with their host society and what they can contribute.

Sina demonstrates a willingness to interact and learn from others in any circumstance, but he also makes some assumptions, which may limit him. He wants to present himself as a person of commitment who stands for his own ideals. He is being challenged to uphold these principles and believes a regular lifestyle would undermine them. Sina rebels against "settling" and conformity. His way of life is to be a rebel. In Iran, he was a rebel against the government. Here, he keeps his rebellious nature.

Though Hiva has no status as yet, his olive empire has outlets throughout Europe. The olive, rather like a political refugee, undergoes many processes to become palatable. Hiva uses his executive role—the invisibility of which deeply frustrates him—to disseminate his ideal of community and cooperation in business. "*To tell you the truth*," he said,

> *I live with my ideas and my beliefs. I am the brains behind my system, and I bring my culture to the business. It is like with olives. They store them, they buy them from the Mediterranean, they add a few different spices. I have a knack with food; I marinate and distribute them. I have a vision of how this can grow and thrive.*[58]

In fact, with Hiva's innate talent for secret dissemination, he and just two others in his homeland distributed forty thousand banned books over several Iranian provinces. When he was arrested, Iranian intelligence were astonished not to find a network of thousands behind this operation.

Darius believes no one is born with more abilities than anyone else. "*It depends on how much effort, how much work you have done to get what you want or reach a destination. . . . It was a hard time, but I was patient. . . . You know, if someone is working, there is a variety of experience; he goes out, he comes in, he creates . . . the first thing is basically to keep himself busy.*"[59]

When I asked for his advice to others, Darius replied, "*All those studies I have done before, psychologically—I will try to work on their mind; to make them understand that they are not alone, they have abilities, and if they want to make changes they don't need anybody to help them; they themselves alone, they can make any changes.*"[60] Regarding the idea of working to make a change, no change happens without an active personal commitment to make it happen. Darius is a more solitary operator than some of my other participants; he is the group's philosopher.

Watan has strong feelings on the subject:

> *Working is very important to me. I feel if I stay at home just one week, I lose a year. When I applied for work here, I wrote a simple sentence: "I don't want benefits—I want to work." After just one week, I received permission to work! Now I have my own restaurant. . . . When I started, I had to work from morning to midnight. Most nights I didn't sleep more than four hours. From 9 p.m. to midnight in the kebab grill, I could only earn £18. I worked six months like that. I tried to learn to cook. I used to take meat home, to practise on. Every night I practised! One day the chef had a fight with the owner and didn't come in. The boss was desperate to find someone—I said, "I can do it." He said, "You've been washing dishes here, you don't know how!" I told him, "Yes I do. I took six months to teach myself the job."*

I started to work—I earned £50 instead of £18, every day. It was hard, but I enjoyed it. But I couldn't earn enough because I didn't have asylum. When the owners know you don't have asylum, they pay you much less. I had to carry on. I didn't want to commit suicide! When things are tough, I have to get through it. I can't say, "I cannot engage with this." I had to carry on—I had no other choice.[61]

My nine participants' active desire to work hard and creatively on their condition made them willing to engage with my project and to put their voices into it. This was how Karimi summed it up: "*Everyone can work, in any circumstances—they can do something for themselves. After managing to escape from Iran and to bring my family with six children here, how could I then say to myself, I can't find work, I can't learn the language?*"[62]

LANGUAGE AND SKILL IN ADAPTATION

"My native language is much stronger here," said Sina. He identified what he considers abuses of the English language: "*For example, here they use a lot of big adjectives— why do they say 'amazing,' 'beautiful'? What do those words mean? Just say 'done'—'I did.'*"[63] His spirituality from the desert informs this perspective: a nomad's use of language is economical and practical. He speaks like a monk, a poet, a pilgrim. He dislikes what he sees as the wasting or abuse of language, which he feels erects barriers between people.

Mastery of language plays a crucial part in a political refugee's adaptation process. For Sina, the possibility of learning languages and using them creatively inspired him to grasp opportunities, in stark contrast with his homeland. Because his mother tongue, an ethnic minority language, is now allowed to become more expressive and articulate, it develops his opposition to the regime that suppressed it, becoming enriched through discourse.

As long as you freely use the internet to learn, perhaps it is not very organised, but you can enjoy learning and make yourself more able, powerful, and useful. Education is not just academic education. When I go out, I have conversations with different people, and I always learn from these interactions.[64]

Sina also relished the opportunity to develop a gift, such as music. For the tribesmen, music is their lifeblood, allowing them to express their rhythms, their ancestry, and their spiritual connectedness with nature and with themselves collectively. In Iran, all nonreligious music—national, classical, or Western—is prohibited. The English families who invited Parya to their musical gatherings played a major role in her joyful adaptation to and enthusiasm for her new world.

Lida's fight for justice became enriched by her more objective understanding of the battlefield from a distance. She focuses now on adapting herself to new ways and people and learning to speak English well. "*I'm still actively trying to change my situation, but the nature of my activity has changed. I see this as a part of my fight for life.*"[65] Lida also takes the opportunity to study and to improve herself—a direct attack on the regime's suppression. Like Watan, she has gained a new perspective: "*When I was there, there were many aspects of the political situation that I couldn't see, but now see clearly, from here.*"[66] The effort of learning a host country's language, such as English, German, or Swedish, serves to broaden a person's base and to enrich his or her perception of the world.

Watan had this to say about his sense of self:

> *The basic thing here is to learn the language. That is the key to everything else. . . . I easily make new friends. . . . .As you know, I'm fluent in English, but I don't know the complicated words so well. For example, in the court I didn't have a solicitor or interpreter but I was able to present my case. I was able to express myself and make my statement. I told them that even if they refused, I would still be the same person. I would be the same person who came to this country. What I told to the court, I followed.*[67]

My participants use forceful words to explore or describe their situation. For example, they say, "must," not "might." The violation of their human rights has shaped their use of language. When it comes to torture, rape, violence, rejection, and misrecognition, my European clients tend to use euphemisms; but political refugees express themselves clearly, boldly, and without hesitation. I feel their emotion and their anger. In their native languages, they differ from English speakers, who are less emotional and more considered. My participants are very direct.

I also observe their natural use of metaphor. Many good poets are born in battlegrounds and in prison, where a heightened awareness develops. Lida and Hiva both speak of "a flood" of protest, of which they are part, which carries them to a place where they can fulfil their destiny. Lida described her escape as a piece of wood in the waves that is brought eventually to shore. Gila speaks of the blood of her husband's courage and martyrdom, which flows in her veins; she will never give up. For Darius, the "flickering light" of hope beckoned him steadily through his dark years of dislocation. Hiva sees the mixture of cultures in the United Kingdom as a garden of many beautiful colours, and his hidden work, marinating and distributing olives, as a way of disseminating ethical business initiatives. "The red London bus," with its cheerful colour and relaxed passengers, liberated Sina from the past. For Karimi, the beautiful flowing rivers of his homeland were places where he was forbidden to speak. Watan put his fiery Zoroastrian courage to work—to roast meat and create his new life. Sara guarded and nurtured her children across the mountains to a promised land and baked bread for her new neighbours—a gestural language reaching further into the home than words.

These are powerful visual images. I found that little has been written about the subjective experience of language and what it means in terms of self-confidence and personal recreation. Repeatedly, my participants described their sensations of trying to connect where there is no common language, and of breaking through the dam. They spoke in terms of birth. A newborn child receives and creates language through the warmth of being loved and recognised. Conversely, someone whose interactions are starved may develop an aggressive character in order to be heard. The situation under the regime in Iran displays in extreme form a human society's starvation by its government.

We also speak about "word play,"—the play of language—as in poetic metaphors and music. This concept is forbidden under most dictatorships. The formation of language and a rich, flexible vocabulary is democratic, or "of the people." Sina told of his sense of release:

> *I feel I am able, er—perhaps I can't express myself in Farsi, I mix Farsi, English and Turk-ish! [laughing] I have strength and ability. I feel the debt I owe to other people. I have this dream; I don't want it to stay only in my mind like a fantasy, I want to act. I hope and I will put it into action.*[68]

"*One hundred per cent,*"[69] said Hiva, "*engage with this society, get close to it. Language is crucial to interaction.*"[70] Through careful attention to the recorded interviews, and through the effort of transcribing my participants' lived experiences, the project helped me focus on this subjective experience of language and communication, and how its mastery can alter a person's perception of "being thrown into the world"[71] and even modify their sense of identity.

With my participants' unanimous willingness to work with me, their use of language, inner and outer, became their instrument of transformation and resettlement. The challenge increased their intellectual clarity. Their freedom of speech is a freedom to breathe: the daily task of trying to communicate and to make oneself understood by word, gesture, or activity. It takes a sustained commitment to overcome the difficulties of learning a language and its cultural syntax.

Language is a commitment: an organic process of communication, connection, and interpretation. The task of assimilating a new language and its cultural nuances shapes a refugee's thought and redefines their world.[72] In this regard, some political refugees, such as Lida's husband, do not dare to compromise their emotional and ideological identity by learning English; they become recluses. Because of their loyalty to their homeland, it is too difficult to cross that bridge. Those who cannot—or refuse to—learn the host country's language withdraw into their own diminished resources.

Language thrives with use and input. Language reveals the human condition and develops through dialogue, passion, and imagery; it expands possibilities and cross-fertilises ideas. My nine participants' suppressed native languages grew richer through freedom of speech in the new country, through the rediscovery of who they wanted to be. The use of language is extended through social networking, with or without media technology.

SUPPORTIVE NETWORK

Most of my participants escaped from Iran with the help of supportive networks that also helped their families reunite—a reality they needed to recreate in the host country. Lida recognises she could never have reached where she is today without the support of others:

I would like to develop my language skills. I want to work and to integrate more with the people here, and to carry on my political activities. I'm thinking of writing a novel! I recognise how important my own community is to me. Without my cousin's help, and without my friends, things could have been very difficult. I feel I belong here. I'm not a stranger here—I don't know why I have this feeling, but here it is! Perhaps it's because I was recognised here, officially.[73]

Karimi expressed his feeling: "*I am forever grateful for the support I received from the government and from people—for all humanity—human loving. I received much respect, kindness, and care. My children are studying, getting a good education. In Iran we were nothing.*"[74]

For Darius on his own, establishing supportive networks was touch and go:

After eleven months not answering, the Home Office just rejected my application. A few of my English friends in Stoke-on-Trent wrote a letter to the Home Office for me. I cannot just, you know, live in a small room or somewhere far from other people; it would drive me crazy, to be lonely like that. That's why I seek contact with more people.[75]

Watan's social networks were largely created through his new close friendships in this country. He would like to be more politically active here. "*Our political parties have meetings in Manchester, Leeds, London—always I try to go.*"[76]

Many family and community networks, deeply embedded by tradition in Iranian culture, were split and set at odds by the regime. A significant aspect of my participants' resettlement is their ability to inspire respect and care, to replant the seeds of extended family, and to reach out towards the kind of connectivity that renews a society's health and vitality. For many, this was achieved through the hardships of surmounting misrecognition and prejudice following their escape.

There is also an onus on the host community to make this a two-way process. Barbara Harrell-Bond showed that host communication competence is essential to cross-cultural adaptation, and that host and refugee communities should co-exist "with no greater conflict than that which exists within the host community."[77]

In other words, the psychological and social health of a host community can make all the difference to a refugee's assimilation.

SURVIVAL GUILT

In general, my participants developed new internal weapons to continue the fight, which in part mitigated their survivors' guilt, with so many killed or left behind. Sina's violated people are never far from his mind. To some extent, he is able to reconcile the fact that he can no longer reach them physically with his "future plan" to do some good in his new extended family. There is a deep concern for the tribe's well-being, and the desire to protect the human tribe as a whole from enemies is profound.

Sara's feelings in battle strove with her parental guilt, which remains with her. Here, she describes her moral dilemma when she had to leave her children:

I felt guilty, a bad mother, I felt shame. My oldest daughter in particular couldn't under-stand, and we had tensions—now she understands. She tells me, "I couldn't understand when I was little, but now I am proud of you!" I remember when my youngest daughter was with me—my oldest daughter thought it was because I preferred the little one. This was so very dif-ficult. Now it is my son who has psychological problems; he keeps telling me, even now, "You left me. You left me." For a mum, it is very difficult to be separated from her children even for one night. . . . Although it is some years ago, it still makes me shake all over. I feel very emotional about it. The situation is right here in front of me. It was very, very difficult, very painful to decide. Painful. . . . And my son who is ill says, "If you and my father hadn't been politically active, I wouldn't be this way." He always says that. He blames us for his problems. Our children respect our humanitarian work, but they don't want to do it themselves.[78]

When I asked Karimi how he felt about not being in the battlefield, he replied:

I always think about this. One day I shall have to go back—not leave it too late, because I will need enough energy. I think that in order to fight we have to be in the battlefield. When I was there, at every moment I felt the people's pain. I feel I should go back one day. The regime must end. To tell you the truth, I feel guilty because I'm not in the battlefield. I said I'm happy here and my family are safe; but always I have this feeling about my people. There is something lacking in my life—I want to be there. For as long as the regime are in power, I want to be among those who bring freedom. From here, I can't go into the streets there, to change the regime. I need to be among the people, reach them, have an active role. Even though at the moment I am also fighting and working hard, I don't have the feeling of being in the front line, while I am here. I am politically active here, at demonstrations against the regime and at meetings; I do everything for those who fight against the regime.[79]

Like Sara, Gila suffered maternal guilt. She keeps her torture in prison secret from her children, just as she did not break under the torture itself. Hiva's intense emotion and guilt at having endangered his family undermined his application for asylum:

My sister and my brother were arrested because of my activities. I was unhappy about that. I felt responsible for their problem. They were arrested because of me. I had this guilt all the time. In Iran, they didn't have financial problems, but now I've put them in serious difficul-ties. When I came here, I thought about them all the time. I couldn't do anything. I didn't have asylum status. I was under pressure from these things. In this situation, I had to face the Home Office.[80]

SENSE OF SELF AND CULTURAL ADAPTATION

Some political refugees such as Karimi and Hiva, through therapy from the Medical Foundation, have been helped to articulate their spiritual and personal crises regard-ing the battlefield and their family members. Specific therapeutic skills are needed, first, to understand their pattern of "self for others" and, second, to help them find and develop those same possibilities in the new society.

The ability to adapt to changing conditions might be our greatest human strength. A political refugee's first crisis on arriving here concerns his or her identity in the new country. As we have seen, some of my participants were granted asylum quickly and could start establishing themselves. Others had to wait, sometimes for many years, which further stretched their inner resources. Relocating to a strange new city from a place of no return was taxing for all my participants, who knew others unable to adapt.

Karimi, who had to make existential adjustments, said:

> *My life here is very good, for these reasons: first—my children are all well educated, and my wife is studying. I can see a bright future. In this country I receive a lot of respect from people. I am happy here. Although I think about Iran—my relatives, people, my brothers, sisters, I can't think only of myself—although I have these feelings about Iran, with the things related to myself and my family, I am content. Here we are regarded as human. . . . I have my own identity.*[81]

Many refugees are advised to identify themselves to the host country as victims of overwhelming suffering.[82] Watan told me that his friends advised him when he went to the court to try to cry. He refused to play the game: "*I can't do those things. I can only be myself. I didn't want actually to pretend to be a victim—not at all. . . . I wanted to have my I.D. to be able to live here.*"[83] His view reminds me of Darius's statement, on being asked to "cooperate" with regime agents: "*I was not that kind of person. I never lived like that.*"[84]

Although Hiva was still waiting for his refugee status, the sense of who he really is, what he creates, and what his values are grew strong and centred as he spoke to me:

> *Because I have my own value, my political value, I don't seek to undermine the values of other people. I create a humane relationship with others. People who work with me want to carry on. I don't think so much for my own benefit as for the collective benefit to everyone. My aim is not for personal success; I cannot compromise my values with profit making. One reason I am successful in business is that my mind is not materialistic; it isn't immersed in money or making profits. My talent and creativity aren't limited to profit.*[85]

This is why I urged my participants to focus on their lived experience and feelings, rather than on intellectual or political discourse. I believed this helped them discover an existential truth within their lives, which their sense of guilt, stress, or inadequacy may have obscured.

Some researchers have made cultural generalisations, such as the assumption that Asians dislike direct eye contact.[86] This inadequate and generalised perception of individuals or their sociopolitical background confines cultural expression to fixed behavioural traits. In Wen-Shing Tseng's view, culture is the dynamic, flexible development of a society's attitudes and value systems to regulate behavioural and ethical codes.[87]

In pluralistic societies, a mosaic of ethnic cultures is embedded. Culture is an instrument of nationality and locality. How would my participants define what culture is, and what it means to them? They all hold strong views about the negative aspects of their natal culture, as well as the universal humane values that sustained them privately and collectively through upheaval.

Perhaps Hiva the olive merchant's image of a garden most clearly describes the phenomenon. He feels stimulated by the mixture of races and cultures in the United Kingdom. It helps him to understand the negative and positive aspects of his own culture and to make personal changes.

> *Sitting at home is just a downhill path. Do whatever work you can! I recognise here is like a garden full of colours. I am a product of my own culture, and I keep those values that are important to me. Being in this society helped me to remove the negative side of my natal culture. The different cultures here are this garden of many colours. They create a beautiful garden. You can benefit from the colours, perfumes, and smells. It is up to you. Learn from those different cultures to develop your life.*[88]

Gender inequality is rooted in the culture Karimi was brought up in. When he saw men and women whom he respected interacting naturally with one another, his prejudices were overcome. An internal personal revolution engenders and develops a grassroots social revolution beyond the front line.

> *Those who say a woman who shakes a male stranger's hand is corrupt are wrong. I've seen many decent, respectable people do that. It doesn't mean that. They kiss a person, but it isn't unethical. I learned; and this changed my view. In Iran they might not shake hands, but they do wrong things. Ethical commitment is important. I really learned from that. You can shake your neighbour's hand and even kiss her, but she is like your sister, you can be like her brother—this is how she thinks. Their commitment and their way of thinking encouraged me to understand this culture. My attitude was wrong, totally wrong. This here is right.*[89]

My participants, however, criticised the individualistic culture they perceived in their new home. In their view, people here are locked in their own interests and do not support or befriend each other easily. Darius is shocked at the way the elderly are treated, being placed in care homes far from their families. *"In a country like Iran, when you get older, maybe your family or other people will be around you to look after you. But in a society like this, you are just on your own when you grow older. When I see this, I sometimes find it painful."*[90]

Others dislike what they perceive as careless use of language and the numbing over-availability of entertainment and casual relationships. I discussed these unexpected threats to their value system with them. Watan feels, however, that relationships here between men and women are *"very much better."*

> *Here, the women are more honest. Living with European women enabled me to learn trust. For example, I wanted to marry an Iranian girl . . . her relatives think, if their daughter comes here, I might marry someone else as well. This is their attitude—that a man might*

have four wives and thirty-six children! Here you can't even manage with one! If I wanted to draw comparisons, I would say that relationships here are healthier.[91]

After Sina, Darius, and Sara had lived here for a while, they began to notice things that troubled them, in particular a lack of respect. Darius said, *"Some of my friends here tell me stories—'what happened to my wife'—their English wife, I mean; she was in hospital, and the doctor was disappointed, he couldn't do anything for her. So they abandoned her, just like that.*[92]

Comparing aspects of their past with the situation they find here, far from their communities at home, might sometimes make my participants feel they lost more than they gained, yet motivate them to do something positive. None of them "romanticise" their past; they want to look forward. For many of them, their ethnicity remains their centre of gravity, which helps their adaptation to Western society. For instance, Sina's upbringing and outlook are tribal: a nomadic society's centre and safety is the good of the community or the "larger self." At the beginning of his new life in the United Kingdom, he rose to the challenge of integrating with a new, individualistic culture and of adapting his own value system. Carrying the cultural identity and sensations of his tribe forward into his new world, he replanted his values and discovered how to grow, educate himself, and develop personally through relationships, engagement in current affairs, his studies in anthropology, and his job driving others around the city. Engaging with the cultural diversity here, Sina learned new language skills and gained a university degree. Like my other participants, he wants his unique journey from suffocation to rebirth to be heard, to bear the torch for his people, and to help wherever he can.

When I asked him what he misses most about his homeland, Sina reflected,

What does it mean for me if I miss it—does it mean I want to go back? No! There is no life for me there. If I go to Iran, I fear they will make me inhuman. They will pay me to be an agent of the regime—dirty work to stay alive. My challenge—I suffered a lot—is to be more human and to keep my values strong. I never want to lose that![93]

Sina's essential quest and quality is linked with the heritage of the tribe and its seasoned "human-ness." It is this humane quality he found in the people he met and befriended since his escape that he appreciates most. The rising of the phoenix from the ashes is not a one-off event: it extends into all circumstances and into all endeavours.

I am moved by Sina and hope to meet him again. He is honest: tribal nomadic life is not all rosy. It involves strong pressures, conflicts, and arguments for the individuals within it. It has a rough and ready texture. It is human, uncomfortable, and profound. It is home.

Political refugees often diverge from their national culture. Their group loyalty and the sacrifice of their personal lives, belongings, and assets to the cause make them somewhat different from the norm. As outsiders, they have a distinct role to play. In their cultural adaptation process, we should recognise an expression of universal rather than local values. Sara said she loves her family members but feels more attuned to her comrades in the party. Karimi misses the battlefield but brings the high principles of the freedom fighter to his engineering skills, to do justice to the job and what it is worth, and to help others. Sina, Gila, and Lida find fulfilment in their care for others. These are positive reflections of my participants' political culture within the new society.

Among political refugees I also find some natural rebellion against authority, which occasionally works to their disadvantage. They are strong minded. They might project onto officials in the new society what they fought against in their homeland, where officialdom was against them.

INTERIOR STRENGTH AND RESOURCES

In general, my participants do not allow themselves to be defined by traumatic events but, instead, by the internal resources they have found to overcome them.[94] They have worked hard on themselves psychologically, spiritually, and socially. Their individual experiences and resettlement have given them this opportunity to develop their resources. They had no choice because too much was at stake—their children, their comrades in the Resistance, their integrity, and their ideology. This pressure accelerated their humanitarian growth and reflexivity, which in some ways they pioneered.

Lida reflects,

> *I have also learned to accept some difficult situations, like the death of beloved ones. Once, I also learned that when I really love someone, I love them as they are—not how I might want them to be. Also, I think I have become calmer; I am more relaxed. They didn't respect my rights in Iran—that made me very angry. It shaped my emotional life—I was short-tempered and sometimes aggressive. But now I'm more laid-back and compassionate.*[95]

Sara also learned to handle her impulsive temper and to learn from others.

"*What would I say I have learned?*"[96] said Watan. "*I have learned humanity. I have learned the reality of life. I have learned not to be aggressive and become more emotional, more open. I appreciate life, even the lives of birds. When I was in Iran, I didn't mind killing birds, but here I couldn't do that. I have learned the value of life.*"[97]

Darius feels he lost a decade of his adult life to the prolonged disruption and stress of homelessness he went through until he got his leave to remain in the United Kingdom. His spiritual practice and visionary patience played an important role[98] in his ability to illuminate his dark years, especially with hindsight. Ana Vanista-Kosuta and Milan Kosuta have found other examples of the transmutation of trauma into inner growth and meaning.[99]

My participants' deepest resource lay in their adaptability and willingness to learn afresh, change old attitudes, and build bridges, as well as in their ability to trust. Trust is regarded as social—an interactive quality that develops through relationships.[100] "Trust is a psychological attitude."[101]

In my field study and therapeutic practice, I have found trust extends through the working relationship to build an individual's centre of gravity, the existential foundation of his or her strength of purpose and hope. In all my participants, this resource was challenged before, during, and after their escape. It was interesting to find across the sample, without exception, an existential shift from self-preservation to "the good of others" as the highest purpose of my participants' political and spiritual activity. Not much work has been done in the literature to investigate this dimension.

HOW DO THEY SEE THEIR FUTURE?

In general, the participants in my study are optimistic. Compared with their past, the future beckons to them and is bright. They all want to do something actively for others and, in some cases, to alleviate their survivor's guilt. Having made the transition in their lives, they are confident of their ability to make changes. This depends on their connection with others in their relationship with the host society. For instance, if rejected by the Home Office, they must live a shadow existence; they cannot make future plans or start a family. The problem of survival continues, but it strengthens their internal resources.

The priority across the sample is to become a useful member of the host society, and when faced with difficulties, not to give up but to keep going. Each participant is aware of his or her place in history; within the loyalty to that wider canvas, they try to resolve local tensions in their family or marriage. They are all eager to work, to expand their adventure of integration with the new culture, and to adhere to their resolute stance against the regime. Those who were political activists in Iran join resistance movements here and continue the fight for human rights and social justice. Those who do not belong to a party cultivate and develop their interior revolution. For all of them, their escape means communicating their message, working hard to become better human beings, caring for and loving others, and contributing to the host society and towards a positive future for their children in the world.

Through the difficulties and releases of their new birth, my participants gained recognition and respect. They faced both internal and external hardships, which challenged and developed their language skills. Through their determination to work and to communicate in English, they created supportive networks, which enrich the host community. Productive employment helps ease their survivor's guilt. Cultural adaptation in the family context is an ongoing process; their children's educational achievements and engagement with schoolmates help the parents integrate, as Sara, Parya, Gila, and Karimi have demonstrated. Their sense of identity remains flexible and grows in line with their integration.

It is difficult for Sina to talk about himself apart from the wider context of the community and its well-being with which he is identified. He feels guilty because his closest friends and relatives were killed or had suffered, whereas he managed to escape. This strengthens his sense of responsibility to do whatever he can for his people. Their poverty increases and they get no support from the regime.

"*This is my ideology for tomorrow,*"[102] said Sina, "*at least by working in cultural and educational activities for others, I want to do everything I can for others, and so I will, in small or large ways.*"[103]

All my participants are sensitive to the constant threat their people face. They distrust authoritative infrastructures. They keep in touch with their relatives and try to assist them, as they now live safely overseas. Although they have settled here, most of them engage emotionally with what is going on in their homeland. They see themselves not as individuals but as part of their ethnic communities. Although physically in the United Kingdom, their hearts are in Iran. This could impede full engagement with the host country, though my female participants who became head of their families are keen to integrate. Children play a positive role in this.

Speaking of his "tomorrow plan," Sina described his desire to do something valuable for others, to benefit them. Because of his gratitude to the community that gave him a new home, he wishes to be helpful and positive, to study communications in technology, and to enjoy his work.

At the time of his interview for my study, Darius—who had by then been granted asylum—made a change for the better in his life. We met informally at the restaurant where he was employed in the kitchen. He had that day secured a good job in translation and administration, and he was jubilant:

> *I'm happy now that things are changing, gradually. . . . I can see a bright future—especially as I am getting this job! And hopefully they are going to contact me. I worked with them today, from 10 a.m. to 3 p.m.; they gave positive feedback, and asked for my own feedback, which I gave; and they asked me if I am happy to work with them and I was. Now, gradually things are going to change for the better. I'm sure a lot of work still needs to be done, you know.*[104]

Gila feels confident that, whatever her situation, she can make a success of it for her and her children and make her stand against the regime:

> *I'm a hard worker. My children and I all work hard. We don't want to claim benefits here . . . because we have freedom here, we can live like other people. They accept us and we have an obligation to pay our taxes. . . . One thing I would like to do: I want to give service to others. I would like to do voluntary work to help others . . . even in a charity shop. I don't want to sit at home; I like to work. This is my nature—I want to be active. . . . I believe if human beings take responsibility and become independent, they can succeed.*
>
> *I love to help others. One of my friends told me of a woman in financial difficulties. I had only £50 in my wallet. Without thinking, I asked her address, and I sent the £50. That week I had no money for myself—I didn't even tell my children. I thought this is a good opportunity for me this week, to understand how people feel who have nothing; I can share that feeling. I love to do these things, even if I don't know the people. Even I heard of someone in Iran, who is in difficulties—I talked to her sister here, and asked, "Is it OK for your sister to accept my support?" I try to save some money. I sent her some because she couldn't*

pay her rent in Iran. Doing these things makes me feel good. It makes me feel more relaxed, and I sleep better.

This is my nature—I have to respond when someone needs help.[105]

Gila would never exchange her small two-room flat in London for the fine house, beautiful park, and stretch of river she inherited in Iran. Here, she is free to teach her mother tongue to her two grandchildren; she also wishes for an opportunity to help young Syrians. "*I can look after two children—I have room. I wish to fetch two Syrian children and bring them here.*" At the end of our interview, she told me: "*What I have said is not only for your project. I have said it before. I feel more relaxed now, after talking about the suffering.*"[106]

I asked Sina to consider this scenario: "Imagine meeting some political refugees who escaped from Iran." I then queried, "What would you tell them, on the basis of your own experience?" He spoke for the group:

The first thing I would tell them is to understand that they have rights here—for example, the health service and the facilities they can use. The second thing is that it is good to work. To work hard is very important. Even if you are studying, that is your work. Find a job and go to work! Try to overcome your communication difficulties—learn the language. There are a lot of obstacles; be ready to resolve them. It is difficult not only for you but for everyone. Everyone has to face these same problems; this is the most important thing. You can't expect everything to be ready for you—you have to be willing to resolve these problems.

Challenges and obstacles await you! The traps are all ready for you to jump into! Some are social, others economic. And you need to beware: there are regime spies here! You must be careful what you say and write. It is your right here not to be followed by regime spies.

My main conflict is with the way everything here is too available. . . . Here, the welfare is of a high standard. This is good, but also it is bad. The whole situation encourages you to have a routine life—go to work and come back home, go to work, and come back home—and then go gambling! You are, but you are not. You are being, but also you are not-being. Physically, you are surviving, you are OK, but what about your feelings, your beliefs, your meaning of life. What about your value system: when you can't reach it, can you live according to your principles? I feel I have to resist the routine situation on a daily basis—to keep my spiritual ideals, through thinking and also through educating myself.

Here, you have many material things, but at the same time, having more creates more problems! You have to choose your value system or lose it. This is about freedom, or going under. It's like being in a flood. If you don't stand with your integrity, the whole bourgeois capitalist value system will actually carry you off, sweep you away. Without my values to stand on, I feel I am dead, maybe not physically but psychologically. Here, I still must go on fighting, though in a different way.[107]

Because he does not "go with the flow" socially, Sina is in a position to observe how people here are also forced to compromise and to forget who they really are. He discovers that he continues to resist "a regime." There is an uncomfortable awareness of the new society's "bombardment to conform." The routine way of life it "imposes" is intolerable for a nomadic tribesman—it is yet another aspect of dictatorship. Projecting here his fear of the regime in Iran, he is determined to remain a free man. It is an existential dilemma. There are probably arguments in himself and with others. He doesn't quite fit in. His pride and purpose drive him further: perhaps that was in his nature, as a boy, back home. Wherever he goes, he will storm the barricades. For him, communication means movement and liberty.

For Sina, as for all my participants, there is no end to the desire to evolve. There is an ideal life in their hearts, towards which they are moving. The phoenix in each case provided an incentive to rediscover their identity. There is a powerful instinctive urge to give something significant back to the community that rescued them. If Sina still lived in his tribe it would be simple: he would marry and give his children to the tribe's long life. Finding himself now distanced from his people, he cannot turn back the clock. His heart is tribal and beats within his extended human family, yet he feels alone. This makes him sensitive to people's loneliness here in Britain.

The nine people in this book were accustomed to communicating ideas in the political forum. The rare chance to open up and discuss the suffering in their private lived experience released them further, bringing them fresh insight and understanding.

Here is their summary:

Karimi: *I feel our family and my future is bright; I am very optimistic.*
Sina: *I want to do something for them. This is my "tomorrow plan."*
Darius: *You can change things if you want.*
Hiva: *When you have no recognition from the Home Office, you can't think about the future.*
Sara: *You must make yourself a useful member of society.*
Watan: *If you face difficulties, don't give up. Carry on, keep going.*
Parya: *I want to resolve my problems with my husband.*
Lida: *I want to work and to integrate more with the people here, and to carry on my political activities. I'm thinking of writing a novel!*
Gila: *Another way is to stand against the regime. This is what I did, and what I will always do.*[108]

NOTES

1. Armin H. Danesh, "Exploring Iranian Political Refugees' Experiences in Britain: The Phoenix Rises from the Ashes" (Doctoral diss., Middlesex University, 2019), 129.

2. Jeffrey Champlin, "Born Again: Arendt's 'Natality' as Figure and Concept," *Germanic Review* 88, no. 2 (2013): 150–64.

3. Hannah Arendt, *The Human Condition*, 2nd ed. (Chicago: University of Chicago Press, 2013).

4. Arendt, *The Human Condition*.

5. Danesh, "Exploring Iranian Political Refugees' Experiences," 129.

6. Karimi, interviewed by A. Danesh, London, 12 October 2015.

7. The Medical Foundation is now called Freedom from Torture.

8. Lida, interviewed by A. Danesh, London, 7 October 2016.

9. Parya, interviewed by A. Danesh, London, 30 November 2016.

10. Parya, interviewed by A. Danesh, London, 30 November 2016.

11. Danesh, "Exploring Iranian Political Refugees' Experiences," 170.

12. Darius, interviewed by A. Danesh, London, 25 August 2016.

13. Darius, interviewed by A. Danesh, London, 25 August 2016.

14. Danesh, "Exploring Iranian Political Refugees' Experiences," 171.

15. Hiva, interviewed by A. Danesh, London, 29 June 2016.

16. Hiva, interviewed by A. Danesh, London, 29 June 2016.

17. Watan, interviewed by A. Danesh, London, 27 June 2016.

18. Donald Woods Winnicott, *The Family and Individual Development* (London: Tavistock, 1965).

19. Charles Taylor, *Multi-culturalism and the Politics of Recognition* (Princeton, NJ: Princeton University Press, 1992).

20. Danesh, "Exploring Iranian Political Refugees' Experiences," 173.

21. Danesh, "Exploring Iranian Political Refugees' Experiences," 176.

22. Sara, interviewed by A. Danesh, London, 7 November 2015.

23. Karimi, interviewed by A. Danesh, London, 12 October 2015.

24. Watan, interviewed by A. Danesh, London, 27 June 2016.

25. Sina, interviewed by A. Danesh, London, 8 August 2015.

26. Lida, interviewed by A. Danesh, London, 7 October 2016.

27. Watan, interviewed by A. Danesh, London, 27 June 2016.

28. Darius, interviewed by A. Danesh, London, 25 August 2016.

29. Darius, interviewed by A. Danesh, London, 25 August 2016.

30. Danesh, "Exploring Iranian Political Refugees' Experiences," 174.

31. Gila, interviewed by A. Danesh, London, 23 August 2016.

32. Gila, interviewed by A. Danesh, London, 23 August 2016.

33. Sara, interviewed by A. Danesh, London, 7 November 2015.

34. Sara, interviewed by A. Danesh, London, 7 November 2015.

35. Sara, interviewed by A. Danesh, London, 7 November 2015.

36. Danesh, "Exploring Iranian Political Refugees' Experiences," 175.

37. Parya, interviewed by A. Danesh, London, 30 November 2016.

38. Danesh, "Exploring Iranian Political Refugees' Experiences," 175.

39. Lida, interviewed by A. Danesh, London, 7 October 2016.

40. Karimi, interviewed by A. Danesh, London, 12 October 2015.

41. Karimi, interviewed by A. Danesh, London, 12 October 2015.

42. Danesh, "Exploring Iranian Political Refugees' Experiences," 176.

43. Danesh, "Exploring Iranian Political Refugees' Experiences," 176.

44. Gila, interviewed by A. Danesh, London, 23 August 2016.

45. Danesh, "Exploring Iranian Political Refugees' Experiences," 177.

46. Darius, interviewed by A. Danesh, London, 25 August 2016.

47. Danesh, "Exploring Iranian Political Refugees' Experiences," 179.

48. Watan, interviewed by A. Danesh, London, 27 June 2016.

49. Watan, interviewed by A. Danesh, London, 27 June 2016.

50. Sara, interviewed by A. Danesh, London, 7 November 2015.

51. Lida, interviewed by A. Danesh, London, 7 October 2016.

52. Danesh, "Exploring Iranian Political Refugees' Experiences," 180.

53. Danesh, "Exploring Iranian Political Refugees' Experiences," 180.

54. Sina, interviewed by A. Danesh, London, 8 August 2015.

55. Sina, interviewed by A. Danesh, London, 8 August 2015.

56. Sina, interviewed by A. Danesh, London, 8 August 2015.

57. Sina, interviewed by A. Danesh, London, 8 August 2015.

58. Hiva, interviewed by A. Danesh, London, 29 June 2016.

59. Darius, interviewed by A. Danesh, London, 25 August 2016.

60. Darius, interviewed by A. Danesh, London, 25 August 2016.

61. Watan, interviewed by A. Danesh, London, 27 June 2016.

62. Danesh, "Exploring Iranian Political Refugees' Experiences," 211.

63. Danesh, "Exploring Iranian Political Refugees' Experiences," 184.

64. Sina, interviewed by A. Danesh, London, 8 August 2015.

65. Danesh, "Exploring Iranian Political Refugees' Experiences," 182.

66. Danesh, "Exploring Iranian Political Refugees' Experiences," 182.

67. Watan, interviewed by A. Danesh, London, 27 June 2016.

68. Sina, interviewed by A. Danesh, London, 8 August 2015.

69. Danesh, "Exploring Iranian Political Refugees' Experiences," 184.

70. Danesh, "Exploring Iranian Political Refugees' Experiences," 184.

71. Martin Heidegger, *Basic Writings*, ed. David Krell (New York: Harper & Row, 1977).

72. Lera Boroditsky, "How Does Our Language Shape the Way We Think?," Edge, 11 June 2009, https://www.edge.org/conversation/lera_boroditsky-how-does-our-language-shape-the-way-we-think.

73. Lida, interviewed by A. Danesh, London, 7 October 2016.

74. Karimi, interviewed by A. Danesh, London, 12 October 2015.

75. Danesh, "Exploring Iranian Political Refugees' Experiences," 185.

76. Danesh, "Exploring Iranian Political Refugees' Experiences," 185.

77. Barbara E. Harrell-Bond, *Imposing Aid: Emergency Assistance to Refugees* (Oxford: Oxford University Press, 1986).

78. Sara, interviewed by A. Danesh, London, 7 November 2015.

79. Karimi, interviewed by A. Danesh, London, 12 October 2015.

80. Hiva, interviewed by A. Danesh, London, 29 June 2016.

81. Karimi, interviewed by A. Danesh, London, 12 October 2015. "I feel our family and my future is bright; I am very optimistic" (Karimi, interviewed by A. Danesh, London, 12 October 2015).

82. Dinesh Bhugra, Tom Craig, and Kamaldeep Bhui, eds., *Mental Health of Refugees and Asylum Seekers* (Oxford: Oxford University Press, 2010); Renos K. Papadopoulos, ed., *Therapeutic Care for Refugees: No Place Like Home* (London: Karnac Books, 2002); Guus van der Veer, *Counselling and Therapy with Refugees and Victims of Trauma: Psychological Problems of Victims of War, Torture and Repression* (New York: Wiley, 1998); Colin Lago, *The Handbook of Transcultural Counselling and Psychotherapy* (Maidenhead: Open University Press, 2011); Christophe Bertossi, ed., *European Antidiscrimination and the Politics of Citizenship: Britain and France* (London: Palgrave Macmillan, 2007).

83. Danesh, "Exploring Iranian Political Refugees' Experiences," 189.

84. Danesh, "Exploring Iranian Political Refugees' Experiences," 189.

85. Hiva, interviewed by A. Danesh, London, 29 June 2016.

86. Fred Bemak, Rita Chi-Ying Chung, and Paul Pedersen, *Counseling Refugees: A Psychosocial Approach to Innovative Multicultural Interventions* (Westport, CT: Greenwood, 2003).

87. Wen-Shing Tseng and Jon Streltzer, eds., *Culture and Psychotherapy. A Guide to Clinical Practice* (Washington, DC: American Psychiatric Press, 2001).

88. Danesh, "Exploring Iranian Political Refugees' Experiences," 190.

89. Karimi, interviewed by A. Danesh, London, 12 October 2015.

90. Danesh, "Exploring Iranian Political Refugees' Experiences," 191.

91. Watan, interviewed by A. Danesh, London, 27 June 2016.

92. Darius, interviewed by A. Danesh, London, 25 August 2016.

93. Sina, interviewed by A. Danesh, London, 8 August 2015.

94. Renos K. Papadopoulos, "Storied Community as Secure Base: Response to the Paper by Nancy Caro Hollander 'Exile: Paradoxes of Loss and Creativity,'" *British Journal of Psychotherapy* 15, no. 3 (1999): 322–32; Renos K. Papadopoulos, "Refugees, Therapists and Trauma: Systemic Reflections," *Context* 54 (April 2001): 5–8.

95. Danesh, "Exploring Iranian Political Refugees' Experiences," 192.

96. Watan, interviewed by A. Danesh, London, 27 June 2016.

97. Danesh, "Exploring Iranian Political Refugees' Experiences," 193.

98. Kenneth Pargament, Harold Koenig, and Lisa Perez, "The Many Methods of Religious Coping: Development and Initial Validation of RCOPE," *Journal of Clinical Psychology* 56, no. 4 (2000): 519–43; Nalini Tarakeshwar, Kenneth Pargament, and Annette Mahoney, "Initial Development of a Measure of Religious Coping among Hindus," *Journal of Community Psychology* 31, no. 6 (2003): 607–28.

99. Ana Vanista-Kosuta, and Milan Kosuta, "Trauma and Meaning," *Croatian Medical Journal* 39, no. 1 (March 1998).

100. Piotr Sztompka, *Trust: A Sociological Theory* (Cambridge: Cambridge University Press, 1999).

101. Christiano Castelfranchi and Rino Falcone, *Trust Theory: A Socio-cognitive and Computational Model* (Hoboken, NJ: Wiley, 2010).

102. Sina, interviewed by A. Danesh, London, 8 August 2015.

103. Sina, interviewed by A. Danesh, London, 8 August 2015.

104. Darius, interviewed by A. Danesh, London, 25 August 2016.

105. Gila, interviewed by A. Danesh, London, 23 August 2016.

106. Gila, interviewed by A. Danesh, London, 23 August 2016.

107. Sina, interviewed by A. Danesh, London, 8 August 2015.

108. Danesh, "Exploring Iranian Political Refugees' Experiences," 132.

7

Clinical Relevance

Armin Danesh

This chapter bridges the world of therapy and the world of the refugee. What is the real political crisis that refugees face? Are they able to regenerate their lived meanings and to survive? What seeds can be sown for a fresh outlook or change in attitude towards them?

To be recognised and accepted by government organisations in a new country, most political refugees face the condition that they must present themselves as victims of human rights abuses. Many mental health organisations that provide therapeutic services for refugees perceive them systematically as victims; their main focus is on what the refugees have lost. My participants' view is different. For them, the mission continues: to bring about positive change in their homeland. In this light, my participants were able to transform their losses into an increased commitment.

For them, there is no greater loss than to have their idealism destroyed. For example, the martyrs and the sacrifice they made continue to inspire and encourage others and to give energy to the struggle for liberation.

SIGNIFICANT FACTORS IN THERAPEUTIC WORK WITH POLITICAL REFUGEES

From my participants' experiences, I summarised the following important factors in four domains: personal/psychological, social, physical, and spiritual (see table 7.1).

Table 7.1   Significant Factors in Therapeutic Work with Political Refugees

Personal/psychological domain
1. Value system and political identity is the essence of their existence.
2. Trauma is mainly related to their ideological crisis.
3. Trust must be reestablished; otherwise, their therapeutic experience may be based on fear.
4. They see things mainly in black or white or right or wrong; they use forceful language to express themselves.
5. Recognition and respect are crucial to their sense of identity.
6. It is essential to recognise and remind them of their internal resources and achievement.
7. Subjective experience of language.
8. It is important for them to use their value system and their desire to work for others as therapeutic resources.
9. Subjective meaning of trauma.
10. They want to do the best for others; alternative might be survivor guilt, despair, and/or depression.
11. Responsibility, motivation, and action are their familiar ground.
12. They have high expectations and tend to set the bar high. They are self-critical.

Social domain
1. Their loss is related to their political task, rather than to material possessions.
2. It is important to them that they establish a social network and be community oriented.
3. Their attitude against dictatorship in their homeland may be projected onto figures of authority in the new country.
4. Working on gender equality is the yardstick in their adaptation process.
5. They are not merely victims or problems.
6. Political refugees are fully capable of dealing with their basic needs and confronting conflict situations.
7. They need to adapt their political identity to their new country.
8. Their views might be extreme because they resisted an extremist regime.
9. They need to learn how to deal with the: cultural, environmental, and behavioural differences in their new country.
10. They prize confidentiality, have the habit of secrecy, and may experience paranoia from having lived under a dictatorship.

Spiritual domain
1. They need to acknowledge their value system, purpose, and meaning.
2. They have a strong sense of self-connection and care for humanity and the environment.

Physical domain
1. They need to be active to maintain a healthy lifestyle.
2. Generally, they are practical and creative.

SUGGESTED THERAPEUTIC PROCESS

The characteristics of this therapeutic process are relational, phenomenological, collaborative, developmental, and educational.

The starting point is of course based on human interaction, rather than on a professional atmosphere. Developing trust is fundamental, through recognising their value system with care and respect. Exploring problems, engaging with and learning from them, the therapist should remind political refugees of their internal strength and allow the work to be focused on those resources. In the process, a common language may develop. We should continue to expand their familiar ground of responsibility and commitment. Their desire to help others may be utilised to strengthen their own self-connection.

As we work on the developmental process of authentic self, we can confirm and support the effort they are making towards the changes they are expecting. I will return later to the concept of authentic self.

Contrary to the Diagnostic and Statistical Manual of Mental Disorders (DSM), which pathologises, diagnoses, and prescribes, this therapeutic process is neither directive nor medical oriented. It requires training and considerable professional competence (see figures 7.1 and 7.2).

It is important to mention that there are many organisations and individual therapists offering therapeutic service to refugees and asylum seekers in the United Kingdom. They do not necessarily follow DSM criteria. Some of them, such as the British Refugee Council, Freedom from Torture (Medical Foundation for the Care of Victims of Torture), and the Baobab Centre for Young Survivors in Exile, have developed their approach to meet the needs of their clients.

The DSM, published by the American Psychiatric Association (APA), is considered the most important reference document for assessing and categorising mental disorders. The DSM provides a common language among clinicians, researchers, the pharmaceutical industry, health insurance companies, and policy makers.[1] There are, however, ongoing debates and criticisms among mental health professionals about the DSM's validity, reliability and utility.[2]

The British Psychological Society (BPS), a highly respected organisation representing more than fifty thousand members, made many criticisms of the new manual, the DSM-5.[3] In 2011, the BPS highlighted biased criteria and a failure to acknowledge the importance of social factors as precursors to mental health problems.[4]

Since the DSM was first published in 1952, some feminist psychologists have contributed to critical analysis of the manual on the basis of philosophical and sociopolitical dimensions. They have emphasised that psychological disorders are linked to the broader sociopolitical, economic, and cultural context.[5]

The DSM displays both scientific and clinical limitations. It potentially medicalises patterns of behaviour and mood and unnecessarily stigmatises individuals. Clinicians should consider their clients' internal resources and resilience, rather than only their perceived deficits. In addition, the sociocultural, environmental, spiritual, and political domains should be taken into account in perceiving human suffering.

AN EXISTENTIAL FRAMEWORK AND
A MEDICAL MODEL (DSM-5)

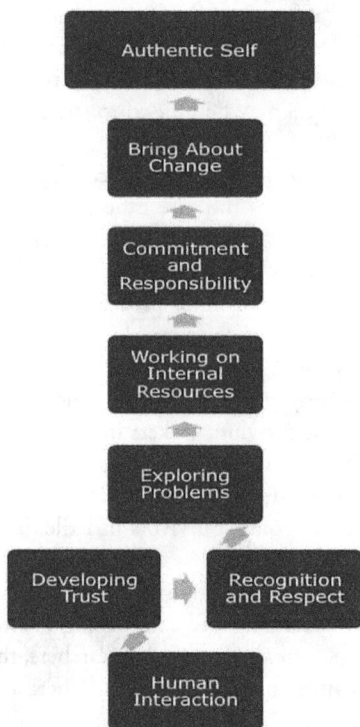

Figure 7.1 Existential Framework: Relational, Phenomenological, Developmental, Collaborative, Educational and Towards an Authentic Self.

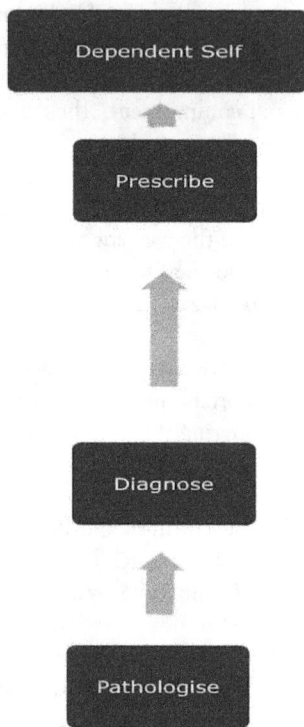

Figure 7.2 DSM-5: Directive and Medically Oriented.

AUTHENTIC SELF

Many writers, from ancient Greece to the Enlightenment, from Existentialism to contemporary social theory, have studied the concept of authenticity. Existentialist psychotherapists have also carried out exhaustive studies in this area. In the past three decades, authors like Charles Taylor, Alessandro Ferrara, Charles Guignon, and Somogy Varga have attempted to reconstruct authenticity.[6] However, the concept specifically as a moral idea is relatively new, understood as being true to oneself for one's own benefit.

IS AUTHENTICITY POSSIBLE?

In this section, I attempt to outline the meaning of authenticity in this study. I will briefly refer to the philosophical foundation as well as the existentialist psychotherapist's perspective.

A number of significant cultural changes in the seventeenth and eighteenth centuries led to the emergence of a new ideal in the Western world.[7] During this period, human beings came to be thought of more as individuals than as socially oriented. At the same time, there was an increasing awareness of what Charles Taylor calls "inwardness" or "internal space." The result is a distinction between one's private and unique individuality and one's public self.[8]

The important issue is that the ideas of authenticity and autonomy are interrelated in many ways. The concept of autonomy emphasises the individual's self-governing abilities. It is connected to the view that moral principles and the legitimacy of political authority should be grounded in the self-governing individual, free from diverse cultural and social pressures.

Another decisive factor was the simultaneous emergence of a distinctively modern concept of the self. This can be seen in the work of Jean-Jacques Rousseau, who argues that the orientation towards life, which should guide the conduct one chooses, should come from an internal source.

The word *authenticity* has become closely associated with Martin Heidegger and Søren Kierkegaard and was adopted by Jean-Paul Sartre and Simone De Beauvoir and by existentialist therapists and social theorists who followed them.

Kierkegaard's work on authenticity highlights the notion that each of us is to become what one is.[9] He criticises modern society for causing "inauthenticity," leading to what he calls widespread "despair," which manifests itself as spiritlessness, denial, and defiance. In Kierkegaard's view, "becoming what one is" and avoiding despair and hollowness is not a matter of solitary introspection but, rather, a matter of passionate commitment in relation to something outside oneself, which gives life meaning. For Kierkegaard, this ultimate commitment was his defining relation to God.

Some existentialists say that the key to becoming authentic is to face our own death and our own limitation. In the dynamic process of opening ourselves to this reality and accepting it, we find ourselves most truly.[10] This idea is based on the view of Heidegger. Heidegger considered the nature of authenticity in his exploration of existence, in which he refers to human existence as *Dasein*. The defining characteristics of *Dasein*'s potentiality-for-being are displayed in the transformative events that lead to the possibility of being authentic. It becomes possible to see the whole of *Dasein*, including both its being as a "they-self" and as authentic being-one's-self.[11]

So the key to understanding authenticity lies in the characterisation of *Dasein*'s being as a relation between two aspects or dimensions making up human existence. On the one hand, we find ourselves thrown into a world and a situation not of our own making. At the same time, however, to be human is to move towards achieving ends understood as integral to one's overarching life-project.[12]

Heidegger sees authenticity as being true not to oneself, but to existence. In other words, authenticity is being open to or facing the givens of existence, including our *thrown-ness* and inevitable death. For Heidegger, the only way to reclaim authenticity is to become transparent to our being-towards-death and to fully accept death as inevitable. He regards authenticity and inauthenticity as two different modes of being.

Sartre's view is that all values are generated by human interactions in situations, so that value is a human construct with no external forces (existence precedes essence). Inauthenticity is often associated with Sartre's "acting in bad faith."[13] Sartre's account of "bad faith" is a kind of self-deception and involves believing oneself to be something while being something else. For Sartre, the project of being in good faith seems impossible, as we are always necessarily in bad faith. The inescapable nature of bad faith seems to leave no possibility of authenticity. However, Gary Cox's summary of Sartre's view states that authentic existence is a project that has to be continually reassumed. A person is only as authentic as his present act. Authentic existence (the sustained project) is an unattainable existentialist ideal. Nevertheless, it is an ideal worth aiming at.[14]

De Beauvoir takes up Sartre's characterisation of the human condition and expands on ideas only hinted at in Sartre's famous 1946 lecture, "Existentialism Is a Humanism," in developing a conception of authenticity. According to De Beauvoir, Sartre's conception of the human being as "engaged freedom" implies not just that each individual finds his or her "reason for being" in concrete realisations of freedom but also that willing one's own freedom necessarily involves willing the freedom of all humans.

De Beauvoir also builds on Sartre's notion of engagement to extend the idea of authenticity. Following Sartre, the authentic individual will be the one who takes up the terrifying freedom of being the ultimate source of values, embraces it, and acts with a clarity and resolve consistent with his or her best understanding of what is right in this context. In this way, the concept of authenticity is a continuation of the ideal of being true to ourselves: we are called upon to become, in our concrete lives, what we already are in the ontological structure of our being.

In my opinion, there is no "fixed" or "authentic" self. The self is always becoming and should be understood as a process rather than a concrete thing.

Following Heidegger, existentialist therapists such as Hans W. Cohn emphasise that there can be no authentic or inauthentic self, only an authentic way of being in the world.[15] For Emmy van Deurzen, recognising our own limitation in facing death is crucial to becoming an authentic self, and it is impossible to achieve authenticity as an entirety.[16] We need also consider how the level of authenticity can vary in different areas of our life.

Most existential phenomenological therapists assist their clients to be aware of their own meaning in life, to act accordingly, and to take responsibility for their actions. They thus achieve greater authenticity. It is a dynamic, developmental, and ongoing process.

My nine participants, who were seeking freedom to make choices in the direction of their beliefs, were aware of the risk and took the responsibility to act. In Heidegger's terms, they projected their life into the future. For my participants, moving towards a high level of authenticity means following their political goals and value system. Their aspiration to individual oneness is related to their responsibility to others. My participants' initial task was not to focus on their own well-being. Their aim was to follow their value system and the meaning of their existence. This project enabled them to follow the path towards their greater authentic self. However, authenticity is not an absolute position or concrete state. In other words, to consider authenticity as a fixed phenomenon leads to inauthenticity. In this respect, authenticity and inauthenticity are part of their everyday lives. The developmental process of authenticity involves the four domains of existence: physical, social, psychological, and spiritual. Figures 7.3 and 7.4 illustrate the "authentic self" and the "united self."

Some scholars formulated the human condition through the interplay of knowledge, feeling, and action (see figure 7.3).[17] My own emphasis on responsibility encompasses these factors in the evolution of the authentic self. In my understanding, one of the pillars of Abrahamic religions is their concept of "heaven" and "hell," through which human responsibility inescapably manifests. Responsibility is central to the thought of philosophers such as Aristotle, Plato, Immanuel Kant, Friedrich Nietzsche, Jacques Derrida, Emmanuel Levinas, Heidegger, and Sartre.[18] In Hannah Arendt's view, responsibility is defined in terms of political presence rather than in legal or moral contexts.[19] The nature of responsibility is both relational and ideological, linking oneself to others to become a united self (see figure 7.4).

Figure 7.3 Authentic Self.

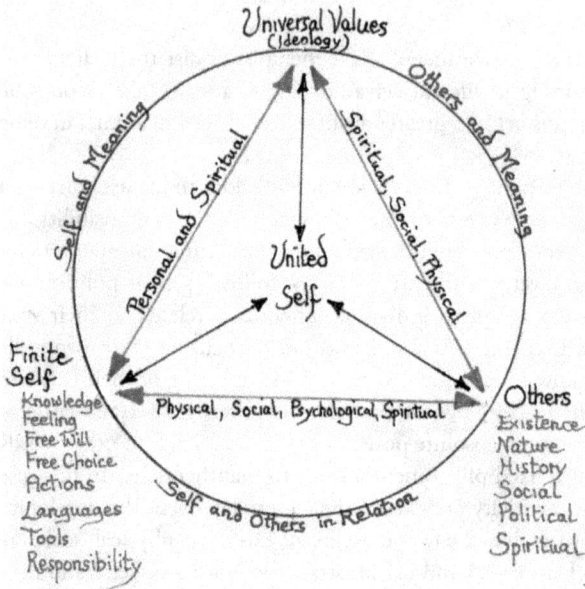

Figure 7.4   United Self in Relation.

HOW DOES THIS STUDY APPLY TO THE THERAPY WORLD IN GENERAL?

I am not in a position to supply a general application of my study or to establish a theory; however, my findings are based on the human capability to confront extreme situations. My nine participants' internal resources enabled them to survive potentially paralysing experiences. The principle is applicable to therapy in general.

Facing loss and trauma, their sense of meaning and purpose—their service for others—enabled them to survive. They wanted to bring about change, to free themselves and others. They came through the "refiner's fire" and rose from the ashes. Their story manifests the human capacity to face difficulties of any kind. They continue to survive and to demonstrate that resilience. They didn't give up. Their purpose in life encouraged them to overcome psychological, cultural, and social obstacles. If we want to make a positive change, we must concentrate on what we have within ourselves, which is real. We are also aware that the dynamic process of change is relational—external, involving others—as well as internal.

My participants exemplify the way we can set our life on a better course: their presence in the therapy situation amplifies this idea. Their story of the human struggle calls to all; if you want to, you can make the change. In other words, for my participants the therapeutic situation is not confined to their own lives. Their desire is to improve the human condition. They demonstrate that if you set your bar—your meaning of life—high, your own personality will identify with and become that liberation. Mainstream psychotherapy tends to focus on the individual, but humans are social beings. The political refugee works towards a human connectivity or field, where the individual may exist and grow.

To desire the common good brings a shift within individuals who feel threatened by others. The invitation to those others removes the sense of threat. The progress of therapy requires a focus on the quality of the therapeutic relationship itself. The shift is from an exclusive biological family to the world of one's chosen ideological or universal family, which includes the former.

I found with my participants that those who kept their positive values intact are integrators. Their desire as political refugees is to bring society together. Sara baked loaves of bread for her new neighbours. Gila wishes to adopt Syrian children. Watan sheltered an African whom he did not know and sent money to a stranger in Iran who was ill. This is their deep mission and message.

This direction in my study, moving from the individual to the wider community, is future focused. That quality of human capability requires recognition, care, and practice. Focusing on individual self-interest cannot satisfy or reach the heart of a political refugee. That quality grows beyond the individual to the wider good. All my participants expressed in their different ways that "my problem does not belong to myself, but to human society."

My participants agree that clients who are political refugees were probably trained to have a clear aim. They are unlikely to feel confused or existentially divided. The ideal to which they dedicate their lives means more to them than any past parental dynamic or factor of upbringing. Some of them are astonished when asked to consider themselves personally.

What is their therapeutic need? For some, ideological trauma may remain the main major issue and may hinder their progress. Additionally, family conflicts that surface in the upheaval of resettlement in a new culture need urgent attention. These are local features in the bigger picture a political refugee carries.

To focus too much on oneself becomes stressful.[20] Relating with others, the existential themes brought into therapy enrich the whole field. When Heidegger says we are in relation with others, it means we bring it into practice. Nietzsche's "be your own God" means to take responsibility at that level. We may say this is common ground for human beings who are political activists and refugees.

When our inner strength is recognised in this way, we join humanity; we join the world. The movement from person-centre to social-centre is towards connectivity, collectively. Human capability is restricted and even suppressed if we concentrate too much on personal self.

As long as "my position," theory, or role weigh heavier than my client's well-being, the therapy will not progress. To make a change, we must move beyond promoting our status. My personal self-regard contradicts my availability to my client. Conversely, as I attune to my client's well-being, the dynamic changes. My nine participants opened these windows:

1. Meaning and purpose
2. If we want to, we can
3. Future focus
4. Social focus

Authentic selfhood rarely exists in isolation—it thrives in the social domain, in the interactive triad, in the adventure of relationships.

The gift for others gives political refugees their energy. They need to work actively for the common good. They may be traumatised not from torture or loss or unforgettable memories but, rather, from ideological crisis, lack of access to those in need, and the threat of isolation. They need to be useful for others.

The ideas they manifest are therapeutic. In judo (which I teach and practice), when people look after each other, they can learn. If one person's strength is used excessively, another gets hurt. When we take responsibility for the group, we develop that combined attention. My participants incline towards collective healing.

In my work with refugees in particular, I find it useful to consider clients within their immediate network and family system, as well as by themselves. I believe—or, rather, hope—that my project will generate or contribute to a wave or resonance through all therapy, not limited to the problems faced by political refugees. They seem to offer their experience so a wider viewpoint may evolve. To be reminded of what they have already achieved and the meaningful sacrifices they have made potentially helps them to tackle the problems they face. In therapy generally, recognising clients' interior resources as an asset can help them overcome personal difficulties. Recognition of capability is empowering.

It is essential to give voice to this reality. They might have lost it for a while when they were uprooted from their familiar environment. Therapeutic care should support their ability to rediscover it, find their existential centre of gravity, and continue to work for freedom.

Dictatorships try to isolate people from each other; but the human design is social, interwoven, and interconnected. This reality helps the individual survive torture and upheaval.

By bringing the human struggle into high relief, the political refugees' real achievement is probably in conveying their progressive message: "We can create change if we want to." The therapeutic world is energised through this focus on human resources and capability.

NOTES

1. Gary Greenberg, *The Book of Woe: The DSM and the Unmaking of Psychiatry* (New York: Blue Rider Press, 2013); Stephanie F. Dailey, Carmen S. Gill, Shannon L. Karl, and Casey A. Barrio Minton, *DSM-5 Learning Companion for Counsellors* (Hoboken, NJ: Wiley, 2014).

2. Greenberg, *The Book of Woe*; Allen Frances, *Saving Normal: An Insider's Revolt against Out-of-Control Psychiatric Diagnosis, DSM-5, Big Pharma, and the Medicalization of Ordinary Life* (New York: William Morrow, 2013).

3. Fifth version of psychiatry's diagnostic code (DSM-5: see the website www.dsm5.org).

4. Allen Frances, "The British Psychological Society Condemns DSM-5," *Psychiatric Times*, 26 July 2011, https://www.psychiatrictimes.com/view/british-psychological-society-condemns-dsm-5.

5. Carolyn Zerbe Enns and Elizabeth Nutt Williams, eds., *The Oxford Handbook of Feminist Counseling Psychology* (New York: Oxford University Press, 2012).

6. Charles Taylor, *A Secular Age* (Cambridge: Harvard University Press, 2007); Alessandro Ferrara, *Reflective Authenticity: Rethinking the Project of Modernity* (London: Routledge, 1998); Charles Guignon, "Authenticity," *Philosophy Compass* 3 (2008): 277–90; Somogy Varga, *Authenticity as an Ethical Ideal* (New York: Routledge, 2013).

7. Lionel Trilling, *Sincerity and Authenticity* (Cambridge, MA: Harvard University Press, 1972).

8. Charles Taylor, *The Ethics of Authenticity* (Cambridge, MA: Harvard University Press, 1991).

9. Søren Kierkegaard, *Kierkegaard's Writings, XII*, vol. 2, *Concluding Unscientific Postscript to Philosophical Fragments*, trans. H. V. Hong and E. H. Hong (Princeton, NJ: Princeton University Press, 2013).

10. Emmy van Deurzen, *Everyday Mysteries: A Handbook of Existential Psychotherapy*, 2nd ed. (London: Routledge, 2009); Hans W. Cohn, *Existential Thought and Therapeutic Practice: An Introduction to Existential Psychotherapy* (London: Sage, 1997).

11. Martin Heidegger, *Being and Time*, trans. J. Macquarrie and E. Robinson (New York: Harper & Row, 1962 [1927]).

12. Heidegger, *Being and Time*.

13. Jean-Paul Sartre, *Being and Nothingness*, trans. H. Barnes (New York: Washington Square Press, 1984).

14. Gary Cox, *Sartre: A Guide for the Perplexed* (New York: Continuum, 2007).

15. Cohn, *Existential Thought and Therapeutic Practice*, 125.

16. Van Deurzen, *Everyday Mysteries*.

17. Anna-Teresa Tymieniecka, ed., *The Origins of Life: The Origins of the Existential Sharing-in-Life* (Rotterdam: Springer, 2012); V. R. Taneja, *Socio-philosophical Approach to Education* (New Delhi: Atlantic, 2005); Eberhard Herrmann, *Scientific Theory and Religious Belief: An Essay on the Rationality of Views* (Kampen: Pharos, 1995); Gerald Corey, *Theory and Practice of Counseling and Psychotherapy* (Boston: Cengage Learning, 2016); Florence W. Kaslow and Robert F. Massey, eds., *Comprehensive Handbook of Psychotherapy, Interpersonal/Humanistic/Existential* (Hoboken, NJ: Wiley, 2004).

18. François Raffoul, *The Origin of Responsibility* (Indianapolis: Indiana University Press, 2010).

19. Hannah Arendt, *The Human Condition*, 2nd ed. (Chicago: University of Chicago Press, 2013).

20. A. Wells and D. M. Clark, "Social Phobia: A Cognitive Approach," in *Phobias: A Handbook of Description, Treatment and Theory*, ed. G. I. Davey (Chichester: Wiley, 1997).

Conclusion

Armin Danesh and Alison Assiter

This book opened with a theoretical chapter challenging one interpretative concept of a refugee. We suggested there that Nyers's theoretical framework, while very interesting, plays into the hands of those who would characterise refugees in a somewhat negative manner. We argued there, and elsewhere in this book, that much of the literature on refugees regards them either as "problems," as caricatured in the excerpt (chapter 1) from George Orwell, or as victims who basically need help. We suggested that these polarised but rather limited views are carried over into the psychoanalytic and mental health fields.

The book, primarily through the case studies and through Armin Danesh's own personal story as a political refugee from Iran, offers a very different picture of the refugee. We do not claim that the case studies in themselves overthrow the commonplace image of the refugee, but they offer an important corrective to the assumed view. The political refugees whose stories have been outlined in detail and depth in this book indicate a view of a refugee as a person with enormous resilience and interior resources, with much to offer whichever country in the world they end up in. It is important to note, as far as all refugees are concerned, that, as argued in the first chapter of the book, each one of them has human rights under the UN Universal Declaration of Human Rights. No one therefore ought to be reduced to Giorgio Agamben's "bare life."

The stories you read here were told by people who faced enormous difficulties in their countries of origin. They managed the escape process in different ways, and they faced, as though reborn, the settlement process in their new country. None of them spent long in the limbo state of "bare life," although some of them failed to get settled status in their host country of Britain. Even those people, however, showed determination and resilience and found worthwhile activity in the United Kingdom. We do not want to stigmatise those refugees who do not manage to settle in the ways outlined here. Nor do we wish to claim, "they did it, so why should others not succeed?" Rather, our intention has been to suggest that these stories ought not to be ignored in the literature. If a person has survived torture and imprisonment in their country of origin and has faced the challenge of moving from one country to another with little hope of going back to their place of origin, then, as we have shown here, those people have enormous strength and resources. We hope that others will derive strength and hope from the accounts presented here. In the rest of this concluding chapter, Armin Danesh reflects on the process of researching the various clients whose stories are told in the book.

The interpretative phenomenological analysis (IPA) framework helped me gain a better understanding of the phenomena (lived experiences) as they present themselves. This method argues that all description constitutes a form of interpretation. In general, the relationship between the researcher and the data generates the insights.

In this study, I could not avoid interpretation at any stage, but I maintained a commitment to grounding my interpretation in my participants' viewpoint. To engage with my participants' experience, I needed to be able to identify and reflect on my own experiences and assumptions.[1] This awareness enabled me to gain a richer body of data.

The research I conducted was close to my heart. From the outset, I needed to recognise the potential influence of my strong motivation and passion for the topic, on the research process and on the participants. What steps would I need to take to lay aside my own experience and assumptions? The viewpoints of both researcher and participants have to be identified and elucidated because of issues of bias. For instance, I was aware of my tendency to focus on the more positive aspects of my participants' narratives. My way to guard against this bias was to monitor my work through my reflective journal and to have my research supervisor check my interpretations and analysis as I went along. My journal is organised into four books, one for each year of my research. In the initial stage of developing it as my doctoral project, I arranged for my supervisor to interview me at the beginning and at the end of my data analysis.

To clarify my view, I formulated my assumptions in relation to four domains—personal/psychological; spiritual; physical; and social. I find that in the personal and psychological context as a whole, political refugees tend to have strong, highly motivated personalities: they take risks to benefit others. In the spiritual context, they are likely to feel linked to meanings beyond the material world; helping others comes before their own personal safety. Political refugees are obliged to change their social habitat. Existentially, they face death and have to avoid arrest. Furthermore, after escaping from their home country, the environmental change to their physical world may alter their outlook. They might need to generate new meanings regarding their life in the United Kingdom. Some who are able to create that meaning survive the change, but there are many who do not.

My reflection on my interactions with participants links their stories. Some of the research material was in the form of discussions arising spontaneously; I acknowledged my participants' creative role in the project. Developing trust was crucial to gaining rich data. When research interviews are conducted on a more formal basis, it can limit participants' ability to speak openly or in depth. The researcher may or may not possess the gift of inviting sensitive information.

Reviewing my life story helped me develop self-awareness and reflexivity, and to be truly attentive to what my participants had to say. My openness and engagement with their stories revealed to me details of my own that I had forgotten. During the research, my self-awareness improved.

A phenomenological approach to my participants' stories helped me recognise that there is no objective truth and that a phenomenon can be perceived in almost unlimited ways, within a wide spectrum. This openness allowed me to consider "grey" as a possible alternative to my own habit of seeing things in black and white. In other words, IPA enabled me to move away from a battlefield mentality to an approach more appropriate to everyday life. As an example, my relationship with my wife changed, because I have realised how essential it is to respect and recognise alternative viewpoints. That realisation brought openness, coherence, and flexibility to the relationship. This indicates a developmental process, which is essentially ongoing. In my view, openness is not simply a "given" but requires commitment in its pursuit. Otherwise, as I have myself experienced, previous patterns of thought can easily reestablish themselves.

I invited Karimi and Sara to the slide presentation of my research. For the first time, my participants saw the result of the contribution they had made. Karimi listened carefully, and when I emphasised the issue of trust, he replied, "*That is very true. The problem of whom to trust is all-important.*"[2] When I showed him how the "threat to their existence" was not only physical but also ideological, psychological, political, and spiritual, this had a strong impact on Karimi, who recognised that his own life experience was being mirrored back to him.

When I moved onto the significance of the findings, he confirmed these when discussing his own resistance to the extreme pressure employed by the interrogators. Although he was tortured, his values and the knowledge that people regarded him as a hero helped him endure it.

Many people other than myself have undergone torture. Thousands were executed; they were martyrs. Those people inspired me. Because of them, I was not truly alone in the prison, even in solitary confinement. I was not alone, because before me, people had resisted in this place, in the prison. It was normal and natural for political refugees to resist.[3]

When we discussed gender ideology, Karimi commented that this was a major obstacle in his path. "*This is so true for me.*"[4] He also said divorce was common among Iranian political refugees in the United Kingdom, due to the men's difficulty in accepting the new role of women. He referred to the positive experiences of many female refugees, arising out of the adaptation process, when cultural challenges were inevitable.

When I moved to my clinical work with political refugees, Karimi agreed with my recognising and respecting a client's ideology and political philosophy, rather than solely focusing on his or her personality. I think this is an important evaluation in existential therapy.

From the beginning of my conversation with Sara, I became aware of her wider concept regarding family. The literature generally emphasises the nuclear family unit. Sara, however, said she felt closer to the members of her party than to her biological family. My participants' ideology comes before blood relationships and extends the meaning of "family." When Sara's children were small and very dependent on her, she was still able to prioritise her activity in the battlefield.

I presented my study and asked her for her view. She said: "*I feel you acknowledged my own identity. I have felt unrecognised in the UK. Most people consider political refugees to be the same as other immigrants and refugees.*" She added emphatically: "*I have been working with Iranian refugees for many years, and the issue of gender equality is crucial.*"[5]

When I asked her if she would like to add anything, she mentioned the importance of work and keeping physically active in the adaptation process.

Something else came up in our conversation: male refugees tend to connect more with other men, among themselves, and also with friends and relatives still in their homeland. This doesn't encourage them to engage with or integrate in the new country.

Regarding psychotherapy, Sara said, "*I had several therapists myself. They found it hard to understand my life or what I've been through.*" She repeated several times: "*They had no idea of the politics or the ideology. They were very nice people; they listened to you, but they had no idea. I couldn't form any connection with them. It is very important to have a therapist you can speak your own native language with.*"[6]

Concerning the issue of trust, Sara said, "*What you did before the interview—setting up a few meetings—helped me to trust you. Without that I couldn't have told you much. I was very open with you—I told you everything.*"[7]

The focus on internal resources is significant. I explored my participants' subjective experiences under such headings as *culture, language*, and *resettlement*. The qualities of political adaptation, self for others, and spiritual crisis were also discussed. I discovered some differences in male and female experiences. In the Iranian misogynist regime, discrimination is institutionalised. As a result of the escape process, the woman's role begins to change. During adaptation and resettlement, women take charge of their families, and men become existentially challenged by the reality of gender equality. The women in my study were keen to learn the English language and to interact. Men tended to live more in the past and to engage with their own community, whereas the women were more future focused and enjoyed making new friends.

I suggest that a clinical model for working with political refugees should consider value systems and political identity. Refugees' trauma is mainly related to their ideological crisis. Respect for this factor is crucial to their sense of identity. The therapeutic model should recognise and remind them of their internal resources. The subjective meaning of trauma should be considered, together with the desire to work for others' benefit. Responsibility, motivation, and action are familiar concepts. The sense of loss experienced by refugees relates to their political agenda rather than to material possessions. My participants' struggles highlighted the vital aspect of gender equality: it is the yardstick of their adaptation process. It is essential to consider these social constructs in all therapeutic practice. Political refugees are not simply "victims," and they are not "problems." They all agreed how important it is for them to be employed.

I found that, in all of them, recognition of their own sense of mission in a free society awoke their self-connection and their ability to act accordingly. In every instance, their dilemma—for example, how to adapt their political identity to the life here, while friends in Iran remained on the front line—reminded me of the uncertainty and angst that authentic living demands.[8]

I learned from the experience of all nine participants that their political refugee status is determined by their conscience and dignity under all circumstances. They recognise that their commitment to life prepares them to confront new dilemmas and to keep their value systems intact.

On their arrival in the United Kingdom, they all felt they were met and recognised, even though some of them experienced a protracted asylum process. They made connections with other people in the new society. They all said it was crucial for them to develop these interactive relationships. It helped them not to brood on the past, and even to develop a fresh viewpoint. My participants want to express gratitude and to contribute to their new social communities in practical ways. They do not put their personal interest before others.

In Iran, their values were suffocated. Even if they have managed to transfer their political activity to the new society, the situation in Iran continues to trouble them. They never feel apart from that reality, though their new freedom enriches their quality of life. Under repression, their collective or ethnic identities were forbidden.

Their message to new political refugees to this country is to understand their rights and their opportunities to establish themselves here, to learn the language, to interact with others, and to work—not just to stay at home. This is bound to help their well-being. They all agree that it is unhelpful to try to direct and resolve refugees' situations in their stead, or to tell them what they should do. They need to find their own way, and others must recognise this.

All my participants found fulfilling work and say that, regardless of the new challenges, they are happy to be in the United Kingdom. They have the freedom to be themselves. They are distressed about the conditions they left behind yet passionate about their own internal revolution and rebirth.

NOTES

1. David Harper and Andrew R. Thompson, eds., *Qualitative Research Methods in Mental Health and Psychotherapy: A Guide for Students and Practitioners* (New York: Wiley, 2011).

2. Karimi, interviewed by A. Danesh, London, 18 October 2017.

3. Karimi, interviewed by A. Danesh, London, 18 October 2017.

4. Karimi, interviewed by A. Danesh, London, 18 October 2017.

5. Sara, interviewed by A. Danesh, London, 15 November 2017.

6. Sara, interviewed by A. Danesh, London, 15 November 2017.

7. Sara, interviewed by A. Danesh, London, 15 November 2017.

8. Ernesto Spinelli, *The Interpreted World: An Introduction to Phenomenological Psychology* (London: Sage, 1989).

Index

adaptation. *See* United Kingdom (UK), adaptation and resettlement in
Africa, 84, 108, 110
Agamben, Giorgio, 12, 14, 16–18, 155
Arar, Rawan, 3–4
Arendt, Hannah, 12, 13, 14, 16, 20; on natality, 115
Aristotle, 15; *Oikos* generic term of, 6–7; "zoe" and "bios" distinction of, 14, 16–18
arrests, 24, 38–39; by association, 103, 131; avoiding, 58; of brother, 58, 59; of close friend, 52; daily occurrence of, 57; by Religious Guards, 53, 55, 56; research participant accounts of, 83, 84, 85, 95, 97, 102, 126; resistance rules governing, 106; of wife, 54
Assembly of Experts, 33
Assiter, Alison, 13, 18, 65, 69, 71–73
asylum: delayed, 119–20; non-asylum status, 123
asylum seekers, refugees differentiated from, 5, 40
authenticity: authentic self, 146, *149*; autonomy interrelatedness to, 147; dictatorships and, 152; philosophers on responsibility and, 149; possibility and concept of, 146–50, *149*, *150*
Azari-Qomi, Ahmad, 33–34

"bad faith," 148
Baobab Centre for Young Survivors in Exile, 145
Beauvoir, Simone de, 147, 148
Bernstein, Richard, 75–76
Betts, Alexander, 7
Bhatt, Chetan, 18
Bhugra, Dinesh, 7
birth theme, 115–18
Bolsheviks, 31
BPS. *See* British Psychological Society
Bradley, Moira "Mama," 47, 67–71
British Psychological Society (BPS), 145
British Refugee Council, 145
Buddhism, 117
Burnett, Angela, 6, 7
buses, gender segregation on, 60, 110

Carter, Jimmy, 25
case studies. *See* research participants
Catholic Church, 62, 67
Central Intelligence Agency (CIA), 24
Chimni, B. S., 4–5
CIA. *See* Central Intelligence Agency
climate change, 3, 16
The Concise Oxford Dictionary, 30
Constitutional Revolution of 1906, in Iran, 24, 27, 41
Council of Guardians, Islam and, 33
counselling, 65

161

About the Authors

Armin Danesh is a consultant psychotherapist, director of a human rights organisation, and chair of a mental health charity. He worked for over thirty years with refugee families who were traumatised or facing extreme crisis, and his doctoral thesis was about the experiences of these political refugees. In addition to teaching phenomenological therapy, Danesh currently supervises psychotherapists, counsellors, and students. Coupling existential themes with politics and psychology is characteristic of Danesh's clinical and academic work; he integrates Western and Eastern philosophical views to shed light on existential issues.

Alison Assiter is a professor of feminist theory at University of the West of England (UWE), Bristol. She is a philosopher and has written a number of books on political philosophy, feminist philosophy, and Søren Kierkegaard's philosophy. Her two most recent books are *A New Theory of Human Rights: New Materialism and Zoroastrianism* (Rowman & Littlefield, 2021) and *Kierkegaard, Eve and Metaphors of Birth* (Rowman & Littlefield, 2015). She is an active campaigner on human rights issues, an editor of the journal *Feminist Dissent*, and has volunteered in an organisation for refugees and migrants.

www.ingramcontent.com/pod-product-compliance
Lightning Source LLC
Chambersburg PA
CBHW050515280326
41932CB00014B/2331